SUNSHINE GIRL

*My Journey from the Soviet Orient to
the Western World*

Dildora Damisch Muzafari

Review

Sunshine Girl by Dildora Muzafari is a uniquely personal yet highly informative story about the trials, tribulations, and triumphs of a girl who grew up in Uzbekistan in the Soviet period. Born in the 1950s in Soviet Central Asia, Ms. Muzafari shares the rich and tragic history of her family which came from a long line of Central Asian intellectuals and was severely oppressed in the Stalinist period. She then provides a first-hand view of Tashkent and the small Uzbek villages during her formative years, the Earthquake of 1966, life in a closed Soviet city during the Perestroika era, the realities of living in East Germany, the fall of the Berlin Wall, the work environment at Radio Free Liberty in West Germany, and, ultimately the profound transformation of her hometown after the fall of the Soviet Union. Told with humor, personality, and refreshing candor, this account adds a fresh and unusual perspective to the collection of narratives about dislocation and immigration, as well as racism and women's issues. Even those familiar with life in the Soviet Union and Eastern Europe often know far less about the five Central Asian republics, and will thus find this book a beautiful and passionate window to that world.

Yet this book is valuable not only as a historical account; it is also the personal story of a girl who grew up in a society where two very different cultures collided — the more modern, secular Soviet one and an ancient, traditional Muslim one - and who simultaneously fit into both and neither. Sunshine Girl follows Ms. Muzafari's struggle to free herself from the social, historical, gender, and racial constraints imposed on her by her society, find her own voice, and reach a place she could truly call home. Her bold, unique, and passionate voice carries the reader through her odyssey which stretches from Uzbekistan to Ukraine, Russia, East Germany, Hungary, West Germany, and ultimately, Michigan. It also chronicles her great love affair with an East German and the overwhelming political and cultural obstacles the couple overcame to be together. This love story is at the heart of the book and will inspire anyone who has had to fight for love.

Perhaps the most beautiful chapter in this book is Ms. Muzafari's touching depiction of her return to Tashkent in 2006 to find it had changed beyond recognition from the place where she grew up. But luckily, the reader will have already been immersed in the beautiful, multicultural Tashkent of the author's childhood, with its aroma of onions and fried dumplings, bright tapestries, bustling markets, and closely-knit communities. Although that Tashkent is no more, it will continue to live in the reader's memory and in Dildora Muzafari's beautiful memoirs. The reader will also be left with the writer's incredible love for life and culture, as well as her plucky grit and determination in her decades-long quest for self-realization.

Always lively and interesting, and at times profoundly insightful, Sunshine Girl is a wonderful read for anyone interested in the struggles of individuals to find themselves in and beyond the context of their cultures. It will also be of great interest to students of Soviet, Central Asian, and Islamic studies, who will have the rare opportunity to see Soviet Uzbekistan through the eyes and heart of a woman personally familiar with the Uzbek, Russian, European, and American cultures, and thus able to present her experience in a multifaceted way that is accessible to the outsider. Last, but not least, Ms. Muzafari's work is a valuable asset to the growing canon of global stories which allow the reader to gain insight into global issues and institutions from previously unrepresented perspectives, and to understand the plight of individuals as they navigate a world characterized at once by vast differences and surprising universal truths.

Laura Kline, PhD Sr. Lecturer in RussianCMLLC

Wayne State University

TABLE OF CONTENTS

Introduction 1

Chapter 1 My Country.. 3

The "Stans"..4

Language...4

Chapter 2. My Parents 7

Studies 15

Love...16

My Mother Dinara..18

Marriage..20

Chapter 3. Childhood.. 23

Musical Theatre and Television 23

The Earthquake of 1966 24

School..29

The Bazaar 39

One Glass for Everybody! 42

About Hygiene..42

Samovars 42

New School, "Internationalism", Russian Superiority....................43

Cotton and the Aral Sea Tragedy 46

Child Labor!...47

Mahalla 47

Islam under Soviet Rule..50

Ramadan..51

Reading 53

The Happiest Childhood in The World...54

A Foreigner at Home..*59*

Chapter 4. Grandma **61**

Vacation in Crimea *63*

Blat...*66*

Train Travel..*67*

Leningrad..*69*

The Kommunalka...*71*

Shopping and Alcohol *73*

Alcohol *75*

Stores...*78*

Chapter 5. Kokand **83**

Crimean Tatars *85*

Village Life *86*

Cotton *87*

Shakhimardan..*88*

Isfara *89*

Village Kids..*91*

Movies *92*

Everyday Music..*94*

The Uzbek House..*98*

Chapter 6. High School **103**

Highschool Sweetheart..*107*

Friends *112*

Uzbek Wedding Traditions *113*

Matchmaker...*113*

The Test Phase *114*

Breaking the Bread..*116*

Girls' Day...*117*

Dowry *117*

The Wedding *118*

The Traditional Wedding Ritual *119*

In the Groom's House *119*

Post-Wedding Rituals *119*

Chapter 7. Friends **121**

Parades *121*

Uzbek Koreans *124*

Russian Germans *126*

Chapter 8. University Entry Exams **129**

Chapter 9. Odessa **137**

Chapter 10. The GDR **221**

Chapter 11. The Wedding **237**

Chapter 12. Baby Indira **247**

Chapter 13. "Gosekzameny" or "State Exams" **255**

Chapter 14. "Posledny god uchyoby" or "My Last Year of College" **261**

Navruz *261*

Carl Zeiss *263*

Chapter 15. Dubna **267**

Abortion *270*

Soviet women *271*

My friend Olya *272*

Uzbek Food *277*

Food *279*

Kids and Different Cultures *281*

Gorbachev *286*

Escaping to the West *296*

Chapter 16. Escaping to the West **301**

Return to the GDR *301*

Freedom *308*

Chapter 17. Radio Liberty **311**

Independence of Uzbekistan *321*

The Aral Sea *323*

Uzbek Women *324*

Understanding Islam *324*

Chapter 18. America **331**

American Patriotism *338*

Why I Decided To Live In America *339*

**Chapter 19. "Ташкент или ностальгия по городу которого нет"
or "Tashkent, Or Nostalgia For A City That Doesn't Exist"** **343**

Alay Market *345*

Shakhantaur *346*

Beshagach *347*

The Square *347*

The "30 Years Of The Komsomol" Movie Theater, Or "The Thirty" *349*

Karl Marx Street *349*

Chapter 20. A Letter to My Grandchildren **351**

Dedication

To my parents Dinara and Muzaffar for always loving and supporting me. It's impossible to thank you adequately for everything you've done, from loving me unconditionally.

You are both the reason why I am so strong.

I could not have asked for better parents and thank you for being in my life. Words cannot explain how much I love both of you!

Introduction

As I begin writing this book, I am on a German train going from Koblenz to Munich. I am moving back to Munich, and this is the 11th time I have moved to a new home.

Sometimes I ask myself who on earth I am and which culture and which country I belong to. On the one hand, after over twenty years in the US, my heart really belongs to America, and I feel like an American. On the other, I am a global person. I belong to the global world of today.

I grew up in the former Soviet Union, where there was a mixture of Muslim and European cultures, then I lived and worked in Europe for more than 20 years, and then I spent twelve years in America. So I can easily say that I am truly global!

All my friends who know my background and have heard my stories about my life and experiences have repeatedly asked me to write a book. A book! My close friends have always been extremely interested in my multicultural background and in my broad experience living in different parts of the world. I don't know if my story will be of interest to readers, but I have decided to write it, and I dedicate it to all my friends around the world.

And I really do have friends everywhere. Wherever in the world I go, even today - to Italy, Austria, Czech Republic, Hungary, Japan, Argentina, France, Russia, England or, of course, the USA - I always see my friends, and they share their joys and sorrows with me.

Visiting friends abroad is quite different than going to foreign countries as a tourist!

Discovering a new culture first-hand is the best thing in the world!

I like it when my friends share their day-to-day lives with me. I also like to go to their houses, meet their friends, go shopping with them at the local farmers market, and dine in their favorite

1

establishments. I also like to see how they prepare their traditional dishes, while sharing their culinary secrets with me!

What could be better than having a conversation with them about their everyday lives, which are filled with the same problems as mine, and then realize that despite our different backgrounds and cultures, we are all the same! We women have families and our kids have endless problems at school, our husbands are always busy with their jobs, our grown kids have even more - and bigger - issues, and so on, and so on. We also share our unhappiness about the impossibility of simultaneously having a career and being good wives and mothers...

It seems that all my friends, regardless of their culture and ethnicity, have the same problems. A lot of things unite us today! How well we understand each other! Isn't it amazing that the world is actually so small!

In 1970, when I was in school, I couldn't even imagine that one day I would marry a German and move with him to Germany. I couldn't have imagined that later we would flee from East Germany to West Germany, and then move to the US, where I would have a wonderful life...

Chapter 1

My Country[1]

I was born in Tashkent, which is both a major city in Uzbekistan and the nation's capital. For many years, Uzbekistan was part of the Russian Empire, and later the Soviet Union. Like the other 14 former Soviet republics, today Uzbekistan is an independent country.

When I tell people in the United States that I am from "Uzbekistan," they always respond "Pakistan"? I try to explain that Uzbekistan is very different from Pakistan, and that Uzbekistan used to be part of the USSR. Then they say, "Oh, then you are from Russia!" Yes, maybe they are right. Everyone saw the USSR as Russia. People often don't know how large the USSR was and how many different ethnic and religious groups there were in that country, which covered one sixth of the Earth's surface.

---

[1] Map Source: Wikipedia (Public Domain)

The Soviet Union was made up of 15 different republics whose populations had completely different languages, religions, and ethnic backgrounds. We didn't have anything in common. We couldn't even understand the language of people who lived only 60 miles away. Sometimes even the cuisines and cultures of other Soviet Republics seemed exotic to us.

During the Soviet period, there was a tradition of holding music festivals featuring ethnic music from the various republics. We usually had entire week-long festivals celebrating Georgian, Ukrainian, Estonian, or Armenian culture. These were extremely interesting events for me! I loved going to concerts and the theater. The beautiful costumes, music, and traditional dances ... everything was so very different from in my culture ... That is why when people ask me if I am from Russia, I have to explain how different Uzbeks are from Russians!

The "Stans"

The Soviet Union was divided into fifteen republics which whose borders were drawn more or less along ethnic lines. Five of those republics were located in Central Asia: Uzbekistan, Tajikistan, Kazakhstan, Turkmenistan, and Kyrgyzstan. The names of all the Central Asian republics end with the suffix "-stan", which means "land" in many Central Asian (and Middle Eastern) languages. Thus, "Uzbekistan" means "land of the Uzbeks," "Tajikistan" means "land of the Tajiks," and "Pakistan" means the "land of the Pakistani."

Language

Today the official language of Uzbekistan is Uzbek, and it is written in the Latin alphabet (like English). However, the history of language on the territory of today's Uzbekistan is rich and complex.

Like most of the languages of Central Asia, Uzbek belongs to the Turkic language group, but has elements of other languages. Historically, Central Asia was characterized by a rich tapestry of Turkic dialects spoken by the various Turkic peoples who inhabited the area. Then, thanks to the Persian empire, Persian became the language of the court for this region. Consequently, for centuries

4

urban intellectuals spoke Farsi, and you can still find many elements of Farsi in modern Uzbek. Arabic words entered the language with the introduction of Islam and were used for religious purposes. From the fifteenth century on, the written language of Central Asia was "Chagatai" or "Old Uzbek". It was the language of a rich literary tradition, including works by the famous poet Ali-Shir Nava'i. Russian words arrived later, with the Imperial Russian - and subsequent Soviet - conquest of the region.

Before the absorption of Central Asia into the Soviet Union, Uzbek was but one of the many Turkic dialects spoken by some of the Turkic tribes in the region. When the Soviet republic of Uzbekistan was created in 1929, all the peoples living in that region were classified as Uzbeks, whether or not they in fact were, and the Uzbek dialect became their official language, squeezing out the other local dialects. Thus, you can say that today's Uzbek is in many ways the creation of the Soviet state. Furthermore, the Soviets switched Uzbek from the Arabic to the Latin alphabet in 1928, then to the Cyrillic alphabet in 1940. After the collapse of the Soviet Union in 1991, there was a backlash against Russian influence, which included eliminating Russian borrowings from Uzbek and replacing the Cyrillic alphabet with the Latin one. Nonetheless, the Cyrillic alphabet is still frequently used in Uzbekistan today.

Chapter 2.

My Parents

My parents are well-educated people. My father was a director for Uzbek TV, and my mom was a university professor.

My father Muzaffar belongs to the 30th generation of a very old family. One of his ancestors was a religious scholar from Baghdad by the name of Sheikh Zayniddin, short for Sheikh Zayniddin Kyi Arifoni Tashkondi ibn Sheih Shahobiddin Abu Havs Umar Suhrovardi. He was born in 1164 in Iraq and came to Central Asia as an Iraqi ambassador. Sheikh Zayniddin, the son of Zia addin Jakhim Sukhravardi sheikh, who was the founder of the Sukhravardiya Order of Sufism, was sent to Central Asia by his father to spread Islam.

When Sheikh Zayniddin approached the ancient city of Tashkent ("The City of Stone"), his camel suddenly stopped and lay down near the Kukcha city gate. This was seen as a sign from above that a Madrasa school for the teaching of Islam should be built on this spot. After his death, Sheikh Zayniddin was buried in the Village of Arifon, just behind the Kukcha gate. The neighborhood is now called Kukcha.

132 years after Sheikh Zayniddin's death, the Great Amir Temur (Timur), the founder of the Timurid Empire and the Timurid Dynasty (1370–1405) in Central Asia, visited his grave and, as a sign of respect for Sheikh Zayniddin, ordered the construction of a mausoleum of the *khanaka* type with a double cupola. Today the mausoleum, which has undergone restoration several times, still stands not far from my family's house. On its façade some *sura* from the Qur'an are engraved, and a giant round seal sits atop it.

Next to the mausoleum there is a *chillyakhona*, an underground monastic cell, which was built in the 12th—13th centuries. Entering it is a special experience. In the summer, it is cool inside, and in the winter, it is warm. When the Quran is read there, you can hear a strange, high-pitched sound. The opening in the ceiling lets in the rays of the sun, which reflect off the walls and illuminate the lower part of the room. The followers of Sheikh Zayniddin could determine the exact time of the day based on where the sun was being reflected. In other words, this part of the mausoleum complex was a type of observatory.

Fortunately, five valuable documents about the family tree of Sheikh Zayniddin, which were sealed and certified by the superior judges of their periods, have survived until the present day. These documents were hidden for a long time during the Soviet period, when it was unthinkable to talk about such an ancestry or to display such documents. If you wanted to have a career, it was better to be of peasant or working-class roots.

Sheikh Zayniddin's family tree stretches over 1200 years, and his descendants live in the Kukcha neighborhood until this day. One of them is my father, Muzaffar Asadullayev.

A large number of the male members of this family have been important people of their times: scholars, theology professors, politicians, scientists, poets, and writers. Even today, all my father's cousins are scholars of mathematics, physics, or philosophy. Like most of his family members, my father is actually very strong in mathematics, but he decided to follow a different path.

Born in 1927, my father had a very good early childhood. His family had money and owned a lot of land in the Old City of Tashkent, including the Kukcha neighborhood. My dad's father and his four brothers also owned summer and winter homes, something not typical for that time. My dad spent entire summers in those summer homes with his many cousins, playing in the gardens, climbing trees… Most of his cousins later became well-known scientists and scholars. Then, in 1940, the Soviet government nationalized the land …

My dad started school when he was six years old. He remembers that he was one of the best students of his class, just like his three sisters and all his cousins. Most of his cousins were older, and my dad told me it was a family tradition to compete and try to be the best at everything.

My dad's mother, Mavjudahon, was the only daughter of Said Ahmad Askiya Eshon. The surname Eshon – as well as Khodja – was reserved for families who are the decedents of saints. These "holy" families became a sort of Central Asian nobility, and as such were highly educated and prominent in the scientific and cultural fields. Thus, it is not surprising that Said Ahmad Askiya Eshon was a theology professor at the Kokaldash Madrasa, a religious school. Ahmad Eshon was a talented musician and poet. My dad's grandmother, Ahmad Eshon's wife Salomothon, was a green-eyed beauty. She was always done up beautifully, dressed to the nines, and adorned in jewelry. She was also smart, and – something extremely rare before the Soviet Revolution in Muslim Central Asia – she was a college teacher.

Besides his daughter (my granny Mavjudahon), Said Ahmad Askiya Eshon had two sons. The older one, Sulton Qozihon, was the judge of Tashkent and spoke seven languages.

My dad's father, Asadullahoja (short for Asadullo Said Eshon) –a grandpa I never met – was the student of professor Said Ahmad Askiya Eshon at the Kokaldash Madrasa. The professor wanted his only daughter to marry Asadullahoja, because he was impressed by his talent and knew that he was also from a very old family. The tradition of preserving old family trees by marrying children from these families to one another still exists today. It is amazing that 70 years of socialism could not destroy such traditions.

My grandpa Asadullahoja Said Eshon had four brothers. The oldest, Fathullahoja, was in charge of the food department of the Administration of the City of Tashkent, and his hobbies were music and art. The second brother, Haybatullohoja, became a famous poet. Known professionally as "Hislat", he is now revered as a classical writer and poet, and a lot of his poems are still popular today as songs. In 2010, my dad published the book *Hislat*, dedicated to his famous uncle. Another brother of my granddad – Habibillohoja –

9

was a translator, who was enrolled in one of the first Russian schools at the age of ten. As a child he used to translate for people in the streets, which was a very common thing during those days. Habibillohoja was friends with a famous Uzbek writer Abdullo Qodiriy who, like many other famous Uzbek writers, was killed by the Stalinist regime in 1937. He owned a large collection of books from around the world. As for my grandpa, he was a famous politician and a talented orator. He was also put in charge of some major construction projects in Uzbekistan. However, in 1932 he was expelled from the Bolshevik Party for unknown reasons. Ultimately, my grandfather and all his brothers were arrested in the 1930s.

In the Soviet Union, the 1930s were a decade of terror and oppression. Millions of innocent people were arrested, exiled, sent to labor camps, or executed. The intelligentsia, which was seen as one of the main threats to the Stalinist regime, suffered enormous losses, and non-Russians were targeted even more than Russians. This attack on the educated classes were extremely detrimental to the intellectual and cultural life of the country, which would not recover for decades. In Uzbekistan, the president and nearly all high-level officials, as well as members of the intellectual and cultural elite, were arrested and executed. They would later be replaced by people who were loyal to Moscow. My own family did not emerge unscathed.

My dad remembers how a major Uzbek newspaper, "Qizil Uzbekiston" ("Red Uzbekistan"), published an article in 1937 exclaiming that "The Eshon family is an old religious family, and this clan still exists in our society! We won't allow them to spoil our new Bolshevik system!"

All three of my father's uncles were arrested in one day.

According to my dad, my grandpa, who held an important post in the government at the time, tried to protect his brothers when they were arrested by speaking out on their behalf in court: "Even though my family was religious in the past, today they all are hard-working, active people, and they serve the Soviet government. Everybody can make mistakes. Take for example Trotsky, a leading revolutionary like Lenin - even he made mistakes." A man by the name of Muminov interrupted my grandfather, screaming: "Did you hear

10

that? He said that Trotsky was a revolutionary! He defends Trotsky! He is a Trotskyite!" At that moment, my dad's young cousin Omonla, who was only 16, tried to help my grandpa, shouting that he was a well-respected person with a high-level government position, and so on. Suddenly the whole crowd attacked both this 16-year-old boy and my grandpa. Holding his four-year-old daughter in his arms, my grandpa tried to explain to the crowd that all this was a big mistake and that he had nothing to do with Trotsky, but nobody wanted to listen. Soon after this, on November 30th, 1937, my grandpa was arrested. He was 51 years old. That was the last time my dad saw his father.

The night of the arrest, NKVD agents confiscated our ancient books, prints, and manuscripts, which had been passed from generation to generation for centuries. Among the books were collections by our ancestors Sayid Norhoja (1778-1863) and Sayid Mahmudhoja (1810-1891). They have never been seen since.

I referred to a "court" above, but there weren't any real courts during the repressive Stalinist period. Instead, there were public meetings at schools, factories, universities, and in neighborhoods, where everybody was supposed to blame those who had been arrested.

Stalin is guilty of the persecution of millions of innocent people. He destroyed the peasantry and exterminated the intellectuals. The intelligentsia is, by definition, the social group that questions, analyzes, and doubts. It was easy for Stalin to get rid of them. Stalin turned one group against the other, using one to destroy the other, until finally all meaningful opposition had been eliminated.

I think Stalin was the greatest criminal in history. Under Stalin, everything was black or white, friend or foe, good or bad; there was no in-between. It was the genocide of the intellectual class, the nation's élites! Stalin used fear to keep the nation in a permanent state of terror and claimed there were "enemies" everywhere in the country. These "enemies", who supposedly were constantly planning to destroy our socialist country, included Trotskyites, kulaks/farmers, cosmopolitans, Jewish doctors, and so on. As long as the nation believed it was under threat, people had no time to think or, most importantly, question. And if people do not question, it is easy to use unrestricted power.

People were terrified, because Stalin's politics made everyone a potential enemy: "The son is responsible for his father." "Those who are not with us are against us!"

This terror has been deeply ingrained in the minds and the genes of Soviet people. Even today, people are fearful of expressing themselves or protesting against the government. There isn't much opposition in Putin's Russia either.

There is no reason to accuse Stalin of harboring hatred for any particular ethnic or religious group. Stalin was a Georgian, and the Georgians suffered as much as, if not more, than any other ethnic group in the Soviet Union. In fact, every ethnic minority suffered under Stalin, including the Chechens, Ingush, Kabardin, Balkars, Kurds, Crimean Tartars, and Jews. Incidentally, many of these "untrustworthy" groups were exiled to Central Asia.

Not only political persecution, but Soviet economic policy inflicted serious damage on Central Asia, and in particular, on Uzbekistan. To finance Stalin's push for rapid industrialization, Uzbekistan was forced to repurpose the vast majority of its land for cotton production. This would ultimately destroy the former agricultural diversity of the republic and lead to the decline of the Aral Sea, which was used to irrigate the cotton fields. WWII brought another series of blows to the region. Factories, along with Russians and other non-Uzbek workers, were relocated here from the western parts of the country as the Nazis approached. Many Russian and Ukrainian refugees were also evacuated to Uzbekistan, all of which resulted in the "Russification" of the cities. Even today, Central Asia is still suffering the consequences of Stalin's policies, which were enacted without the least consideration for the cultural and economic integrity of the region.

My dad's family did not know the whereabouts of their father for many, many years. Only during the Khrushchev period in the late 1950s could people write the KGB to find out what had happened to their relatives. My dad wrote and received a response: his father had been innocent and was going to be rehabilitated. My dad met with a KGB general who gave him documents stating that my grandpa had been unjustly imprisoned and should have been released. Interestingly, my dad also found out that those who had arrested his father were later arrested themselves. In all these cases, people were put in prison on fabricated charges. Human life was worth nothing...

My grandfather Asatullo was a talented man who spoke Russian well. He managed to earn some money during his time in the camps and send it to his family. It turned out that he worked as a lumberjack near the town of Arkhangelsk in Siberia. My dad also learned that his father had sent letters with poems he wrote about how he longed for his family. Later my dad's sister, my Aunt Muharram, memorized these verses, and knew them by heart until the end of her life.

Once, when I visited my family in Tashkent, my dad's younger sister, my Aunt Muhtabber, read those poems to us, her eyes full of tears ... She was trying to recall her father's face, but she couldn't, because she was only four years old when they took him away.

So, back in 1937, my grandma was left alone with four kids aged 14, 10, 7 and 4. Luckily, they had been well off before the Stalinist Terror, so they had the house my granddad had built and their gardens. For the first couple of years they managed by selling fruits and vegetables from the garden, and then ... their furniture. But soon the Soviet administration nationalized the land of these "enemies of the Soviet People" and built a school on my family's former property. What an irony it is that in order to get by, my grandmother got a job helping with the construction of that school!

Also ironic is the fact that this school, now called "School #40," is still standing and has additional history with our family: my sister and my nieces attended it! Later, during the 1990s, my dad's cousin Olamgurhon, the son of my granddad's famous brother Hislat, was the principal of the school.

After the arrest of my granddad, my dad was considered the son of an "enemy of the people," and was not allowed to join the Communist Youth Organization, the "Komsomol".

The situation got worse when Nazi Germany invaded the Soviet Union in 1941. Suddenly, everything and everyone had to serve the needs of the troops on the frontline. Officials searched the houses and property of ordinary citizens and confiscated anything useful for the war effort.

When the war broke out, my 14-year-old father was working at a corn mill, so he was able to take some of the flour dust left on the machinery. He would tell us about the agony of waking up hungry and going to sleep hungry. His family did not have any meat during the entire war.

In the 1940s, the winters were extremely cold. At night the temperature would fall to below -20°F, but luckily, people rarely got sick. My dad believes this could be due to the fact that people were active and did not eat much. The main sources of sustenance were black bread and simple soups, as well as some herbs during the warm seasons. People used whatever they could get hold of to cook meals in the soup kitchens. At one point – as my dad recalled – they brought in truckloads of little turtles from the Hunger Steppe, an area known for its brutal climate and dearth of living creatures.

The hunger of those days is still deeply engraved in psyche of the older generation.

In 1944, my dad and his mother fell seriously ill with typhus. They lay in bed for two months, and everybody thought this would be his end. But by a miracle - and also thanks to some quinine one of their neighbors had given him, he survived the illness. Then he went looking for work right away and was once again getting up at 6 am. He sold homemade cigarettes, worked as a builder, and performed all kinds of trades.

During the war, there were masses of refugees from the western regions of the Soviet Union. Uzbeks remember the war as the time when a million hungry, filthy people invaded Tashkent. The city was unable to accommodate so many refugees, but people still kept pouring in on the trains and making camp in groups right at the train station or in the dusty streets in the brutal heat of the sun. My dad's family rented some of their rooms out to people from Ukraine for a little cash. People were desperate for what little food and money

14

they could get in Tashkent, which has been called "The City of Bread" ever since.

There was also a lot of theft during those days. People stole everything, even ration cards, which were the most important asset in those days! A ration card provided you with the comfort of a quarter pound of dark bread per day for a month!

My dad remembers an incident at the bazaar: people had caught a thief and were about to call the police. Suddenly, a one-handed war veteran cried out: "Let's give him justice ourselves!" A group of men bent over the unlucky thief and started pounding on him mercilessly. All my dad could hear was grunts and moans.

One of the upsides to the war was that a number of famous theatres and film studios were evacuated to Tashkent. For a few years, the citizens of Tashkent had the privilege of seeing things like "Teve the Milkman" by Sholem-Aleykhem (also known as "The Fiddler on the Roof") with the original cast. Unfortunately, the director Solomon Mikhoels was later put to death by the Stalinist regime.

In 1945 my father was evaluated for military service, but luckily the war soon ended, so he was able to stay in Tashkent. Many of our other male family members fought in the war, and some never returned home. By 1945, those who had survived started coming back. Some of them were seriously injured, but they were alive.

Although the immediate post-war period was full of joy and jubilation, another tragic event occurred: a month after the war ended, at the age of 56, my grandmother died in my dad's arms.

Studies

In 1947 my dad enrolled at the Aviation College, but soon he had to withdraw because he needed to earn money to support his sisters.

Later, a cousin of his returned from his studies in Moscow and started working at the Mukimi Classical Theatre. This is when my dad first discovered the world of the performing arts, as this cousin invited him to various shows. My dad liked theatre a lot, but still had to work and earn money.

In the late 1940s, the first University of Art was founded in Tashkent, where you could study art, cinematography, and directing. In 1949, the first theatre classes opened, but interest among the locals was not great. Remember Muslim culture, where a man was to be the authority in the family and not some entertaining performer! Consequently, the university offered a reward of 20 rubles – a substantial sum at the time – to those who brought in new students. Uncle Najibullah talked my dad into enrolling; another uncle by the name of Sulton, who had a good position and a decent income, as well as my dad's elder sister, offered money to help out. By the way, this Uncle Sulton – although an admirer of the arts – had another interest in this whole deal: he liked my dad a lot and wanted him to marry his daughter Bariyahon.

So my dad finally began a career in the arts. Actually, at that time – he was 22 – he didn't even really know what it meant to be a director …

For quite some time he hid the fact that he was studying theatre and made everybody believe he was studying mathematics and science, like so many of his famous ancestors …

Love

My father Muzaffar was a tall, good-looking young man with blue eyes - quite unusual features for an Uzbek. I can imagine how lots of young girls would have been crazy about him … During his last year of studies, he finally met the girl destined to become my mother.

My dad said to me: "Imagine, it was a freezing cold winter day, and I was getting off a bus. It was really slippery, and I fell and bumped into a young lady. It was your mom! I told her how very sorry I was, and she just smiled in response! After that we parted. Even today I remember her beautiful smile", he would say. "I thought about her nonstop, and I really regretted that I forgot to ask her her name. I had no idea where to look for her!"

At that time, my dad's best friend Armugon was dating a girl by the name of Halima from the Pedagogical Institute. One day he asked Muzaffar if he wanted to go with him to see his girlfriend. "Can you imagine my surprise, when we entered the room and I saw HER next to my friend's girlfriend?! We both smiled like very old friends. Naturally, she remembered me, even though the accident had happened two months before. At that moment I was the happiest person in the world!" my dad would say. "It was love at first sight! I had never before seen such a beautiful girl in an Uzbek silk dress: starry eyes, white skin, and a long, long plait of hair arranged beautifully around her Uzbek cap."

But she was not easy to win over. She was a super-successful student – one of the few students who had been granted a Stalin Stipend – and she had a lot of admirers! Poor Muzaffar so wanted to ask her out to the movies ...! But it wasn't easy to invite her for a cup of tea or ice cream, not to mention asking her out to dance! Dad was a poor student at the time and every ruble he had was already allocated for something.

Mum graduated from college with excellent grades, and they offered her a grant to do her PhD in Moscow! Meanwhile, my dad was working on thesis, and they sent him to the city of Khorezm to produce a theatrical piece, which was very successful.

When my dad graduated, they offered him jobs in several places, including as a lecturer at his own College of Theatrical Arts. But he – at the age of 27 – was so full of excitement and energy that he wanted to try something new and different, so he chose the position of Director at the Bukhara Theatre in the city of Bukhara. Once located on the Silk Road, Bukhara (which means "lucky place") boasts a rich cultural, intellectual, and religious history that stretches over five millennia. Today it is the fifth largest city in Uzbekistan.

So there my parents were in 1954: they had fallen madly in love, but found themselves far apart from one another. Mum was studying in Moscow, and dad in Bukhara. Over the course of the next couple of years, he was very successful and toured a number of cities in Uzbekistan and neighboring states with his theatre.

During the Soviet period, every student had to work for three years after graduation wherever the "government and party" sent them. Only after that was a person allowed to choose their own career path. So after three years in Bukhara, my dad returned to his home city of Tashkent.

My Mother Dinara

My mother Dinara was born in 1929 in the provincial capital of Kokand, a city located in the Fergana Province in Eastern Uzbekistan, which dates at least back to the 10C.

My mom was half Uzbek and half Bashkir. Her mother was a specialist in agriculture from Bashkiria who was sent to work in Uzbekistan, where she met her husband in Kokand.

Later you will understand why I am describing my mom's ethnicity in detail. My mom was a talented student, so she was sent from Kokand to study in the republic's capital, Tashkent. When my dad met my mom, she was studying pedagogy and physiology.

My dad and mom didn't have a lot of opportunities to see one other. When my mom was in Tashkent, she was 5-7 hours by train from my dad Bukhara, and it was expensive for my mom to go there - even as a student. As a young specialist, my father had to spend a lot of time on his new job and didn't have much vacation. Despite all of this, they tried to take advantage of every opportunity to see each other.

My mom was obviously a talented student, because after graduating, she was sent to Moscow to do her PhD. As Moscow was the capital of the USSR, it was very prestigious to study there!

During the Soviet period, Russian was the official language of the Soviet Union. To be able to study at a good university or have a career, you needed to know Russian well, but since my mom grew up in a provincial city, she did not know Russian at all. She always told me how hard it was for her to study in Russia. She would often spend more than 12 hours at a time at the Lenin Library, the biggest library in the country. She wanted to be the best student there, just as she had been in Uzbekistan. Sometimes she felt faint from too much studying and because she was always hungry.

It was very typical for Soviet students to be in this condition. Even though they usually got small stipends from the government, they always had money problems. The food at the school's "stolovaya" (student cafeteria) was not very expensive, but students tried to save their money for other things, like books, clothes, and transportation.

During the three years she spent in Moscow, my mom was never able to visit my dad. My dad managed to visit her a couple of times, because he was already a young professional earning his own salary. The cheapest way to get from Tashkent to Moscow was by train, but it took four days in one direction!

My dad decided to make a surprise visit to Moscow for my mom's graduation. He organized a graduation party, secretly invited all her friends and professors, and bought her beautiful flowers. Then he entered the classroom when she was in the middle of her thesis defense. Can you imagine how surprised she was?! I am pretty sure that at that moment she was the happiest woman in the world! After the party, my mom's friends told my dad that she had been dreaming of a graduation party, but couldn't afford one.

My mom got a job as a professor at the local university in her hometown of Kokand. Once again, my parents were far apart from one other: she was in Kokand, and he was in Bukhara. In a couple weeks my dad would have his first premiere, and my mom knew how important it was for him. She told her friend Zhenya, who she knew from Moscow, and who was now teaching in Bukhara, "Now it's my turn to surprise him!" Zhenya bought front row tickets for the premier, as my mom had asked. When my dad came on stage and the performance began, my dad suddenly saw my mom sitting in the first row. He was very surprised and amazed! What a beautiful smile on her face! At that moment they both realized that they needed to be together!

But it wasn't easy to do. You have to understand the Soviet system, where everything was decided for you. When you graduated from the university, the government would choose your job for you. The government would decide where to send you, and you had no right to say "no", otherwise you wouldn't get your degree.

My dad always wanted to go back to Tashkent, because his entire family was there and because my mom, as a talented

19

specialist, had better chances to have a successful career there. They decided to do everything they could to move there.

For my dad it was easy to get a job in Tashkent. In 1956, a new project was underway to create an Uzbek philharmonic theatre, and they needed a young professional to lead it. My mom, on the other hand, faced a lot of problems; the dean of Kokand University was proud to have my mom on the faculty and didn't want to hear about her decision to leave.

The second biggest problem - if not the biggest - was my grandma. Dinara was her only child, and she was dead set against this marriage. My grandma's dream son-in-law was a scholar like her daughter. She didn't consider my dad's profession serious. He was an actor! How could her daughter, who got her PhD at the best university in the Soviet Union, marry some actor?!

Dinara was a very popular candidate for marriage in provincial Kokand. A lot of young men were dreaming of marrying her. The candidates included the director of a big factory, young scientists, and other young men from respected families. Who was my dad, but a stranger without a serious profession?

Marriage

After moving to Tashkent in 1956, my dad had two jobs. He was teaching at the university and working as a producer at the Tashkent Show Theatre. With money saved up from his job in Bukhara, and full of enthusiasm, he began building a house in Tashkent. And guess what? He built the house on the same land where his family's summer residence had once been located. In accordance with Soviet-era standards, the land had been subdivided into smaller parcels, but nonetheless, he got about 350 square yards for a small house with a small garden.

Like most houses in Tashkent, ours is built of brick in the traditional style: clay mud mixed with straw and formed into bricks, then dried in the plentiful sunlight. Once the brick walls have been erected, they are plastered with a layer of the same clay mud, so that even when an earthquake strikes, these houses don't completely fall apart– they just crack here and there. My own father made the thirty thousand bricks for our house himself!

Finally, in October 1957 my parents were married! They celebrated the event first in Kokand, then in Tashkent. And what a wedding they had! Through his work at the theatre, my dad had a lot of artist and musician friends, all of whom wanted to perform at his wedding. Many of them were very famous, like the dancer Mukaram Tugunbayeva and classical musician Mamurjon Uzoqov. Such a wedding hadn't been seen in Tashkent for a long time!

The celebration took place outside our not-quite-finished house, and my mom was freezing, so she had to wear a heavy overcoat. The weather in Tashkent was unusually cold that day - even the water froze. Luckily, no one slipped on that happy day!

A very tiny and weak little baby, I was born on May 6 of the following year. At that time of year, green apples and apricots start to appear. Now everybody tells me that that's why my brown eyes have a greenish color.

Chapter 3.

Childhood

Musical Theatre and Television

At the age of 30, my dad was the Principal Director of the New Musical Theatre.

In 1957-1958, he helped organize a new tour of Uzbek performances to various cities around the Soviet Union. It was the tradition at the time to have programs with elements of different ethnic cultures representing the various regions of the Soviet Union. Organizing the "Week of Uzbekistan" in Moscow was especially important for my dad's career. He wanted to create something completely new and hitherto unknown to Uzbek culture …And there was not much time, so he worked day and night to make this a groundbreaking event for Uzbekistan, for his theatre, for its ensemble, and for the spectators in the nation's capital!

One of the main elements of the show was a troupe of 40 dancers. Although my father was not a choreographer, he was the one who made the major decisions regarding the repertoire, the costumes, and the cast. Even the show's name, "Bahor" (spring), was his choice.

The careers of many talented and now well-known young artists started - or got a major boost - from working with my dad on this program. Musicians like Kahramon Dadayev, Bahtyor Aliyev, the drummer Nozir, and the composer Muhamadjan Mirzoyev were members of this group.

Most of the dance performances were later named for my dad's three daughters. The first famous dance from the "Bahor" program was named after me – "Dildora" – and is being performed today. It is quite popular!

23

Qunduz Mirkarimova, one of the famous dancers from that show and my father's good friend, performed one of the new dances on TV in late 1958. The melody reminded my dad of an Azeri song and an Azeri girl by the name Gulnoza, who he had studied with in the university. That's why he named both his newborn second daughter and the new dance "Gulnoza". Miss Mirkarimova became very famous thanks to this dance and performed it many, many times.

The most important element of the new performance was the music. Pop music as we understand it today did not exist in Uzbekistan; nevertheless, my dad and his friends managed to create something for everybody...

Many superstars of Uzbekistan, as well as of the Soviet Union, were "born" during the preparation for the "Week of Uzbekistan" in Moscow, including Klara Jalilova, Botir and Luiza Zakirov, and Junus Turayev!

After this tour, my dad worked for the newly created Uzbek TV station. He liked the concept of working in real time, as well as innovation, daily updates, and new technology. The biggest part of his career was television. His focus has always been the culture and traditions of Uzbekistan.

The Earthquake of 1966

A key moment in my life and the life of my city was The Big Quake.

On April 26, 1966, Tashkent was hit by a strong earthquake (7.5 on the Richter scale). Aftershocks shook the city for months.

I remember vividly how I woke up very early in the morning - between 5 and 6 am. Outside I saw a glow, as though the city around us was in flames. I was sleepy and had a hard time understanding what that glow could be: was it an unusually bright sunrise or were sparks flying from electrical wires? And then there was this grumbling underground. It sounded like a lot of heavy bombers were flying at a low altitude. We children decided a war had broken out, and we all ran outside. It was a very chilly morning; all our

24

neighbors were there, barely dressed, most were wrapped in blankets. There was terror in everybody's eyes …

The city's center lay completely in ruins, and most houses and buildings were flattened. I saw one house still standing, but one of the walls missing, so you could see the inhabitants' entire lives in front of you. At night they tried to cover the open side of the house with blankets.

Thousands of people had lost their homes. The city was transformed into a giant tent camp.

We moved out of our house, which was actually intact, but for safety reasons we stayed outside as much as possible, because the aftershocks continued for a long time. Luckily, spring was approaching, so it was pretty warm and sleeping outside was possible. I remember that we children got very used to this situation and to camping outside. Whenever we were inside, we would listen carefully to what was going on outside. When the domesticated birds and animals started making terrified noises, we would run out of the house. The peacocks, in particular, would screech like cats. For some miraculous reason, these creatures could feel the shocks coming long before we humans did! Later, we stopped running out at the first sound of an animal screeching and instead, would watch our ceiling lamps sway. Only when the swaying reached a certain intensity would we interrupt our dinner and run … I don't know why, but it seemed to us that the aftershocks mostly occurred towards evening.

By the way, on one of the nights that we spent outside, I suddenly woke up and felt something stinging and moving in my ear! My parents and I panicked, and they rushed me to the emergency room. There they carefully rinsed my ear, and out came an insect similar to a June bug. Then they plugged my ear with cotton. OK, everybody was relieved and off we went.

But suddenly the stinging resumed, and I started crying again. My parents ordered the ambulance to turn around, and again we were at the emergency room. Again they inspected me and guess what: they discovered another creature in my ear – this time, an ant! The doctor could not believe that two cases of insect intrusion into the same ear occurred on one night! Or did the ant get in when they were plugging my ear with cotton?

The Soviet state wanted to use the earthquake to show the whole world how well "friendship" worked in our country. Suddenly Tashkent became international; there were workers and volunteers from Russia, Ukraine, the Caucasus, the Baltic States, and even Finland. A project called "The Construction of the Century" was launched, and within a few months, new buildings had appeared on the empty lots. Complete cities within Tashkent, like Chilanzar, emerged.

They created a "model Soviet city" with wide, shady streets, parks, fountains, monuments, enormous plazas for parades, and armies of apartment blocks. By 1970, about 100,000 new homes had been built, many of which were filled by the workers, many of whom had settled in Tashkent with their families.

The city was already quite international even before the earthquake. With people from 98 different nations and ethnic groups living in Tashkent, what ethnic group wasn't represented? One could easily have called Tashkent "Noah's Ark". It was normal to find Armenians, Jews, Greeks, Tatars, Uyghurs, Koreans, and other ethnicities here. We knew some words - or even entire phrases - from many of those languages, because people were talking in their native tongues at home with their families. There were also many different kinds of Jews: Ashkenazi, Bukhara, Gorski, Crimean, etc. Ultimately, Tashkent was becoming the "Tower of Babel".

Within a year after the earthquake, the city outgrew its borders, and entire new neighborhoods with high-rise apartment buildings appeared. We used to call these new neighborhoods "Russian towns", because we Uzbeks had never lived in multi-storied buildings.

At the time of the collapse of the Soviet Union in 1991, Tashkent was the fourth largest city in the country, and a center of learning in the fields of science and engineering.

Thanks to the 1966 earthquake and Soviet redevelopment afterward, very little is now left of Tashkent's ancient history, including the traces of its significance as a trading center on the historic Silk Road.

The entire country stepped in to help Uzbekistan during those tragic days. Many children from Tashkent were invited to summer camps and scouting camps in the best parts of the Soviet Union! I was among those who got to spend their summer in a camp near Moscow.

The preparations for my departure were rather hasty, and they quickly got me (a girl!) a rucksack for my travels! It was a hardy khaki-colored military rucksack, which only a Soviet soldier could have hauled on his back. I was very ashamed to walk around with it – or even to be seen standing next to it. But this big ugly rucksack was just the beginning of all my troubles and adventures ...

On the plane from Tashkent, the children around me were anything but Uzbek; instead, they were Russians, Jews, Ukrainians, and Armenians. I turned out to be in the minority! Soviet solidarity was intended to help the suffering Uzbeks, but perhaps because of their traditionalism, few Uzbek families wanted to let their children go to summer camp in Russia! Or maybe ordinary people didn't even know about this opportunity for their children, and it was only members of the local "Soviet nomenklatura" who had quickly figured out ways to mix in with the "suffering crowd" and send their children.

On the bus I already felt that everyone - the other children and the Russian caretakers alike - looked down on me. How in the world did this Uzbek girl show up among these select few, and – to top it off – with this ugly rucksack! Their arrogant attitude towards me did not change the entire month.

It was the first time in my life that I was separated from my parents for a lengthy period of time.

On the bright side, I recall that our camp was near the edge of the woods, and every day I anxiously waited for the breakfast to be over so I could go for walks or play games in the woods. For the first time in my life, I experienced miles and miles of green fields and endless, dense forests. These were things I had only known about from movies and fairytales. How fragrantly the pine trees smelled, the moss, the flowers…there were so many new aromas. And how frightful, how terrible the woods looked: at any moment bears or wolves could appear! Best of all I liked the flowers. One was called "Ivan & Maria" because of its two-colored petals; there were also "True Blue Clocks" and "White Chamomile"… How I wanted to dive into the fields of flowers! Later as a child, I would always draw fields of flowers, pine forests, and orange squirrels. My most favorite motif was the woodpecker. He was such a strange fellow: brightly colored, walking up and down the trees, and knocking the hell out of them with his persistent head!

That summer in Russia a whole new world opened up for me. A new understanding of nature, new smells, the color of the endless Russian fields … The impressions of those days are still very alive in my memory. Later in my life, when we lived near Moscow, I looked for those places, those landscapes, and the images from my childhood, but I could not find them.

There were Russian children from Moscow in the camp. They were friendly and curious, and asked a lot of questions about Uzbekistan, our customs, and our traditions. One weekend, the parents of one of the girls from Moscow came to visit and invited me to their house in the city. What a nice gesture! I gladly agreed to go with them for a day.

Moscow! High-rise buildings everywhere, thousands of cars and millions of people!

The hosts treated me to sweets I never had seen in Tashkent. Such bright and colorful candy wrappers! To this day I remember the taste of those candies: caramelized corn or nuts. Later as an adult I looked for those candies in Moscow, but I never found them again.

I loved talking to Muscovites. I loved their curiosity, and I loved the interesting way of life in the capital city. Compared to the provincial upper-class kids from Tashkent, Muscovites were open-minded, educated, and – most important of all for me – not so arrogant and snooty.

Back to reality: One of the Russian girls from Tashkent envied me because I had local Russian friends and was popular with them. Her name was Tanya, and one day she falsely accused me of stealing. I got blamed and punished for a theft I had not committed! What an injustice! I immediately demanded to be sent back home to Tashkent. When I faced that girl back home in Tashkent, I believe she was thoroughly ashamed of what she had done.

The parents of my girlfriend from Moscow came to say farewell and even offered to let me stay with them for the remainder of the summer break, but I was so deeply insulted that I refused. What a sad ending to an otherwise wonderful time in summer camp.

School

I started school in September 1966 at the age of 7.

By then I was already very different from the other girls in my neighborhood. My parents sent me to a specialized school where English was taught starting in first grade. This school was located in downtown Tashkent, and I had to take a bus and a tram to get there, which took almost an hour each way. The school was considered the best in town and people called it "the English school". My parents wanted their first child to receive a well-rounded, top-notch education. And thus, I ended up being the only Uzbek among children from Russian, Ukrainian, and Jewish families, who considered a good education very important and prestigious. On top of all this, I was to take violin lessons at the best music school in town! But why music, why violin? Didn't my parents know that I totally lacked a musical ear?? Didn't they know that an Uzbek girl was not supposed to become a famous musician?? The only thing everybody knew, I guess, was that a violin is more prestigious than a piano.

However, here I was travelling miles across town to one of the most beautiful buildings in Tashkent, the former mansion of the Russian Governor of Turkestan, then called The Palace of Prince Romanov! During the 19th century the Grand Duke Nikolai Romanov, first cousin of Tsar Nicholas II, was banished to Tashkent for some illegal dealings. His palace in the city center has housed a museum, a school, and, now, the reception hall of Uzbekistan's Ministry of Foreign Affairs.

My school was located in a large, older Stalinist-era building, constructed in Socialist Classical Style with high ceilings, big

29

windows, and a number of pretty impressive Greek columns. This mass-produced architectural style became a status symbol, so that every self-respecting Soviet town insisted on having one. Our classrooms were big.

There were three first grade classes, 1A, 1B and 1V (the Russian alphabet goes: A, B, V, G, D …)

I was in 1V along with about 20 other students. My desk was in the middle of the second row. They put me next to a Russian girl by the name of Natasha, and the two of us sat at the same desk in the same spot through 8th grade!

Unlike in America's schools, in the Soviet Union, students stayed together in the same class and followed the same schedule. There was no individually tailored curriculum, as in the US, where each student follows his or her own path. Regardless of our individual capabilities and needs, we were all stuck together and had to learn the same material, which was prescribed by the Ministry of Public Education. Nobody in the communist system cared about your individuality or your personality with its specific strengths and weaknesses. Instead, you had to be like everybody else, and not differ in any way. Otherwise, no High School diploma for you!

By the end of high school, everybody had to know the basics of calculus, although only a few of us, if any, would need it later on in life. It seemed to me that the majority of my classmates were more inclined toward the humanities, so you can imagine how hard it was for us and how we suffered from the pressure to learn math and science. But who cared? O Lord, how many lives have been "disfigured" by a system so invested in leveling us all to a single common denominator!?

In my class, the Jewish kids stuck out because of their exceptional abilities. It was obvious that their parents helped and encouraged them so they would be well-rounded. One girl by the name of Roufa was my good friend for many years. She was a straight A student. When we started learning the alphabet, she could already read and write. She was good in math, too. And naturally, she attended music school after school. She would also read pretty

30

advanced books, and I enjoyed her company and our interesting conversations.

Since my school was far away from my house, my parents "hired" a young man from the neighborhood to accompany me to and from school. Oh, how ashamed I was to have this poor fellow at my side and an ugly and bulky violin case in my hand! Oh, how I tried to avoid being seen by my classmates! I always ran a few yards ahead of the young man and convinced my parents that he should carry my "heavy" violin case. I told my classmates that I didn't know the fellow and that he just followed me around to impress me. I felt very bad for him and was very embarrassed by my behavior.

My violin teacher, a tall red-haired man by the name of Yosif Savelievich, repeatedly asked my parents, "Why do you torture your child? She has no ear for music!" I had a girlfriend who also hated violin lessons, and the two of us would often come up with various tricks and ploys to interrupt the lessons. Luckily, this torture did not last very long. Within a year, I was expelled from violin class. But then my parents wanted me to take piano lessons. It turned out, however, that it wasn't very easy to buy a piano in the Soviet Union back then! Then, when we were visiting my mother's hometown of Kokand on summer vacation, my parents spotted a piano for sale in one of the stores. They immediately bought it and had it transported 150 miles back to Tashkent. From then on, this huge black "chest" occupied one of the most honorable spots in our living room, and for many years it was the symbol of my sadness.

And so then not only I, but my two younger sisters had to study piano, too. It was not fun at all. It's not like in the US, where you arrive at your piano teacher's house, do a little *plim plim*, and leave the check, then off you go. No, Soviet music teachers were eager to make little Rostropoviches out of you - or at least little Van Cliburns. They were very strict and merciless. We had to attend piano lessons three times a week and – why?? Because on the weekends there were solfeggio musical theory lessons! I absolutely hated all this, because I did not understand it a bit!

When I was in second grade, I had to go to my teacher's house for music lessons, because she had a baby and preferred to teach from home. I went twice a week after school. Sometimes my classmate Katya, who lived nearby, came with me. And I clearly remember how, when there was some time left before the lesson (which happened a lot), I would go to her house to wait a bit. Just like that she would open the fridge and eat something right in front of me without offering me anything, not even a piece of bread. I knew that Russians had different traditions and didn't offer food to guests, but she should have known that after spending the day at school, I was just as hungry as she was. The same thing often happened at my girlfriend Roufa's house: she would quietly sit down and eat something while I would wait in the corridor. Even her mother and grandmother, who would witness the scene, would not offer anything, not even a cup of tea. So once again I realized that there are huge differences in our cultures. Uzbek families would offer their guests the best, most delicious food they had, rather than give it to their own children. Uzbeks have always been famous for their tremendous hospitality. One of our former neighbors liked to bake cakes, and every time she made them, she would share half of them with her neighbors. She really liked doing this and would always ask if they were good. After the earthquake, she moved to Moscow and tried to do the same thing there, but her gloomy and reserved Russian neighbors looked at her as if she were insane. Her son tried many times to explain to her that Russians don't do this, but she couldn't grasp this and would always respond, "We have to share our food with our neighbors just like we did in Uzbekistan".

Each time I entered my Uzbek friend's house to ask her to come out and play, her mom would give me a handful of raisins or nuts, or, when she didn't have any of those, she would give me a piece of bread. When you enter an Uzbek household, the hosts will always ask you "Choy ichasizmi?" ("Would you like a cup of tea?")

Hospitality is the most important law in Uzbek life!

So there I was, on my 30-minute walk along meandering narrow pathways and through empty overgrown lots to my piano lessons. Lord knows what dangers were lying in wait there for me, an 8-year-old little girl. Twice I escaped from some troublemakers by a miracle. What was the point of all this? For the sake of the "Dance of the Little Swans" by Tchaikovsky? I remember having to go outside to use the toilet during one of my lessons at the musical school. At the entrance, a man exposed his male organ to me, and I was scared to death. To this day I am still very afraid of walking through dark city streets. This fear and those memories will probably stay with me until the end of my life. Again, why was all this necessary? Why did we have to satisfy the whims of our parents? In the winter, when our living room wasn't being heated, I still had to sit at the piano and practice my lessons. Oh, how I wanted to sit in the warm family room with everybody else and watch TV, drink tea, or go outside to run around with the neighbor children. Oh, how I hated music lessons. I went through five years of torture and still did not become a great pianist. Only my parents were happy; they were vicariously living out their unrealized dreams through me.

The reason why they are so many famous Russian musicians today is that every other family sent their children to music school. This is still the case today!

Luckily, for all of first and second grade my father (or one of his assistants) would pick me up from school and bring me to the nearby TV studio, where my dad worked. This was apparently the only way to supervise me after school. So for an entire two years, I got to spend time at the TV studio. The first thing I would do was rush to the buffet with a "carte blanche" from my dad. The attendant had to satisfy all my requests. I was really hungry and would order everything on the menu, but it would turn out that I couldn't eat it all and had to call my dad for help. This got too expensive for dad, so later he changed the rules, and I was allowed only one modest dish, like sausage and green peas. Sometimes I would get a glass of lemonade and some pie for dessert. Ever since then, I hate sausage and lemonade! After lunch, I would sit down at the huge desk in my father's office and do my homework. Usually I "finished" it quickly and was then free to roam the studios, peering into every department and studio where different shows were being broadcast. The make-up and costume rooms were my favorites. After a while, everybody there knew me. One day the director of the children's department invited me to play a part in one of the children's programs, which was being broadcast live on the air! I was given the role of the daughter of a poor man who was being put in jail by his rich boss. When they carried that poor fellow away, I was supposed to "cry" loudly into the camera. But on the day the program was aired, I don't know why – maybe due to overexcitement or fear, instead of crying I laughed into that camera! And that was the end of my merry little career as an actress. My dad got a "great" critique from the director of the children's program …

I loved to venture out with my dad when they recorded various musical programs. Usually the video shoots took place in the prettiest parts of Tashkent: in parks, in front of fountains etc. Most of the programs were about Uzbek music and Uzbek dances. The first shoots were usually very interesting, but for some reason they would repeat them over and over again, and I got bored. It was only interesting when the dancers or musicians would try to get my attention and my dad's – by styling my hair in a fashionable way, telling me how much I looked like my dad and that I would have a happy life, etc. … Everybody wanted to get on my dad's good side so they could be on his shows as often as possible.

On one occasion, the famous ballerina Galya Izmaylova told my father that I had all the necessary ingredients to become a good ballet dancer and pointed out my "long, beautiful neck" to my dad. Oh, how I loved her for those compliments!! And hoped this compliment from a famous ballerina would inspire my dad to send to ballet school. It was my dream to become a ballerina! The best times of my childhood were when my dad took me to ballet performances and recordings! I imagined myself in a pretty tutu skirt and ballet slippers! I always tried to get as close as I could to the dancers and touch those beautiful ballet costumes and the ballet equipment. But to my great disappointment, every time I raised the question of ballet school, my father answered: No! I was an Uzbek girl, and Uzbek girls were supposed to do serious things, work in serious professions! Nevertheless, I begged and cried, and finally my parents promised me to let me attend the soon-to-be-opened school of figure skating!

But I had to wait for a long time: the figure skating school only opened when I was done with school.

Becoming a ballet dancer was one of my life-long dreams, but unfortunately, it was never realized!

One of the most fascinating things for me was music. I could spend hours watching an orchestra play and following the magical movements of the conductor's baton. It seemed to me that you didn't need anything more than that magic stick to create the most beautiful melodies. I decided that anyone in possession of the magic stick could be a conductor! So the only thing I wanted from Santa Claus was a magic stick for New Year!

By 3rd grade I was travelling across town between my home and school on public transportation. Once, on a cold winter "morning", my mother woke me up very early (as usual) and then went back to sleep. When I stepped out of the house and walked towards the bus stop, I realized something was wrong: there was nobody there! It was bitter cold, I was in rubber boots (we did not have good footwear back then), and after my first bus ride, I had to wait another 40 minutes for the tram. The adults around me looked all worried and sorry for me. They couldn't understand where I was going that early in the morning. My knees felt stony, my toes were hurting from the frost, and snow was falling nonstop. I walked alone down the empty streets and alleys. How great was my disappointment and confusion when I found the school was closed! It turned out I had been sent off to school several hours early. I had to turn around and walk back the same way I had come. My friend Rutha lived close to the school. Her parents were shocked to see me all alone at 5:00 am at their door! Thank God they realized I was freezing and offered me some hot tea. I sat there gulping the warm, sweet drink, unable to believe that a little earlier I been near death out there, all alone in the frost and snow.

How desperate and alone I felt in that moment! What anger I felt towards my mother who, without looking at the clock, had sent me, a 9-year-old girl, out into the cold! For her it was very important to get up and get to school on time; education and responsibility were very important to her. When I came home from school that day, she did not even ask how I managed. She did not apologize for mistakenly sending me off to school in the middle of the night.

On my way to school I often stopped at my friend Rutha's house; we would walk to school together, and we often walked back together after school. She was Jewish. We usually talked about something serious like a book she had read or last night's TV show.

Rutha was a really ugly girl and had a lot of pimples on her face. Even the pretty dresses she received from her relatives in the U.S. couldn't make her look good (Jews often received packages from relatives in Western countries.)

Besides the "khalat" (or robe) which we wore at home, we Uzbek girls had just two everyday dresses and one dress for holidays and special occasions. In the summer we wore simple cotton dresses, and in the winter, pale flannel ones. We had two types of school uniform for two different seasons. As to shoes: we had just two pairs, plus house slippers. That was pretty much it. We couldn't even dream of dresses from America!

The European Jews spoke Yiddish, but the Bukharan Jews spoke a dialect of Persian. I always felt uncomfortable when the parents or relatives of my school friends spoke in their native languages, which I didn't understand. There were reasons for me not to trust them completely. Recently, when I saw an old picture in a German castle entitled, "The killing of Christian children by the Jews", I was reminded of what I had been taught as a little child. My Uzbek relatives would perpetually warn us children not to get too close to Jews, and would tell us horror stories about their customs. The stories went like this: Every year before Passover, Jews would call non-Jewish children to their houses, lock them up, and feed them nuts and raisins. After feeding them for 40 days, they would put the poor children on a table with a linoleum tablecloth and start poking them with needles. Then they would use the drops of blood for the preparation of their matzah bread.

I was so impressed by these stories, that until I was 15, I never ate any of the matzah they offered me, and I felt uncomfortable when I visited my school friends and they spoke in their language. Maybe they were conspiring against me???

The custom I had been told about was called "blood libel." According to ReligiousTolerance.org, "blood libel" began as "an unfounded rumor in eastern England, that Jews had kidnapped a Christian child, tied him to a cross, stabbed his head to simulate

36

Jesus' crown of thorns, killed him, drained his body completely of blood, and mixed the blood into matzos (unleavened bread) at time of Passover."

The Bukharan Jewish community of Central Asia is extremely old and unique. Jews from the Middle East and Morocco came to Central Asia via the Silk Road and settled mainly in the areas of present-day Uzbekistan and Tajikistan. For centuries the Bukharan Jews have managed to preserve their identity and culture, in spite of oppression and persecution, as well as separation from the rest of the Jewish world.

After school, my girlfriends and I usually walked to the bus stop through a maze of small streets and ended up at the Besh Aghach Central Square. "Komsomol Lake", Tashkent's "Park of Recreation and Leisure", was located there. It was a real artificial lake!

All Soviet towns had "Parks of Recreation and Leisure"; they varied only in size. The layout was always the same, and the statues in them were always the same. There would sometimes be a statue of the writer Maxim Gorky, the writer Alexander Pushkin was always in the same thoughtful pose, and there was always at least one statue of Lenin. I hated all the statues and portraits of Lenin. Every town and village had one, every railway station and every airport had at least one, if not two, every official building had either a life-size statue, a bust, or both and above every desk of any importance you could see an oil painting of Lenin in a suit and tie. All over the country, the statues of Lenin were identical: either Lenin, hand in pocket, faced the world nonchalantly, or he stood with squared shoulders and a clenched fist, with one raised arm pointing into the distance. The images of Lenin were like those of Christ all over Europe. The significance of Lenin for the Soviet people was perhaps similar to the significance of Christ for people in other countries.

Parks of Recreation and Leisure were typical creations of the communist system. People could go to them on weekends, holidays, and in the evening to relax and have fun with the entire family. It was very pleasant to paddle around the lake in a boat – especially, as they say, on hot summer nights. However, I never managed to take a boat ride on that lake, either because it was considered too great a luxury to go out with the entire family or because Uzbeks just did not do that. In general, it was not customary for Uzbeks to relax and have fun with the entire family. The only form of entertainment Uzbek families practiced was visiting other families. The typical Uzbek family is big, with lots of aunts and uncles, brothers, sisters, and cousins … Just think of all the birthdays, weddings, childbirths, etc... In other words, there were lots of occasions to celebrate, and there was simply no time for cultural events, parks and the like, outside of the family and the home.

But I went to school with children from European families and always heard about their adventures in the parks. We had several parks in Tashkent: Pushkin Park, Gorky Park, and Thelma Park. For some strange reason, there was not a single park dedicated to an Uzbek celebrity. Obviously, the "Park of Recreation and Leisure" was a European concept. There were rides, small stages, music pavilions, carousels, ice cream kiosks, and cafés. In some parts of the park you could hear music being played, and people danced on open-air, fenced-in dance floors. I remember how once, when relatives were visiting from "the countryside", my parents decided to show off a little bit and went with us to a park. That was quite something! We girls got to dress up in new dresses and shoes! Tons of people were strolling along the paths in the park, showing themselves off and checking people out. Then we went to an ice cream shop and had a big portion each. They served the ice cream in little metal cups (not like the china at home!), and the ice cream seemed even tastier because of them.

Unfortunately, we were not allowed to use the giant swings. We were reminded that Uzbek girls don't do that and that we had to behave modestly.

Once my grandmother took me to the park at "Komsomol Lake," and we had "European Food." Not the standard Uzbek dishes which you could get on every corner and which we were tired of eating at home. For us, an exotic European meal was a simple meatball with mashed potatoes and green peas. Wow, plus a glass of terribly sweet lemonade called "Buratino", the Russian name for Pinocchio. At that moment, I felt like I was travelling abroad, and I knew I would brag about this trip to the neighborhood children who were never taken out anywhere. Uzbeks usually do not eat out, and eating at restaurants was expensive during the Soviet period. Imagine a 15-ruble restaurant bill on an average salary of 100 rubles!

Going to a restaurant also meant drinking alcoholic beverages and dancing, which Uzbeks did not do. The music in restaurants was loud, and some people danced while others were eating. Couples dancing in public is something very foreign for Uzbeks. We just perform our national dances, in groups, at weddings and other family occasions.

The Bazaar

How I loved to walk around our bazaars! We have the Shaykhantur, Farhad, Turkmen, and Hospitalny bazaars, and there is even a Russian bazaar, the Allayskiy Bazaar.

At Besh Aghach Square you could find one of the biggest markets, full of kiosks, stands, tents, and wagons. From every direction you could hear young men loudly shouting, "Posht! Posht!" ("Watch out!"), as they carried and transported goods. There was Uzbek music everywhere, a monotonous and wailing sound. You could watch artisans and craftsmen doing their work right there: smiths, carpenters, and potters … You could see storage chests of all sizes, with shining bands made of various metals. There were also traditional Uzbek cribs and beds ("beshek").

At the market you could find anything an Uzbek household would need for daily life: tablets, basins of all sizes, pitchers ("kumgan"), buckets … and thousands of "samovars" (Russian teapots). You could also see colorful handmade "suzani" (embroidered wall tapestries) hanging on wooden fences, as well as carpets & rugs made of wool, cotton, or silk. You could smell the bazaar as soon as you entered it! There were shish kebabs everywhere! And every Uzbek bazaar has dozens of eateries and food stands. You won't go hungry! You can have excellent food at any time! Shish kebabs, samosas, mantu, lagman…

You could watch the cook prepare incredibly long "lagman" noodles. Right in front of you, with quick, skillful movements, the cooks, mostly men, would whirl the dough around, transforming it into a very thin strands of dough. When Russians or people from other parts of the Soviet Union visited Tashkent and its bazaars, they felt just like they had walked into the fairy tale "1001 Nights." There were people of countless nationalities and ethnic groups, so it was like a modern-day Babel, as I mentioned earlier. You could buy fresh milk and dairy products from the Germans (the Volga-Deutsch...); Korean women would sell rice and spicy marinated vegetables like kimchi.

Each year in late April you could buy the first strawberries and yellow or red sweet cherries at the fruit stands of the Meskhet-Turks. Imagine the incredibly colorful spectrum of such ordinary items as dried fruits: raisins of all shades, from amber to dark red, yellow apricots, dark brown *uruk* cherries, anthracite plums ... And the colors of the bazaar would change depending on the time of the year. Towards autumn, they would turn to orange and yellow: the orange of persimmons and the red of pomegranates, cut open and on display so you could see their centers and sample them... the yellow of quinces, oh, so intense in smell ... Later, this aroma, the aroma of quinces, would haunt me, but neither in Europe, nor in America could I ever find anything as tasty and aromatic as the quinces in Tashkent...

Further on, there would be rows full of nuts, pistachios, and almonds in all varieties of refinement: salted, sugared, and honey-covered. After that, mountains of halva, gold-colored halva made from sesame seeds, and darker halva with poppy seeds or dried dark apricots ...

The way people bargain and haggle at the bazaar is a story in itself. Oh, the Uzbeks are great hagglers! It seems the ability to haggle is something Uzbeks inherit genetically. Starting in early childhood, my father would take me to the Kukcha Bazaar in our neighborhood and teach me how to bargain. Without this skill, he didn't think a woman could survive in this world. As soon as you would enter the bazaar, you would hear the merchants shouting, "Come closer, I'll give you a low price! It's all from our home garden..." There were all kinds and pitches of voices: tenor, baritone, bass. The stronger voices would outshout the elderly and the women.

There would be voices shouting from all sides. Some merchants would be standing in front of mountains of watermelons, others would be sitting in their carriages with honeydew melons. There were many different kinds of melons, and I was amazed at how my dad could tell one from another. Depending on who you were and how you looked, the merchants would address you as follows: "Qyzymkha" ("little daughter"), "Holadjon" ("auntie"), or "Amakidjon" ("uncle"). If you looked Russian, they would add a Russian accent to their speech, which sounded so funny! The best way to get a lower price as a customer was to pretend that you were leaving and the items in question were not interesting to you. Or you could say, "Give me a lower price, and I will take a lot of them!"

The best thing, of course, was to address them in Uzbek; they would immediately see you as one of them. Since I looked different from a typical Uzbek, everybody was usually surprised when I spoke in pure, fluent Uzbek. The merchants would comment, "Look at how well this Russian girl speaks our language!"

The first advice my dad gave me was to go around the entire bazaar and find out what the prices were. Then you were supposed to approach a merchant with relatively low prices and offer him half his price. If the merchant refused, you were supposed to turn around and pretend you were leaving, and then they would give in and sell you the goods at your price. What could they do? "There is so much competition here," my dad said. His advice helped me so often later in life.

One of the central bus stations was located on Besh Aghach Square, along with the big bazaar. Busses would leave from there to go to all corners of Uzbekistan. One of the most important things for me at the Besh Aghach Bus Station was the dozens of kiosks where all sorts of "pirozhki" were sold. The Russian word "pirozhki" means "small pies". They can be filled with fish, cottage cheese, jam, cabbage, mushrooms, chopped hard-boiled eggs, or meat. These pies are served alone or with soup at lunch. My favorite was piroshki with liver! As they were the least expensive ones, I could buy more of them for the little money I had! My parents didn't spoil me with pocket money.

One Glass for Everybody!

And there was "gazirovka," the refreshment for everybody: sparkling water in mobile water tanks with syrup dispensers. They would pour some syrup from a huge upside-down glass cone into your glass and then top it off with sparkling water from the tank. I usually chose the dark red syrup for my lemonade, but you could also choose plain sparkling water, which cost you just one kopeck! Flavored drinks, i.e. lemonades, cost four kopecks, and quite often when you paid with a 5-kopeck coin, they would not give you the one kopeck in change. Elderly people, sometimes couples, would operate these refreshment stands. I remember how some of them talked among themselves in a strange foreign language. Later I realized that it was Yiddish.

About Hygiene

They had a funny system for washing the glasses: they placed them upside down on a sprinkler system with 2 rings of sprinklers. A turn of the handle, and the glasses were sprayed clean with fresh water. It took just a few seconds, that was it. And surprisingly, the glasses were always clean! And no one got sick! Imagine how many people used these glasses during the day, and they used plain cold water for cleaning! Later, the human-operated stands were replaced by vending machines and sadly, it was often impossible to use them because the glasses had disappeared.

Samovars

Even today, samovars are considered an integral part of any Uzbek household. They are used to boil water for tea.

The Russian word "samovar" means "self-boiler". A samovar is a metal vessel which you fill with water. Samovars are made out of a wide variety of metals: copper, brass, and even silver. In Uzbekistan, our samovars were usually made out silver or nickel. Sizes and designs varied, from "40-pails" (400 liters or 100 US gallons) to 1 liter (1 US quart) in size, from cylindrical to spherical in shape, from plain iron to polished brass to gilded in finish. Samovars come in different body shapes as well: they can be shaped like urns, craters, barrels, cylinders, or spheres. A typical samovar

42

consists of a body, a base and chimney, a cover and steam vent, handles, a faucet and key, a crown and ring, a pipe, chimney extension, and cap, a drip-bowl, and a teapot. The pipe is filled with solid fuel to heat the water in the surrounding vessel. A small (6 to 8 inches) smokestack is put on top to ensure airflow. After the fire is put out, the teapot can be placed on top of the samovar to be warmed by the hot air passing through. The teapot is used to brew the "заварка" ("zavarka") - strong, concentrated tea. The tea is served by diluting the concentrated tea with "кипяток" ("kipyatok") - boiled water - from the main part of the samovar. Samovars are particularly well-suited to tea drinking in a communal setting over many hours. The Russian expression "to have a sit by samovar" means to have a leisurely talk while drinking tea from the samovar. This is similar to the German "Kaffeeklatsch" and Turkish Nariel culture or (superficially) the Japanese tea ceremony.

New School, "Internationalism", Russian Superiority.

When I was in 4th grade, a state committee found out that my school was in disastrous shape. Then there were rumors that they were planning to build us a new building in a more central part of the city. There were even rumors about us getting our own swimming pool… And so starting in 5th grade, I had to commute to the new school, which was located behind the Allay Bazaar. In connection with the move to the new building, my class became even more Europeanized. One new classmate spoke English fluently. He was of a Macedonian background and had lived in Australia. Who would come from Australia to live in Uzbekistan?? Moreover, our new teacher, who had also just arrived from somewhere in Russia, also spoke fluent English, so we had the rare opportunity to listen two people conversing in perfect English! But Lidia Mikhaylovna – our new teacher– was a very arrogant woman who made no secret of the fact that she was not thrilled that they had sent her husband, a military person, to Uzbekistan, rather than to a more central place in Russia. Unfortunately, her attitude towards us locals was typical: she looked down on us, which meant most of all me, as I was the only Uzbek in the class. She even did not notice my existence. It did not matter how well I performed and how well I prepared for tests - I always got Cs. Just because I was a local. To be a local to the Russians meant I was a second-class person.

Back then, a lot of political and military leaders from the "center" (Moscow or Leningrad) were sent to the "periphery". Officially, power in the Soviet Republics was exercised by local people or by the local Communist Party organization. But in fact, the true high-level authorities in the satellite republics were Russians. The first secretary of the local Central Committee was always a representative of the local ethnicity, but the second in charge, the secretary of ideology, was a Russian, and he had the real authority. A similar scenario existed in the Soviet Army: the people serving in any given place in the Soviet Union did not belong to the dominant ethnic group there. Uzbeks did not serve in Uzbekistan. Georgians did not serve in Georgia. Ukrainians did not serve in Ukraine. The reason was very simple: should it ever become necessary to use military force against the local population, it would be far more difficult and dangerous to order Armenian soldiers to shoot Armenians, than to have this job done by Georgians or Azeris. Moreover, a soldier who is not part of the local culture doesn't know the local language and the local mentality. This is how the Russians kept control over the Soviet republics.

Like other empires, Russia exploited her peoples politically and spiritually. Even though officially the Soviet republics were called "sisters" and said to be equal, we were never equal. The consequence of not being Russian was officially sanctioned discrimination in education, politics, professional life, and so on. The ethnic minorities of the Russian Empire, especially in central Asia, found their cultures, their sense of national identity, and their ways of life being destroyed. In Uzbekistan, as in other republics, the local history dating back to the period before the October Revolution simply wasn't taught. Of course, before the Revolution in Central Asia, almost everyone was illiterate. Thanks to Lenin's ethnic policies, elementary and secondary education was conducted in both the local language and Russian, as were newspapers, magazines, books, radio and television programs. Film studios produced movies directed by local directors based on scenarios written by local writers. And there was 100% literacy in Uzbekistan.

But Russian control over the republics was total, as it had been in czarist times.

The Russians have never tried to respect or understand different cultures. Both the USA and the Soviet Union were multi-cultural societies, but with huge differences. Different peoples came to the US from other places, whereas the majority of peoples in the Soviet republics were natives, locals. It is one thing to deal with racial, religious, and cultural prejudices in a country of newcomers, where people have broken with their roots and started a new life; it is a very different issue to deal with people who have lived side by side for centuries, fought against one another, and whose cultural stereotypes are set in the cement of history. The former is what is called a melting pot. The immigrants who came to the US were thrown into a melting pot and came out as Americans. In the Soviet Union, the nationalities problem was never resolved.

There are many reasons for what some consider to be the totally unexpected eruption of nationalism after the collapse of the Soviet Union, and one had to do with the lack of cultural understanding consistently demonstrated by Russia. I remember how Leonid Brezhnev, the general secretary of the Communist Party, announced in 1972 the birth of a new historical group of people, the Soviet People. Instead of acknowledging, diagnosing, and resolving the nationalities problems, slogans about "the eternal friendship and brotherhood of the Soviet peoples" were proclaimed everywhere. Centuries-old ethnic divisions, which were rooted deeply in the hearts and minds of millions, were intensified by Stalin's deliberate divide-and-conquer tactics and the stupid economic policies of the Brezhnev period. The hurts festered and bled beneath the surface. So when *glasnost* took the lid off, they exploded with a special fury and violence.

The Russians always believed that they were the supreme race and were worth emulating. In reality, we hated all the Russians living in our country. They were so arrogant. For example, the Russian newcomers worsened what was already a bad housing shortage. Local people who had had to wait for years for new apartments saw themselves pushed even further back in line by these invaders. To make things worse, the Russians made no effort to learn the local language. They never respected our culture, and my classmates frequently laughed at Uzbek music. They would always say with arrogance: "We Russians had to come here because the local people were very backward. The Uzbeks needed education, science, engineers, and doctors, and they could not provide for themselves, so they asked us Russians to come and educate them and help them develop a new way of life." They behaved like colonists! That is why most Uzbeks hated them; even my parents prohibited me from speaking in Russian, the language of the infidels, at home.

Cotton and the Aral Sea Tragedy

The Russian colonial approach was most apparent in Soviet Central Asia. They transformed Uzbekistan into a cotton-growing appendix to Russia. Cotton rules supreme here.

Tremendously labor-intensive, cotton picking has been the job of women and children. Students were released from classes from September through December and from March to April to pick cotton. The cotton "plantation" occupied over three million hectares of land on which fruit, vegetables and grain could have been grown. Soviet agricultural policy even led to the destruction of the incredibly beautiful and bountiful Fergana Valley, which was famous for its delicious apples, figs, and pomegranates. It was the most fertile land in all of Central Asia, and before the October Revolution it fed the entire region.

Moreover, the beautiful and unique Aral Sea region was turned into a place of disease and death. Once one of the four largest lakes in the world, the Aral Sea is now one-tenth of its original size thanks to Soviet irrigation projects. The fishing industry which once prospered on the Aral Sea has been destroyed, leading to unemployment and economic loss. Moreover, pollution from the unrestricted use of fertilizers and pesticides has led to ecological problems and diseases, such as leukemia and sterility. Isn't this an obvious case of colonialism? And even though the Soviet regime, which caused the problems, is no more, the people of Uzbekistan are still suffering the consequences and must clean up the mess.

Child Labor!

It was and still is completely normal to see children working in the cotton fields. Just look at the headlines of newspapers and news agency reports about Uzbekistan from back in the Soviet time. And the same is true today:

- "Students and State Employees Are Deployed to the Frontlines of Cotton-Picking"
- "Exhausted Children Collect Cotton"
- "Every Autumn the Time Comes for the Students of Uzbekistan to Do Their Duty in the Cotton Fields"
- "Food Shortages, Cold, Dampness, and Hard Work from Dawn to Dusk - That's What They Get Instead of Their Legally-Guaranteed Education"
- "The People of Karakalpakstan, Including the Younger Students, Toil in the Fields, But All the Revenue from the Export of the 'White Gold' Will End Up In the Purses of People in Tashkent, While the Local People Suffer from Poverty"
- "In Qashqadaryo Province Everybody Is Forced to Pick Cotton, Even the Military"
- You Will Find Government Employees, Students of Universities, Colleges, and Schools in the Fields"

Even today cotton is one of Uzbekistan's most important exports. Nobody cares how it is being harvested. Why don't international organizations speak out about this? Why are companies buying Uzbek cotton today, despite the use of child labor and forced labor?

Mahalla

In school I sat next to Natasha, a very beautiful Russian girl. But she was sad all the time.

Her mother was divorced and worked as an accountant for our school.

Natasha often had bruises on her face. She told me that her mother and grandmother beat her for the slightest mistakes or for bad grades in school. They lived in the Chilanzar neighborhood, one of the areas of Tashkent that was built after the Big Earthquake of 1966. Mostly "Europeans", i.e. non-Uzbeks, lived in that area. Natasha was my "window" into that other world. Their way of life and relationships between people were totally different than what I experienced at home and in my Uzbek neighborhood. Girls could easily stay out late with their friends, and they could be friends with boys. In my world, the "mahalla," boys and girls were not even supposed to get close to each other. The word "mahalla" derives from the Arabic word "mahalli," which means "local". The *mahalla* is a centuries-old autonomous institution organized around Islamic rituals and social events. After the Soviet period, *mahallas* were regulated by law. They were also given the authority to oversee a range of activities within the territory of the *mahalla*. *Mahallas* are now organized as committees, with a chair who runs the day-to-day business and has administrative support. Although by law the *mahalla* committee's activities are supposed to be controlled by general neighborhood meetings, in practice, the administrative government authorities control their activities. Today key government officials participate in the repression of individuals and families that the state deems suspect. They cooperate with law enforcement and other authorities to gather personal information on members of the population. In breach of the right to privacy, family, and home, they keep files on those considered suspicious by the government, including "scandalous families" with disobedient children, and pass on this information to the police and the executive authorities.

In my *mahalla,* a girl and a boy could not be together. In the Russian neighborhoods, boys and girls simply played together, took walks in parks, went to the movies, and fell in love… I listened to Natasha's stories about her first rendezvous, her first kisses. Oh god, how I wished to be in her world and in her environment just for one day and feel like a free human being. In my world, all day long I was told that a Muslim girl must not have wild emotions, must not feel free, and must not feel any of the things I felt when I was listening to Natasha's love adventures. A Muslim girl does not make her own

48

decisions or seek control. She is trained to be submissive, humble, and docile... If you are a Muslim girl, you "disappear" until there is almost no "you" inside yourself. In Islam, you are not supposed to become an individual, and many people, especially women, never develop a clear sense of their own individual will. Instead, you submit. That is the literal meaning of the word "Islam", "submission".

The main goal of Uzbek parents was training their daughters to be quiet inside, so that you would never raise your eyes, not even in your thoughts, not even inside your mind. Despite this upbringing and despite the environment I grew up in, I knew I was different; something inside of me always resisted the Uzbek way of raising girls. There was always a small spark of resistance and independence in me. I was always rebelling against the traditional subjugation of Uzbek women. Although the Soviet Union had proclaimed the liberation of women, it didn't result in sexual liberation, but in an even greater form of patriarchy. Maybe this was a reaction to the stark contradiction between the behavior demanded by Uzbek families and actual daily life in Soviet society. Even as a child, I could not comprehend or accept the downright unfairness of the rules, especially for Uzbek women. I couldn't understand Islam: how could women desire to be treated so unfairly? Later, as an adult, I got very angry at a religious ceremony when I heard the mullah saying that a woman's testimony is worth half that of a man's. I couldn't believe it!

Natasha and I were living in different worlds, although we were growing up in the same country and in the same city. In the society I inhabited during the day, people lived extremely openly, and there was equality between men and women. That society was extremely different from the culture I had to return to every day after school. Even though our country had declared itself anti-religious, in daily life things were different. In Uzbek families, Muslim traditions were very strong, and it was especially hard for women. Russian parents and Jewish parents developed the talents of all their children, boys and girls alike ...In Uzbek families, it was the opposite: talents would be suppressed ... ("it is against our culture, our religion").

49

I can vividly recall from my childhood the sight of elderly Uzbek women completely covered in their burkas, with thick, black, horse-hair veils covering a woman's entire face. Yes, in the 1960s you could still see women in burkas, which the Russian Bolsheviks had "torn off" women in Turkestan, freeing it from feudalism back in the 1930s. There was also the characteristic squeak of their Uzbek boots in rubber galoshes … The sight of this "object" coming at you with no eyes or any other visible features, plus that strange noise… It was a fear-inducing experience… I get the same feeling today when I see Arab women completely covered in black. In our country, the expression "dumping the veil" meant "becoming an emancipated woman". But in fact, although Uzbek women behaved in public as if they were emancipated, as soon as they entered their houses, they became subdued Muslim wives. I could never understand why, after 70 years of communist development and a policy of liberation and equality, it had proved impossible to eradicate the tradition of humiliating women in Muslim society. Uzbek women, like all other women in the Soviet Union, received a higher education, could have careers, became professors, actresses, etc. But as soon as they came home, they would put on their "burkas," which turned them back into submissive Muslim wives.

Islam under Soviet Rule

During the Soviet period, the government waged a war against all religions, including Islam. In the Central Asian republics, which were traditionally Muslim, the government persecuted those who continued to practice their faith by excluding them from government positions, branding them as nationalists, and even imprisoning and executing them. Thousands of mosques and religious schools were closed, their property was seized by the state, and books written in the Arabic alphabet were burned. Nonetheless, Islam was not completely eradicated from the region. Moreover, even where religious belief was successfully eliminated, the three main religious and cultural rites of circumcision, the religious wedding, and the Muslim funeral ceremony were still almost universally observed by Uzbeks. Many people also continued to celebrate the major Muslim festivals. So, for example, although fasting was rare during Ramazan, Eid al-Fitr, the Festival of the Breaking of the Fast, was commonly celebrated with an "iftarlik" ("fast- breaking party"). Friends and neighbors would send "iftar" ("fast-breaking food"), which was carefully prepared to ensure that it did not become "haram" (unclean). Many also attended the mosque for morning prayers during Eid al-Fitr. The Soviets attempted to replace some of these religious rituals with secular alternatives, such as civil weddings and funerals and agricultural festivals, which fell at the same time as traditional Muslim festivals. In addition, according to locals, "the Soviet government would always schedule the best TV programs during religious holidays." However, these efforts had limited success, and only among the more urbanized and Russianized Uzbeks. Perhaps more successful was the continuous atheist propaganda campaign, which students were subjected to at all levels of schooling. Courses on scientific atheism were mandatory, and students are asked to write papers on subjects such as "My Relationship Towards Religious Holidays and Towards Religion Itself." Apparently, if an essay were anything but antireligious, the student would be kept after school for a talk and asked to rewrite the paper. There would also be repercussions later, when he or she was applying for a job.

Ramadan

I remember how on religious holidays from far away you could hear the "karnai", giant pipe instruments, being played in the town squares. Along with that, from every direction you could hear – and even feel - the playing of the "doyras", Uzbek hand drums.

Certain foods were being sold everywhere:

- *Funtikmi* almonds

- Cotton Candy, which tickled our faces and melted away in our mouths like a sweet cloud

- Salty *kurt* (1-inch diameter balls made out of dried sour milk)

- *Parvarda* (Uzbek caramels)

- Roasted sweet corn

- Red rooster-shaped candies on sticks (our version of lollipops)

High above the ground there would be a tight-rope walker holding a pole for balance. He would wear black velvet pants stuffed into high soft boots and a sleeveless red velvet jacket with gold trim. He would walk high in the sky, waving his pole, then sit down on the rope, turn and do somersaults ...

Ramadan was also a month of family togetherness. The streets would be filled with people: big families on their way to visit relatives. There was feeling of unity and a deep sense of community.

Ramadan is the holy month of fasting. During Ramadan, observant Muslims refrain from eating, drinking, and engaging in sexual activity from dawn until sunset. Fasting is intended to teach Muslims about patience, humility, and spirituality. As I remember, only some of the old people would keep the fast, but they did so without praying. I think they did it more of out of sense of tradition than out of religious feelings. In those days, only a few old people would attend Friday prayer in mosques. We children were sure that the old people went to the mosque just to keep themselves busy. Usually after Friday prayer they would go to the *chaykhana* (tea houses) to talk. We were taught - and believed - that being religious was a sign a person was poorly educated and backward. For all the twentieth-century trappings of Soviet ideology - its scientific grounding and its claims of being objective and rational, in fact it was basically neither new nor modern, just a relic of an extremely ancient and primitive spirituality. Officially the Soviets abolished God; nobody could become a member of the Soviet Communist Party without being an active atheist. Lenin was our god. ... and our one and only religion ...?

I remember the "nikoh", the Islamic ceremony where you are legally bound to your spouse by the mullah. People would secretly invite an imam to celebrate the *nikoh*. Almost all Uzbek families did it, but they had to do so in secret. I am pretty sure that the government knew about it and just ignored it, because they knew that *nikoh* was more of a traditional thing than a religious one.

Similarly, during Ramadan my parents always went to the *Iftar*, the fast-breaking parties. People would cook the best Uzbek meals and treat their neighbors for *Iftar*. The "Hayit Palov" is one of the favorite dishes to make for *Iftar*. It's an extremely delicious meal made from lamb, carrots, and rice. *Palov* has to be eaten with your hands - actually your fingers. You form a little "spoon" with the four fingers of your right hand, scoop up a little pile of *palov*, move it to the rim of the big plate, and press it into a small ball, which can then be shoved from the "spoon" into your hungry mouth with your thumb. It requires quite some practice to learn how to do this without dropping a single grain of rice! You have to just put aside your sense of refinement and enjoy the *palov*! Often the host himself feeds the most honored guests with his own hands! On the plate of *palov*, it is customary to put some baked goods like "Bogirsoq" (plain donuts), "Hushtuli" (small bits of dough fried in oil and covered with powdered sugar), or "Chak-Chak" (bits of dough glued together in various shapes with honey).

I just loved to sample the sweets and treats sent by our neighbors. They were all different, as each family had its own special recipe. We loved the "religious" holidays, although we had no idea what they all were about. The most important thing for us children was to get dressed up and visit friends and family. And of course, we liked the money given to us by relatives, so we could go and buy sweets like roasted nuts and rooster-shaped lollipops.

Reading

As an Uzbek girl, I always felt like an outsider in my school. The teachers would make it clear that I didn't belong by openly disregarding me, and my classmates - through their arrogance toward me. I was different from everyone else not only during class, but even during breaks. Everybody else would discuss the TV programs or movies they had watched the previous evening, but I had nothing to add to these conversations because I hadn't seen the programs. In my family it was forbidden to watch Russian movies; they were considered immoral, as there was kissing and embracing on the TV screen. Those films taught nothing but debauchery. For me, watching TV was a luxury, and I was only allowed to watch kids programming on weekends for just one hour. My mother thought reading books was something holy. We children never sat around without doing something useful. Mom's favorite expression was: "Whenever you have a minute of free time, grab a book!" And so we read books our entire summer vacation!

The Soviets were great readers. They read everywhere imaginable: on the subway, on elevators, on buses, on trains, and in parks. By the age of 12, I had not only read all of Russian children's literature, but all of Western children's literature as well: Mark Twain's *Tom Sawyer* (actually all of Mark Twain's books), Rudyard Kipling's *Rikki-Tikki-Tavi*, Lindgren's *Pippi Longstocking*, Robert Stevenson's *Treasure Island*, Lewis Carroll's *Alice's Adventures in Wonderland*, *The Invisible Man* by H.G. Wells, Sherlock Holmes, works by Jerome K. Jerome and Charles Dickens... We were usually given long lists of books to read for our summer break, which lasted three months (from June 1st to September 1st). Of course, there was a lot of Soviet literature with tons of communist ideology on that list, but there was also Western European literature. We read a lot of American authors such as Mark Twain, Dreiser, Faulkner, Steinbeck, and Hemingway. Later when I told Americans that we had read all these authors in school, I found out that most of them had never read any of them. I am pretty sure that the average Soviet citizen knew more about American literature than the average American.

"Western Literature" was even a subject in our school curriculum during the 6th, 7th, and 8th grades. We read books, wrote essays on them, and even learned some excerpts by heart. For example, we knew parts of Goethe's *Faust*. As you can imagine, at 13 we did not understand much of *Faust*, Gogol's *Dead Souls,* or Tolstoy's *War and Peace*... How could we, at 14, understand much of this serious literature, when our hearts and minds were occupied with boys and fashion? I think they taught us Soviet literature because it was full of communist ideology, but why the western books? Maybe just to occupy our minds with something, so that we would not think of anything else and would not be interested in life abroad. This approach seemed to have worked.

The Happiest Childhood in The World

As a child I always believed the Soviet slogan about us being the happiest children in the world. Everywhere children were dying of starvation and by contrast, we had "the happiest childhood". We proudly became members of the "Young Octobrists" and "Young Pioneers" youth organizations. And we proudly wore little red star-shaped pins with the image of young Lenin as a curly-haired, blond boy. We all wanted to be like him. We were constantly told how talented he was, and how he started reading at 5! Oh, how many days of our happy childhood were spent learning verses and stories about Lenin by heart? Then, in 5th grade, we were thrilled to join the "Pioneers". Before that, I was always jealous of the kids who wore red kerchiefs, the badge of the Young Pioneers, around their necks. This organization was the Soviet equivalent of Boy Scouts and Girl Scouts.

On April 22, a beautiful sunny spring day - and Lenin's birthday - we were brought out onto Tashkent's Red Square dressed in our school parade uniforms. There we solemnly swore the "Oath of the Pioneers": to love the Soviet Union and to live, study, and fight according to the teachings of Lenin and the Communist Party. Then we were solemnly presented with our Red Kerchiefs... and at that very important moment a wasp stung me right by my eye! Could that have been a sign from above? Instead of celebrating this festive occasion, I had to return home with a swollen face and eye.

Still, deep in my heart, I was proud of my country.

Through the Young Pioneers, Soviet kids got their first practical instruction in the commandments of communism, the national religion. Ideology was strong in the Soviet Union. Of course, when they teach you day and night about how tainted capitalism is, about how people in other countries are suffering from unemployment, and about how children around the world are always hungry, you naturally become a patriot of your own country. The communists offered their people economic equality (everyone was equally poor!) and some stability and security. They also forced everyone to reject God, their own ethnic history, and their cultural traditions, and then replaced all this with an ersatz religion, communism.

We were offered hope in the future, a guaranteed ration of food, and steady advancement in our careers. In return for this, we had to demonstrate trust in the system, participate in all kinds of gatherings, and show that we were one of them. By no means could you show much of your personality.

As a member of the Pioneers, you had to go to a lot of meetings, where they would criticize students with poor grades, as well as individualists. Already at the age of 10 you could actually start your career as a chairperson of the Pioneers (in school) and later (in college) – of the Komsomol. The most talented children and young people would usually distinguish themselves in this way, and later they would become secretaries of the Communist Party. Any even slightly talented person would be co-opted by the system and kept busy. Outstanding, talented people were offered paths to realize themselves as industry leaders or political leaders, but only under certain conditions: You were made keenly aware by the powers-that-be that you had to be loyal to the system to reach those dizzying heights. If you served the system, everything would be good. I was an energetic person myself and was active in the affairs of the Pioneers.

Throughout my time in school, I was a Young Pioneer group leader, and I helped younger students in their activities and organized various events. I remember how on one occasion we as a group had to criticize a girl whose family was religious and who went to church regularly. The system actively persecuted churchgoers. Any unsanctioned interest in religion was perceived as a threat to public wellbeing. When I recall this event today, I feel sorry for the poor girl who had to suffer because she and her family were different. During the communist period even children had to "pay" for their failure to be like everybody. The Soviet State highly valued the use of public criticism. Yet they did not seem to understand how devastating constant regimentation was to children. Even children couldn't have individual interests. We could have hobbies, but we had them collectively. Hobbies were organized for Soviet children on a group basis by the State, through schools, unions, the Pioneers, and other organization like "Pioneer Houses". There were, for example, clubs for students interested in stamp-collecting, model airplanes, dance, archaeological and natural studies, camping, art and many other things. There was no chance for somebody to pursue a lone interest. And even if someone wanted to do so, they probably didn't have enough room in their overcrowded apartment for the necessary privacy to do so. And even if they had privacy, I doubt they would be allowed to use it.

Individualism was suspect in the Soviet Union and was seen as a form of dangerous self-indulgence, bourgeois mentality, and a lack of solidarity. All questioning of communist ideology had to be stifled at birth! Anything related to isolation was suspect.

In the early seventies I remember how Angela Davis visited our school. What an event! She was an American political activist associated with the U.S. Communist Party, the Civil Rights Movement, and the Black Panther Movement in the late 1960s through the 1970s. It was an honor to have somebody like Angela Davis in our school. To honor her we prepared a demonstration attacking the capitalist system in the US. Brainwashed by the Soviet media, we really believed that Angela Davis was the victim of the American system. We could not even imagine that in fact, she was being prosecuted for committing murder in the US. She was tried and later acquitted of involvement in the Soledad brothers' August 1970 abduction and the murder of Judge Harold Haley in California. Later I learned that it was not only we Soviet children who were mistaken about her; John Lennon and Yoko Ono wrote the song "Angela" for their 1972 studio album "Some Time In New York City" to show their support. Mick Jagger of the Rolling Stones wrote the song "Sweet Black Angel" in her support. The song was released in 1972 on the album "Exile on Main Street".

In those days, the Soviet media broadcast story after story about the downside of life in the United States: unemployment, homelessness, crime, police violence, poverty, discrimination, and drug abuse. I remember an unemployed man named Bill, who was shown on Soviet TV sitting near the White House protesting. For some reason, our people loved to follow Bill's fate. I remember how we discussed his life during breaks at school. All that was ideology. I imagine that the picture Americans got from their media about the Soviet Union at that time was not the most positive one, either. No doubt there were reports about dissidents, alcoholism, drugs, and corruption. When we were watching programs about the decline of capitalism, we would shout from every corner, "We live a better life than anybody!" But if you asked people how they knew – Had they gone there? Had they seen the US with their own eyes - they would answer, "Why travel there? It is crystal clear anyway! We just know!" And no one would question in return: "How do YOU know?" We were so brainwashed by communist ideology that we believed everything they told us.

At the age of 14, I joined the powerful *Komsomol*, "The Communist Union of Youth". I was quite determined to become a worthy member and wanted to take active part in its activities. If you were an active member of the *Komsomol*, all doors were open to you in the future. You could go to a good college, and a good job in industry or the government was guaranteed for you. Active *Komsomol* members had special privileges and priority for promotion. For example, during the early days of *perestroika*, when private enterprise was cautiously being introduced, the *Komsomol* was given special privileges in opening businesses, justified by the idea that they were giving youth better opportunities. At the same time, many *Komsomol* leaders joined and headed the Russian Regional and State Anti-Monopoly Committees. As a result, many *Komsomol* activists were given an advantage on the business ladder. Many oligarchs are former *Komsomol* leaders.

It was not easy to join the *Komsomol*. You had to have good grades in school and be well-educated politically. I remember how during the admission interview, which took place in the central committee's office in Tashkent, they asked me questions about the political situation in the world, and I had to properly blame the capitalist system for all the problems on the planet. We were so excited and emotional before that interview. I repeated the main bullet points from the organization's statutes. And in fact, not all of us were accepted as members on our first try. It was so embarrassing to get accepted only the second time around. Later I met former Soviet citizens in the West who claimed to not have been members of the *Komsomol*, but I think they were being disingenuous. There was simply no way of getting a high school diploma or a proper college education without being a member; nor would you have any reasonable future in the Soviet System. I tried to be very active; I was interested in politics and in my community. There was just no other way to be an active member of society. I was active in the international politics section. In fact, I was interested in everything international from when I was young. My favorite subjects in school were foreign literature and world history, and I had the best grades in geography. Back then I felt that in the future, I would see the world and the world would be open to me.

A Foreigner at Home

I have always been curious and attracted to new things. Of course, constantly being rejected by my own countrymen made me long for a place where I could feel comfortable. From early childhood I knew that I was not like everybody else. I hated going to visit Uzbek families and hearing them calling me "the yellow girl" ("Saruq"), which is how Uzbeks call anybody with fair skin. To be called "Saruq" (Yellow), "Ourys" (Russian), or "Tatar" was a deep insult in Uzbek society. That's how they called the infidels. People called me these names my whole life - when I was walking down the street or playing with children in my neighborhood... I hated walking along the streets of my *mahalla*, as I was always greeted with looks of hatred and mistrust. Uzbeks do not like any foreigners, even the Tatars. Even though the Tatars had always lived nearby, were our neighbors, were Muslim like us, were clean and orderly, and made the same delicious food. The only difference was that they were blue-eyed and fair-skinned. Maybe Uzbeks envied them for their looks. Envy often causes hatred... I never ever wore the traditional Uzbek dress, made of *atlas* silk, because people, including children, would ask the stupid question, "Who dressed this Russian girl in our national dress??" Oh, what names they called me as a child, because I had a fairer skin and light brown eyes? All the other children had darker skin and dark brown eyes. Once, when a neighborhood boy called me Tatar, I hit him so hard that I broke his skull. Most of the time, however, I did not respond to provocations or insults, such as being called names. I was above all that, and I believed that I would soon get away to a place where I wouldn't be a foreigner at home.

I despised all the Uzbek feudalistic traditions, the arranged marriages at a young age, and marriages among relatives. Marriages between cousins are very common and are often seen as the safest unions possible: they keep the wealth in the family, and any conflicts are quickly resolved by the couple's relatives. Since I attended a school with children from various backgrounds, I started hating differentiation by nationality or ethnic background early on. Even today it makes me furious when I hear people from the former Soviet Union talking bad, for example, about the Jews. It seems like an illness. It makes me angry, when I hear former Soviet people - now naturalized Americans – saying nasty things about African Americans. Where is the eternal friendship we were educated about in the Soviet Union? Why do people put themselves above humans from other nations?

I recall a conversation that took place when we were visiting relatives. Two of my aunts were talking about me with great concern: Who would take that poor fair-skinned girl as a wife? Will she ever get married at all ...? I was sure that even if there was an Uzbek man who was willing to marry me, I would never marry him because of his attitudes towards women. I always admired my father for treating my mother respectfully and honorably, and addressing her in the plural (polite) form of you. He always cooked meals for us, knowing that mother had to work a lot and did not have the time for all of us children and the household. It was very unusual for a man to prepare food every day. Their relationship was very unusual for Uzbek society. They discussed their jobs and had interesting conversations. I recall them talking about a new TV program project for hours. I can imagine how often my dad had to listen critical remarks from his relatives and friends: "It is not a man's duty to help his wife! Why then marry at all...?"

Chapter 4.

Grandma

My grandma on my mother's side was an extraordinary woman. She was a Bashkir with blue eyes and light hair. I obviously inherited her light skin color – along with my father's light skin, so they often called me the Sun's Daughter.

Grandmom was a very active lady. For a long time, she could not come to terms with the fact that her only daughter had chosen an Uzbek and, on top of that, an Uzbek with an unconventional profession in the field of art and music. Finally, in the late 60s, she moved to Tashkent from Kokand, but refused to move in with our family and help my mom, who could actually have used some assistance with the kids. Instead, grandmom requested we buy her a little house at the other end of town where the Tatars and Bashkirs lived, because she did not want to live among Uzbeks. She would usually visit us once a week, if, of course, she had no other travel plans. She was a very active traveler. She was also a member of the communist party cell in her neighborhood. She participated in all kinds of activities, and would often travel to vacation destinations in the fall. We kids were always excited for her to visit, because she would bring us special treats. We loved her big red, red apples, as famous as the "almatinskiye" apples from the Tienshan Mountains, and very aromatic. I was her favorite grandchild; she often took me to her house for the weekend and made delicious pancakes for me. I just loved them: small, fried in butter, and topped with sweet cream. Nowhere else did I experience such a tasty treat!

In the spring she would take me to strawberry farm, where we would pick an enormous amount of juicy strawberries. Then we would make jam, and grandmom also made her strawberry liquor. In addition to her other trips, she would visit a woman she knew in

Leningrad, and when I was finishing 8th grade, she offered to take me with her. Before that I had gone to Moscow twice: once in summer camp just after the Big Earthquake of 1966 and then again with my parents in the early seventies to visit my mom's friend. Unlike Tashkent, Moscow was a living, bustling, and very crowded city. There were people everywhere all the time; it was chaotic, and people were pushy as they waited in lines for stores and museums. I will never forget our visit to the biggest grocery store in the Soviet Union, the Yeliseyevsky Gastronome, named after its prerevolutionary owner. The building, originally a late 18th century classical mansion, was beautiful, and its stunning interior boasts chandeliers, stained glass, and ornate wall decorations. I was shocked to see barrels of black and red caviar and an array of different kinds of smoked sturgeon, beluga, and lox. I enjoyed the heady aromas of freshly ground coffee and mountains of oranges, bananas, and even pineapples. There were also shelves full of different kinds of salami, sausage, ham, and cheese. At that time Moscow was well-supplied in terms of food and clothing. I remember how people coming back to Tashkent from Moscow always brought unusual and tasty things like oranges, lemons, and chocolate. At the same time, if you went just 50 miles outside of Moscow, you would see people waiting in line for bread who had probably never had caviar in their entire lives.

My classmate Olya often had food and sweets in her school lunch, because her dad was a senior train attendant who regularly traveled between Moscow and Tashkent, and thus had access to Moscow's delicacies. Oranges, something absolutely luxurious for us Tashkenters, were nothing special for her. Olya was one of the first girls in our school to wear tights, something we had never seen before - and she even had them in different colors. When I visited Moscow with my parents, my only wish was to go the famous children's superstore "Detsky Mir" ("Children's World") and have my parents buy tights for me! When we arrived at the store, I got dizzy from the huge selection of toys and clothing! I had never dreamed of such clothing! I was dazzled by the selection of tights and wanted all of them – like Olya – from white to red! My parents only allowed me to get one pair, so I decided to get the Poisonous Green ones, because Olya didn't have this color. Imagine how poor we were, if even tights were considered a luxury item! Later, when a "spekulyantka" ("black marketeer") came by our house selling patterned children's pantyhose, my mother bought them for my younger sister, but not for me. I cried and tried my hardest to persuade her to get me some. She explained that they were expensive - 5 rubles (and the average salary was 100 rubles/month) and that had I already gotten some (remember those green ones from Moscow...?).

Back when we were in Moscow we also went to GUM, the huge shopping center on Red Square across from the Lenin Mausoleum. GUM was a consumer mecca for visitors to Moscow. What I remember is huge crowds, long lines, and people from all over the Soviet Union. Outside of Moscow the country was struggling with shortages and lacked basic things like toilet paper, but here, and only here, could buy anything. I also remember hundreds of people waiting to get into the Lenin Mausoleum, the resting place of Vladimir Lenin, Russia's one and only mummy. The Soviet people considered it an honor to visit this place. I was glad my parents were wise enough not waste time waiting in line and damage their child's soul by making her look at the preserved dead body of Lenin.

Vacation in Crimea

The trip to Moscow was actually a side-trip on our way to Crimea. Located on the northern shore of the Black Sea, the Crimean Peninsula is known for its vineyards and its "sanatoriums", which is Russian for "resorts". There are miles and miles of beaches and popular resorts, where thousands of Soviets would spend their vacation.

During the Tsarist period, members of the aristocracy had residences in Crimea. We visited some of them, including Livadia, the summer residence of the Tsars and the astonishingly beautiful Prince Vorontsov Palace outside of Yalta, built in English renaissance style. Some of the other old aristocratic villas and palaces have been turned into sanatoriums for the working people.

It was a privilege to get vacation vouchers to a resort, which were usually distributed by the trade unions in factories and other institutions in accordance with your service record and achievements. These vouchers were mainly given to workers and activists in heavy industry and agriculture, as well as government officials. Some people, however, managed to get vouchers through their "blat" networks. And then there were thousands and thousands of very ordinary people just like us, who went there hoping they would be able to find reasonable accommodations. Some came from very distant, cold northern areas, such as the permafrost regions. A vacation at the Black Sea was considered a great luxury, even if you only managed to get a humble accommodation. Interestingly, there weren't many real hotels in the Soviet Union. My parents rented a room for the four of us in a big apartment that had many rooms. Often the locals would rent out part or all of their homes to vacationers in order to earn some extra money.

In the morning we would go to the beach, where people lay packed shoulder by shoulder. It seemed they were trying to charge themselves with enough sunshine to last them for the rest of their lives. We rarely went into the water because none of us could swim. Due to the lack of lakes or seas in the country, Uzbeks have no chance of learning how to swim. And in fact, swimming is not even part of our culture. I remember how once when I wanted to go "swimming" with my girlfriends in the one and only swimming pool in town, my parents wouldn't let me, because an Uzbek girl is not supposed to show up in a swimsuit and do immodest things like swimming. Not being able to swim caused many difficulties for me later in life. Oh, how I wanted to dive into the Black Sea during that vacation and experience what it feels like in the sea! It was the first time in my life that I was near the sea! The only thing my mom allowed me to do with seawater was rinse my throat with it every morning. Yes, the Soviet people were very into natural things and used a lot of natural remedies. They would bring their children to the beach for the entire summer vacation, believing that would allow them to recharge their health for the entire year.

Instead of going to the beach, my family went shopping. Maybe there would be a better selection here than back home in Tashkent. Or maybe we went shopping simply because when you went on vacation, you had to bring back a present for every relative. Mom was busy buying yards of silk to make traditional dresses out of. A piece of silk was considered a very valuable present! In the hot climate in Uzbekistan, silk clothing was very comfortable. Ironically, the part of the country that produced silk and cotton could not get enough of its own local products! Uzbekistan only produced the raw materials; processing took place in other republics of the Soviet Union. The central government in Moscow would also sell our products abroad and earn foreign currency, which stayed in Moscow and didn't benefit the hard-working and poor local people of Uzbekistan.

One day we visited my dad's colleague in the "Uzbekistan Sanatorium", where only high-level government and industry officials vacationed. Judging by the size and luxuriousness of his suite, the person we visited must have been really important. When they served us tea, the table was bursting with sweets that I had never seen before! In contrast, our family had to squeeze into a single room. That guy and his wife lived in incredible luxury, and I experienced a deep feeling of injustice. That seemed to be normal in a country where all were equal!

Another incident comes to mind from that vacation on the sea. In the room next to ours there was a family from Siberia. The husband was a pilot, and his wife - an amazing blond beauty. One day she returned from somewhere in tears. I remember the pilot, a tall and formidable guy, rushing off to settle something. Later may parents explained to me that they had been promised a room in a sanatorium, but in exchange, the sanatorium director wanted to sleep with the wife. We don't know how the story ended, but the couple soon left. In the Soviet Union, it was normal for Russian women to resolve problems by sleeping with men. It was well-known that when Stalin was alive, his Minister of Internal Affairs Lavrenty Beria would drive around the city and if he saw a beautiful woman he liked, he would order that she be snatched off the street and brought to his apartment. There was no way to refuse Beria's "affections" if you didn't want to end up in a labor camp for years.

In Crimea I became friends with a girl of my age from Yakutia, and we had a good time together. She had a lot of pretty clothes and accessories and changed them often. Once she asked me why I always wore the same dress, and she offered to me one of her dresses as a present. I felt so ashamed that I avoided her from that moment on. In Uzbekistan it was normal for children to have just one set of everyday clothes. Rarely did girls had several dresses, and usually they were the children of important officials, people we called "the rich".

Blat

As I mentioned above, my grandmother took me on a trip to Leningrad for summer vacation. The train ride from Tashkent to Leningrad lasted 4 days. During the summer, trains were usually packed, and to buy a ticket – or rather to *get* a ticket – required using your connections. There was always somebody in a large family who had "blat" ("connections") at the train ticket offices. *Blat* was a very common practice in the Soviet Union.

The word *blat* dates back to the times of Catherine the Great. Goods, jobs, or offices were allocated by the tsarina and recorded on *blats* or "sheets of paper" (i.e. lists). The German word "blatt" ("leaf" or "sheet of paper") was used instead of the Russian one, as there were numerous foreigners from Holland and Germany among Catherine's advisors; moreover, she herself was German. Eventually, *blat* came to mean "connections." In a mismanaged and corrupt economy, favors and connections were the only way to get by and get what you needed: tickets, documents, appointments, clothes, food…anything. Calling a friend or a relative in an appropriate position was the most normal thing. You even needed *blat* to see a good doctor and get the proper treatment. If somebody in the family was expecting a baby, you would activate your entire network to find a good, reliable doctor who had friends among the doctors in your hospital. If you delivered your baby in a hospital without such special arrangements, the medical staff would barely take care of you. Several of my friends and relatives had newborn babies who got infections and suffered permanent damage, because at the time of delivery for whatever reason nobody took proper care of them. Maybe the doctor who promised to be there was absent, or the person who promised to help with their *blat* was too late in contacting the hospital doctors and nurses. Anyway, without *blat* you were nothing in Soviet society.

Blat was also an integral part of business practices. Black market principles functioned well in Soviet factories and institutions.

Spare parts, materials, and services were all provided in exchange for other favors and goods. Of course, the Soviet propaganda machine claimed we were fighting *blat* and condemned it as corruption. But most people were more realistic: although it was unethical and certainly didn't accord with communist ideals, you had to rely on it to get along in life. A Soviet famous proverb says, "You don't need one hundred rubles, you need one hundred friends."

… So using our *blat*, we got train tickets to Leningrad.

Train Travel

My grandmom and I traveled in a train car that was divided into compartments, each of which held four people who had so many suitcases and packages, that it seemed as if they had moved in permanently. Sometimes you could even see laundry drying on lines in long-distance trains.

People usually prepared carefully for their travels and took a lot of food with them. They mainly ate fried chicken for the first couple days and then dried or smoked lunch meat for after that, as there were no refrigerators on the train. Most people didn't eat in the restaurant car because it was expensive. Eating was our favorite pastime on the train. People would take out what they had prepared and share it with their neighbors in the compartment. But most of all I loved stopping at the stations along the way where the locals would sell fresh fruits and vegetables, as well as hot food. Something as simple as a cooked potato with butter and dill seemed to me to be the most delicious feast in the world. But to buy things, you had to get off the train quickly, find what you wanted, negotiate a bit, and then jump back on the train… When we entered Russia, things became even more interesting, as the food became exotic for us: red and black currants, raspberries, and black sunflower seeds, which didn't grow in Uzbekistan. I really looked forward to every new stop. How could you miss this fun!

Besides eating and talking endlessly, which the Soviet people loved to do most of all, we played a lot of cards on the train. When you walked along the train past the open compartment doors, you could also see men in pajamas playing chess and sipping from their beautiful glasses of black tea. Every Soviet man seemed to have a portable, folding chessboard or backgammon set in his traveling kit. Foreigners seeing men in pajamas getting off the train to buy something at a station might have thought something was wrong or that they needed something urgently before bedtime, but in fact, it was common for most of the men to wear pajamas the entire time of their travels.

We loved the endless rounds of tea on the train. The female conductors in their railway service uniforms tea would serve it in glasses with beautiful ornamental metal glass holders. They would also stoke a big samovar, which was typically built into the corner at the end of the corridor of each train car. You would be offered this hot black amber-colored tea with sugar cubes all day long. The Soviet people's favorite thing was to get together and drink tea. And of course, we didn't just drink tea - we would also talk nonstop. Russians love talking for talking's sake! During the four days of traveling you would usually get to know everything about your fellow travelers; they would share their entire lives with you. Over time I had several of these four-day journeys, either to/from Moscow or "Peter" (even during Soviet times Leningrad was called "Peter"). The time went by fast, and it was not boring. I learned a lot about people through their stories, stories of all sorts of different kinds, but few were happy! Oh, how I loved those journeys.

Unfortunately, however, it was hot on the train. The temperature outside could be as high as 114°F, and there were no air conditioners, but nobody complained. And nobody complained about the long lines to the bathroom. We weren't spoiled at all! Every day brought a new landscape to look at. Not far outside of Tashkent you could see the Kazakh deserts, and in the distance, you could watch the slow-moving camels. Then came the steppe, which was slowly transformed into Russian forests, and for miles and miles there would be no sign of civilization. Then there was the mile-wide Volga River. Every time I saw it, I was delighted at its size! The bridge we passed over was at least a mile long. The Volga is breathtaking, and it's hard to believe it's just a river, because in places you can't see the other shore, just endless water. I remember watching big ships sailing here and there.

The Volga River is beautiful, and the landscape along its banks is one of the loveliest and most typically Russian. The houses are typical Russian wooden huts, called "izbas". Between the villages you could see fields full of men and women with shawls around their heads, working side by side. The streets in the villages were full of chickens, ducks, and geese. The landscape was new for me: flat, green meadows and forests everywhere, going on for miles and miles. I have never seen so many trees in my life. My country was dry, hot, and not really green. In Uzbekistan there are mainly bare mountains, the steppe, and deserts. You rarely see green fields, and even fewer forests.

And so, after four days of interesting travels, we arrived in Leningrad.

Leningrad

When you are in Leningrad, you feel like you are in another country. Much more European than Moscow, Leningrad is a beautifully preserved European city. Every day my grandmom and I walked around the city and marveled at its architectural treasures. The builders of this city were all foreigners: Rastrelli, Rossi, Quarenghi, Rinaldi, Brenna De Thomson, Matarnovi, and Trezzini de Lugano etc. Montferrand's St. Isaac's Cathedral is the third largest in the world; it took 40 years to build. The imaginations of Italians gushed forth in Russia like waterfalls. Carlo Rastrelli designed the 2 million square foot Winter Palace on the Neva River with 1050 rooms and 117 staircases. In the village of Tsarskoe Selo, now called Pushkin, Rastrelli designed the Catherine Palace, one of the most lavish and stunning structures in Russia. And on the banks of the Moyka and Fontanka canals, Rastrelli and his followers built palaces for the aristocratic families, including the Yusupovs, Stroganovs, Golitsyns, and Sheremetyevs, and erected some of the loveliest churches in the land. These Italian architects brought with them a Mediterranean love of colors that warmed the cold light of this land, where even the blue of summer is grey with impending cold.

The Hermitage Museum is part of the former Winter Palace. Dazed and amazed, I looked at hundreds of damascene sword blades, a cape studded with 1,000,000 pearls, and brocade dresses that took several years to make, along with dozens of crowns flashing with emeralds, diamonds, and topaz. There were silver sets created by the finest craftsmen, plates from Sweden, Dresden china, and porcelain from France.

The other thing that impressed me was the famous "white nights", which take place in June, when the sun barely dips below the horizon. It does not get dark; instead, the nights stay "white" through the morning hours. During white nights, the streets of Leningrad are usually full of people walking down Nevsky Prospect or sitting outside in cafes, enjoying this natural wonder. At first, it is hard to get sleep during this period, but after a while you get used to it.

In Leningrad there were visitors from all over the Soviet Union, many of whom were standing in line for something. Standing in line - even with children - for hours on end to go to a museum was nothing out of the ordinary. How could one visit Leningrad and not go to most of the museums? My grandmom and I stood in line to visit the Hermitage for several hours, and when we finally made it to the front of the line, we were so tired that we weren't able to go in. One needed several days to properly see all the exhibits in the Hermitage! Standing in line, I noticed that for some strange reason, people were sneaking in ahead of us. It turned out that they were foreigners, and I found out that they paid more and were treated better. I was so angry: why were they so special that they didn't have to wait in line like we did?

I think that even today, foreigners pay different prices for tickets than Russians. You can only find this kind of "discrimination" in Russia. I remember how my Russian-born friends who were visiting from the US would tell their children not to open their mouths, so that nobody would notice their accents and realize that they weren't Russian citizens. Nobody wants to pay extra for museum tickets! But there are always incidents when US-born Russians are found out, because their Russian-American parents didn't teach them proper Russian...and then they would have to pay triple the price! However, it is understandable that the Soviet State subsidized tickets for cultural and sporting events for its citizens. The prices for tickets to the theater, cinema, and sporting events were really low. Every Soviet citizen had access to affordable tickets for cultural events, such as the philharmonic, theaters, concerts, and exhibitions. I remember how, when I was young, we regularly went to all kinds of classical music and theatrical performances, because the school curriculum included cultural education. My music school even provided us with free tickets to concerts of the philharmonic orchestra. We often had to discuss the concerts we attended in detail and write essays about the concerts or operas we saw.

My parents were often able to go to concerts and performances thanks to my dad's work. He often got invitations or free tickets to cultural events. Imagine my surprise and shock every time I see ticket prices for musical events in the West! I have to pick and choose carefully when it comes to going to cultural events because they are so expensive here. The Soviet people were used to going to a lot of performances and exhibitions, and standing in line was no problem for us. Therefore, going from museum to museum and standing in line with my grandmother was a matter of habit.

The Kommunalka

One of the most impressive things in Leningrad was the "kommunalka", where we stayed with my grandma friends.

A "kommunalka" is a communal apartment. Large pre-Soviet-era bourgeois apartments were subdivided by the Soviets into multiple single-room dwellings with shared kitchens, toilet rooms, and bathrooms. Larger rooms were often divided into two or more little bedrooms with thin partitions that didn't even reach the ceiling, so you could hear every little noise your neighbor made!

The communal apartment was intended to be the birthplace of the communist personality, the new communist society. People had to share their living space; private space and property were supposed to disappear, and family life was to be replaced by communist brotherly coexistence. The (not-so-)private life of the individual would be under permanent community surveillance and control. So the Bolsheviks believed that communal living would make people more fundamentally communist in their behavior.

In every communal apartment, there were shared responsibilities and duties. Every family had its assigned day for

71

washing clothes. In the morning there were queues to the bathroom. *Kommunalka* life caused a lot of conflicts and gave birth to a new type of "Soviet personality"! The permanent shortage of living space in the Soviet Union caused many people to accept life in *kommunalkas,* in spite of the terrible conditions, where everything belonged to everyone. You were lucky if you had good, polite neighbors, but that was something unusual, as most of the men in Russia were heavy drinkers.

I never saw a *kommunalka* in Uzbekistan. And luckily, the *kommunalka* we stayed in with my grandmom's friend in Leningrad was a decent one. One neighbor was an old lady from a noble family which actually used to own the flat. The other neighbor was a nice, well-educated elderly man. Each time my grandmom and I were in the kitchen, he would join us and offer us tea. Later, he started inviting my grandmom into his room for tea. His room was very interesting, full of pictures and other old things. He told us they were from his youth, when he studied in Paris and spoke several foreign languages, including German, English and French. His father had been a professor of the University of St. Petersburg. After the Revolution of 1917, they first fled to Harbin in China and then to Istanbul. However, for some reason, they eventually returned to Russia. After the war, the Stalinist regime sent his father to the labor camps, and he never returned. What an irony: the professor survived exile, war, and the Siege of Leningrad, only to die in peacetime in the Stalinist labor camps!

I was very fascinated by the story of this lonely elderly man in Leningrad. How many other Soviets had had a similar fate? The day before our departure from Leningrad, he asked my grandmom to marry him and stay with him in Leningrad. When she asked me my opinion, I was angry: at 15 years old, I found this situation questionable, even indecent. How could elderly people fall in love and move in together?? Love was for young people like me! I thought that even 40 was really old. I was very upset, and I told my grandma not to do stupid things. I was very jealous and could not imagine life in Tashkent without my beloved grandma! Today I feel sad about my childish behavior and egotism. My grandma might have been happy with that man; they wouldn't have been lonely anymore. And since my grandmom was very European, she would have felt at home in a great city like Leningrad.

Usually, our understanding of things comes too late, and only later in life do we realize how much we did not give to our parents and grandparents.

The next year we stayed at another friend's home. In that *kommunalka,* there were only two families. The neighbors had left for the summer; they were staying at their "dacha" ("summer house in the countryside"). A *dacha* can be anything from a mansion to a one-room cabin, and sometimes would lack infrastructure like running water, gas, or electricity.

Dachas were a very important part of Soviet life. Because of the permanent shortage of various types of food in the 70s and 80s, many families survived thanks to their home-grown produce. They grew all kinds of vegetables and fruits at the *dacha,* and would stock up on potatoes, cabbage, and preserves. People in the Soviet Union also ate a lot of bread. They ate bread with everything. Even with potatoes and pasta. Bread was relatively cheap, and it would fill your stomach. I remember how our parents always encouraged us to eat everything with bread.

Shopping and Alcohol

We usually cooked preserves for the winter. We would make desserts, such as compotes and stewed fruits made from apricots, apples, and berries; we would also make fruit jams. My favorite jam was strawberry, because my grandmother and I would make it together. I remember my grandmother stirring and tending to a big kettle of jam for hours on an open fire out in our yard. In the evening, we would cover the berries with sugar, so that by the next morning a lot of juice would have come out. We would then cook the berries all day long in the juice. Oh, what a wonderful strawberry aroma would fill the air! It was customary to exchange jars of jam with our neighbors. One had the best apricot jam recipe, another made the best fig jam, and yet another one – the best cherry jam. My grandmother's trademark was her famous strawberry jam! Jam was one of the most popular products of the peoples of the USSR, because it was an integral part of one of the most important and

73

entertaining customs of the people, be it Georgians, Azeris, Ukrainians, Armenians, Russians, Uzbeks – having tea!

Today, regardless of where I go to meet friends and family, the first thing they do is offer me a cup of tea. And a cup of tea with jam is an even greater pleasure! You don't just drink tea, you also get the sweet aroma of the jam, and you have long conversations … We Soviet people did not need much, not even bread; it was enough to sit and have a chat over tea. The Russian word "sbor" means gathering, which is one of the most meaningful of all Russian concepts.

We would also make vegetables preserves. Most of all I love "eggplant caviar" spread on fresh bread. We used to produce gallons of eggplant caviar! Marinated tomatoes, cucumbers, patty pay squash, and sauerkraut were the perfect appetizers for winter dinners! In order to have the preserves ready for winter, you had to spend a lot of time at your *dacha* during the summer and fall! Many people spent every weekend working on their garden plots, even though it would take hours to get there. But time was something we had plenty of. And we had to stock up on supplies for winter, because the government-controlled food industry did not meet people's needs.

The first time I heard an entire family singing was in Leningrad, when my grandmother took me to the house of her girlfriend. I was stunned and amazed as I listened to the whole family singing their hearts out and shedding tears during the songs. When the neighbors of our host in Leningrad left for their *dacha*, we had the whole house nearly for ourselves. Often our host's son and family would visit, and every time they did, there would be a big feast with tons of food and vodka. Usually the night would start with eating and drinking and talking a lot about everything, then the singing would start, with the entire family joining in. They sang not only folk songs, but recent Soviet hits, as well as patriotic and revolutionary songs. Russian songs are very beautiful and have wonderful music, even the revolutionary ones - if you don't listen closely to the words.

This custom of gathering and singing is something truly Soviet, and many emigrants have maintained this tradition abroad. Wherever there is a group of Russian-speaking people, sooner or later they will start singing, all of them. War and patriotic songs have become part of the Soviet-Russian soul. Russians can be very warm-hearted people, very full of emotions, especially when they are drunk from endless rounds of vodka.

The second thing that struck me was that women drank vodka, and in breathtaking amounts. Back home in Uzbekistan, women rarely drank alcoholic beverages. If they drank, it was purely symbolic - a little bit of wine or sherry, not those big 100-gram glasses of vodka (equal to about two shots)!

Alcohol

Alcohol was a big problem in the Soviet Union, and still is in Russia today. Because of this, life expectancy is much lower for men - and fell to below 60 years in the 1990s. At that time, alcoholism was responsible for nearly half of all deaths among Russian men of working age. Heavy drinking has long been a tradition in Russia, and has been cultivated by all Russian governments, whether Czarist or Communist. History shows that the state has contributed substantially to the problem through a monopoly on the production and distribution of (often cheap) alcohol, which made alcohol a major source of government revenue. On several occasions, the Soviet government attempted to fight alcoholism, but without any success. Brezhnev tried to introduce certain rules and limitations, but kept drinking heavily himself. An anti-alcohol campaign was launched in the mid-80s by Gorbachev, who fought hard against drunkenness and even razed vineyards. This campaign earned Gorbachev, who was the General Secretary of the Communist Party of the Soviet Union, the nickname "Mineral Secretary". When people celebrated weddings or other family events in Uzbekistan during the Gorbachev period, they served alcohol in a typical Uzbek way: in teapots! The young men serving the drinks would ask you what kind of "tea" you would like: "green tea" = vodka, or "black tea" = cognac? Your choice! Although Uzbekistan, as a traditionally Muslim country, should have saluted the anti-alcohol campaign, it was simply unthinkable in the context of the Uzbek tradition of hospitality not to serve a popular beverage. Drinking together helps people forget the problems of daily life; it is, in fact, the easiest way to find a common language, and it often helps people advance in their careers. However, alcohol is responsible for a lot of marital problems. I remember when my mother was the chairwoman of our *mahalla* women's council, she often had women coming to her at night asking her to help resolve family conflicts. In most cases, the problem was alcoholic husbands beating their wives and children and insulting older family members. Poor Uzbek women! They not only suffered at the hands of their mothers-in-law and other members of their husbands' families, but also from beatings by their husbands. And these men were convinced deep down in their hearts that they were good Muslims! What a paradox! Almost every other man in our *mahalla* was a chronic alcoholic. Alcoholism was one of the biggest social problems we inherited from Russian dominance in Central Asia. Alcohol cost "pennies," but it provided the government a sizeable income. It caused a lot of trouble for people, but it also "helped" people forget their problems. What a paradox!

One day my friend from Kyrgyzstan tried to explain to me why, when there was a national discussion about a law permitting polygamy in the 90s, many women were for it! She told me that this law would give many women the opportunity to have a somewhat normal husband and a healthy child. Otherwise, there was little chance that they would ever get married, because so many of the few available men were drunks. And this was thanks to the Russians! Maybe they were right from a woman's standpoint?

I remember a lot of conflicts in my family when my parents came home after parties. My dad's body luckily - or not so luckily - cannot tolerate large amounts of alcohol, so after each party he would be sick all night long. He repeatedly promised my mom not to drink any more, but he was never able to keep his promise. It is simply impossible for a man who is a guest at a party to avoid having a couple drinks. You can't tell your host that you don't want to drink. The host would not accept your refusal, saying, "Do you respect us, do you respect our elders?", or "You have to drink for this!", or "Don't you respect our children?" "Why can't you share a drink and toast to our …?"

Russians and Soviets had to drink to everybody's health, to our great country, to peace on Earth, etc. If you refused to drink, they would question whether you were a man or not.

Although people knew he couldn't tolerate alcohol, my poor dad had to go through this again and again. (Another kind of "peer pressure".)

On Sundays after prayer, men would gather in *chaykhana* tea houses, jointly cook *pilav*, talk, laugh, curse world imperialism and, of course,...have some vodka to support their good spirits. Why not, it's that simple.

Whenever there are two men together, it's already an occasion to have a drink. Send one of the kids off to the store to get a bottle of vodka, and there you have your entertainment! Guzzle your booze and forget about the problems in daily life. Forget about the wife at home, who, after a full day's work, has to cook, do the laundry, feed the kids ... Most men in the Soviet Union were very macho.

Where was Soviet ideology, which trumpeted the equality of men and women? "Women and men are truly only equal in Russia. Only in Russia do they have equal opportunities with respect to employment and get equal pay for equal work." It was very common to see groups of women in grey, dusty, worn overalls, felt boots, and woolen scarves wrapped around their heads doing heavy repair work on railway tracks. In reality, there was no equality or freedom for women!

In Soviet society there was no way not to drink. Even in Uzbekistan, alcohol is widely consumed by men and women alike, although they call themselves Muslims. There was simply no feast without alcohol.

When I was in Leningrad, I was most surprised by the quantity of alcohol men and women were able to consume! And it took a while for them to get drunk. What "training" does it take to be able to drink like that, or was it just in their genes? They would drink entire liters, men and women alike. After the excess and after the singing, there would usually be family conflicts. And a little while later, many would pass out right there on the spot. It was the same story, the same process each and every time. And this would happen at least once a week. Luckily, my grandmother had an excuse not to drink: she said that she was Muslim and couldn't. So during one of the parties at our host's house in Leningrad, we simply left. We –

the feast- and party-proof people from Uzbekistan – simply could not get used to the scenes of alcoholism in Russia.

There were many alcoholics sleeping in the hallways and on the streets of Leningrad. In Tashkent we saw scenes like that, but they were very rare. Foreigners visiting the Soviet Union also had to deal with this culture of drinking. I can imagine how difficult it was for them when they visited Russians! If you were invited to dinner at someone's house and didn't drink with them, you would be insulting both them and their culture. So most businesspeople would be told before their trips that the success or failure of a business trip generally depended on how well they played the drinking game with their partners. The rules of the game included: Don't put a glass with alcohol in it back on the table. If you open a bottle of alcohol, you must keep drinking until it's empty. A latecomer must drink a full glass of alcohol, the so-called "penalty" glass, to catch up with everyone else. Those who were lucky enough to have a good reason to avoid drinking might get away without having to do so; otherwise, they would be gently…

Stores

I loved going shopping with my grandmom in Leningrad. She was a shopaholic.

At 13, I bought my first ever foreign personal care product, a bottle of shampoo from Poland! Cosmetics from Poland were a big deal then, as there wasn't much to choose from among Soviet products.

In the 70s everything was difficult, even the simplest parts in daily life. We had a primitive selection of soaps. Our Soviet mascara was so bad, that after washing it off, your eyes hurt as if they had been "shoe-shined". Soviet fragrances like "Lilly of the Valley", "Moscow Lights", "Red Moscow", and "Red Poppies", etc., had a very sharp smell and sat unsold on store shelves. French cosmetics were also sold in the Soviet Union, but prices were astronomical compared to the average salary. So we were happy when something from Poland or the Baltic republics came along. Oh, how happy I was after that purchase of Polish shampoo! It had such an amazing smell, and it was shiny and sparkled like mother of pearl! What a difference! Back home in Uzbekistan, girls and women used to wash their hair in sour milk! Yes, sour milk! And so did my grandmother, who had strong, dark blond braids until her very last day. They would just soak their hair in sour milk, walk around like that for an hour, then rinse it off with warm water. That was it!

Can you imagine a hot summer day on a full bus or tram in Tashkent? It was suffocating! Our hairstyle was simple, just braids - a good girl had 40 of them! No haircut, not even a forelock. A girl had to look and behave modestly, submissively. Long black hair was the ideal of beauty among the female population in Central Asia. We did everything to have long, thick hair, and were interested in every bit of advice from other girls or women on how to get it. Besides traditional sour milk, we washed our hair in beer, rice water, egg yolks, and whatnot...Imagine walking around for entire days with our hair soaked in sour milk and wrapped in a towel, or pressing the juice of "usma" leaves (something like "basma") into cups and using it to dye our eyebrows, drawing them in beautiful, seagull-shaped arcs! We believed that dying your eyebrows with *usma* juice would make them as black and as beautiful as our hair! *Usma* grew in every garden, but squeezing out the juice from these rather dry leaves was torture, so whenever there was a little bit of extra juice, we would also put it in our hair.

Every girl wanted to attain the Uzbek ideal of beauty: black eyebrows, long, strong black hair ...

But all this did not help me: I was fair-skinned, and I had light brown hair. That's who I remained: the sun's daughter! My friends laughed at me and told me not to waste my time coloring my hair - nobody would marry me anyway! I did not care; I was used to being different. I was different my whole life.

Imagine, until adolescence I didn't know anything about shampoo, and when I first used that Polish shampoo, I felt like a super model! Back at school, everybody gazed at my shiny hair and listened to my story about the shampoo, a word they had not heard before. Now I was the star!

For several years my grandmom and I would go to Leningrad for summer vacation. Before the last trip, I had the opportunity to earn some money working for the Research Institute for Sericulture. I worked in a lab with two of my girlfriends cutting silkworm cocoons in half. Initially it was not very fun, but over time I got used to touching the cocoons, opening them by the hundreds, and putting the insects in the proper boxes. It turns out there were certain features on their bodies which allowed you to determine their gender, and thus sort these guys by their role in the research process.

The silkworm industry, along with the cotton industry, was well developed in Uzbekistan. There even was this Research Institute for Sericulture not far from my home. The job was not very pleasant, but I wanted it, because there weren't any jobs for teenagers. It was not customary to work before you finished high school; in fact, to do so was frowned upon and seen as a sign of poverty. However, I was lucky because my girlfriend's father worked at this institute and helped get us a job. And the job paid pretty well, so I accumulated a good sum of money for my summer vacation. This time I had money in my pockets!

There were always lines in the stores in the Soviet period, because everything was in short supply. This was especially true during the Brezhnev period, which was nicknamed "the period of stagnation". When something was not available in the stores, we would say it was a "deficit". And the only thing abundant in the Soviet Union was "deficits". Everything was in short supply: clothing, household goods, furniture ... even food.

People tried to get by with their so-called *blat*, the private and special connections through family and friends. Let's say, for example, you want something delicious for a special occasion, like salami. So you call your *blat* at the grocery store, and they would tell you when to come to a designated spot, such as the back entrance to the store, to get the desired items.

After seeing the empty shelves in grocery stores, foreigners were amazed at the tables full of food at private parties in people's homes. The Soviets, especially the women, were skilled at getting hold of food and other items. Theoretically, you could get anything you wanted in the Soviet Union, you just had to know somebody, who knew somebody, who knew ...

The capital cities of Moscow and Leningrad were always better off, as they were prioritized in the supply chain, so people from all over the Soviet Union would come here to shop. It was absolutely normal to see people arriving by train or plane from Moscow or Leningrad with their hands and luggage stuffed with such ordinary things as bags of lunch meat, kilograms of cheese, bundles full of oranges, sweets ... or just toilet paper!

So compared to Tashkent, Leningrad seemed to like a shopping paradise, a land of plenty.

Each summer when we returned home to Tashkent, we would bring something special that we had bought in Leningrad. That year we got lucky and managed to buy a pineapple – there was a one per person limit on them! You would never see pineapples back home. I imagined the happy eyes of my siblings when they saw this wonder.

On several occasions, my grandmom and I stood in line for hours to get some coveted commodity like imported boots from one of our socialist brotherlands. Sometimes, after getting in line, we would find out that the goods wouldn't arrive until the next day, so we had to come back several times during the day to hold on to our spot in line. What a triumph, what happiness, when you actually managed to get hold of a DEFICIT item! All the standing and waiting was suddenly forgotten!

All my hard work with the disgusting silkworms paid off! I was able to buy myself a Finnish winter coat, East German boots, a Hungarian purse, and Polish cosmetics - things none of my girlfriends had back home.

Despite the concept of equality in all things, which the Soviet system tried to inculcate in us, we girls were still just like girls everywhere else in the world. We were told: "You make your first impression with your clothes, but your second with your brains." But we wanted to be looked at and appreciated! We wanted to be different, better, and prettier than all the others. So we dreamt of wearing something imported!

It sometimes happened that you would be wearing the same imported (!) coat from Finland or dress from the GDR, but that didn't trouble anybody. It was the fact that you were wearing something imported that made you happy - and everybody else jealous.

For three consecutive summers my grandmom took me to Leningrad, and these trips transformed my mind and my vision of my future. I very much wanted to live in Russia, where everything seemed so advanced, so full of opportunities to see new things, to learn and to study. I loved talking to Leningraders, going to theatres, and experiencing the spirit of Europe. I was very attracted to all this.

In Tashkent there was a permanent conflict going on in me. I was not accepted as an Uzbek, so I was a foreigner at home. Then there were the feudal traditions, the constant reminders that I was a Muslim girl, and the constant oppression of women both at home and in society at large. So I decided in childhood that I wanted to leave. I experienced wanderlust, and Moscow and Leningrad seemed like very good places for me. In Leningrad I even talked to a couple universities to find out the details of their entrance exams.

Returning home after our last trip to Leningrad, I firmly decided that I would leave Uzbekistan after I finished high school. But I still had two years of high school to go!

Chapter 5.

Kokand

Uzbeks rarely travel far from home; they usually spend their vacation at home, because there are always a million everyday problems to be dealt with. Moreover, travel with a large number of children is neither easy nor cheap, and there are usually 5 – 6 children in Uzbek families.

That's why my parents could only afford trips within the borders of Uzbekistan - and to those places where there were family members who could accommodate us.

My mother's hometown was Kokand, and we would often spend several weeks during the summer with our many relatives there.

As someone who had grown up in Tashkent, the city of Kokand seemed really exotic. The milestones of civilization seemed to have occurred here even later than in Tashkent. Most people lived in mud houses just as they had 100 years ago, and many women covered their faces and never sat in a room alone with men.

They did not mix Russian words into their speech as in other places. Their language was very beautiful; they even addressed their children in the formal plural form.

One felt the great respect people had for older people.

The food they offered us was also different. The bread the baked in their tandoor clay ovens had a slightly bitter taste to it, maybe because they couldn't afford high quality flour. But all the food was organic, and all the ingredients were grown right there in their gardens.

Each time we visited our relatives, my mom's uncle would grab a chicken or a rooster and slaughter it right in front of us. Within minutes, they would make a rich, tasty soup for us. At other relatives' houses, they would even slaughter a sheep in honor of our visit.

When they sent us children to the garden to fetch some vegetables for the meal, we saw every kind of produce you can image: corn, pumpkins, and tomatoes of all sizes and colors, from sweet-sweet yellow ones to miniature maroon ones to giant ones called "Yusupovsky" tomatoes. There were peppers of every kind, from sweet red and green ones to extremely hot ones. I remember how we munched the crisp little cucumbers with salt and freshly baked flatbread. At my request, my aunt immediately pickled some of them with garlic, dill and basil. The very next day these quick-salted cucumbers were ready to enjoy, and we children grabbed them straight out of the pot.

Those gardens had a very special aroma, which has haunted me all my life. Only last year when we were visiting friends in France who had a wonderful garden did I realize that it was the aroma of fig trees. Yes, indeed, there had been a lot of figs of various sizes and colors in Kokand!

And there were pomegranates, a wonderful heavy load on those gentle trees.

Almond trees, pistachios, a hundred kind of peaches … and, of course, grapevines!

We did not have this abundance and variety at home in Tashkent. Even the corn which we baked on the fire at night was so different.

Our relatives always greeted us as if we were the most honorable guests from the capital; to them we were something special, more advanced!

We did not wear those long robes and underpants; we did not have the traditional 40 pigtails like the local girls. Once my relatives tried to braid my hair into 40 pigtails, but had to stop at 20 because I was so impatient. Something very new to me were the so-called "askiya", contests of wit (and humor) that took place in *chaykhana* tea houses, and which were very common in Kokand.

84

Tea houses are an important component of Uzbek life; they are a kind of men's club where men not only eat and drink, but also have smoke a little "grass". And they often hold the *askiya* contests there. They start with one guy saying a funny phrase, which the next guy "picks up" and completes ... and soon, everybody is roaring with laughter! And Uzbek laughter is so uproarious, that even people on the street outside are startled by it. Making fun of something or somebody is a popular tradition. You are not supposed to take it seriously, just respond with another joke. The laughter was so infectious, that we kids would laugh along with the men without even understanding exactly what they were talking about.

Crimean Tatars

Crimean Tatar village weddings made a tremendous impression on me. In Kokand there was a huge population of Crimean Tatars. They had been forcibly relocated here from Crimea in 1944 under Stalin, when the Soviet government declared them and the Chechens traitors and deprived them of their autonomy. In 1957, the Crimean Tatars began collecting signatures for a petition to allow them to return to their homeland on the Crimean Peninsula. Some of their leaders were arrested and confined to mental hospitals; others were killed. In 1967, the Presidium of the Supreme Soviet issued a decree on the 'Rehabilitation of the Crimean Tatars', but under its terms, they were still not recognized as a legitimate ethnic group, nor were they allowed to return home.

Only after the fall of the Soviet Union did the Crimean Tatars return to their homeland in Crimea, which was part of Ukraine.

For the first time in my life I met Crimean Tatars in person in my uncle's neighborhood in Kokand. They looked like Turks, and their language is actually close to the Turkish language.

Since we mainly visited Kokand during summer vacation, we children took advantage of the fact that that was wedding season and would sneak in and watch the weddings and all the traditional rituals associated with them. Crimean Tatars are Muslims like the Uzbeks, but their wedding traditions are different.

Their music is totally different; they play completely different instruments. Besides the bass, rhythm guitar and drum, a Tatar wedding band will play an accordion, a violin, trumpets, a clarinet, and duduks (a special flute). Later in life, when I heard Klezmer music in Europe, it reminded me of my childhood and the Crimean Tatar weddings. The heart-breaking sound of the clarinet, in particular, is deeply engrained in my mind, with all of its melancholy and longing for the Crimean homeland.

There was so much sadness in every conversation with the Crimean Tatars. They would always talk about their homeland, and I felt how beautiful it must have been there and how deprived and uncomfortable they must feel in the villages around Kokand. They were hard-working people; they would work in their vast fields.

Another sweet memory about the Crimean Tatars is their national dish and one of my favorite foods. Chee-börek (or Chiburekki) is a fried turnover shaped like a half-moon and filled with ground minced and onions.

Village Life

Life was very simple around Kokand, and socialism was only visible in the existence of the schools, the district committees, and the *Komsomol* youth organization. And of course, the big, red slogans on buildings and all along the roads praising the Communist Party, calling for maximum efforts on the 5-year plan, claiming that People and Party are one, etc. There was only one advertising entity in the Soviet Union: THE STATE!

I always had the feeling that the people there lived two lives: some actively participated in government, but most lived according to their traditional way of life, just as their ancestors had for hundreds of years: cooking food on an outdoor stove, baking bread in tandoor clay ovens, sending the children to collect brush from the fields… And there were no indoor bathrooms.

While Soviet cosmonauts explored space, life went on as it had for centuries in the villages of Uzbekistan.

Cotton

Another aspect of "socialism" in Uzbekistan was the exploitation of women and children in the cotton fields so the republic could meet its economic goals for Moscow.

From spring to fall they would drive everyone, from small children to nursing mothers, out into the fields. And for what? To deliver on the republic's promise of six million tons of raw cotton.

As I said before, cotton harvesting was the work of women and children. Children in the provinces didn't attend school from September through December. Furthermore, the cotton industry created one of the most powerful criminal organizations in the world, one that corrupted both the government and the party structures. Almost the all the government and party leaders of the republic conspired in falsifying cotton production figures. As Moscow ordered the republic to produce more and more cotton, the Uzbek government reported miraculous growth in the amount of land irrigated, as well as record improvements in production, but most of these numbers were fabricated. The Uzbek leadership used exaggerated figures to get the central Soviet government to allocate substantial funds to Uzbekistan. Nonetheless, cotton production brought no revenue to the working people, and it took over large areas of land that could have been used to grow fruit, vegetables, and grain. As usual, the ordinary folks suffered the most.

I always hated the nasty chemical smell and the white powder that covered the ground in the villages and in the fields. Later I realized that they were carelessly sprayed pesticides. Pesticides were used in large amounts - they were obviously cheap. The ordinary people were not spared in any way when it came to meeting the party's goals and winning yet another medal or award for the republic's leader, Rashidov. It was obvious that the level of education of children "out in the provinces" was much lower than that of children in urban settings. The children and their teachers in the countryside simply did not have time for education, as they had to work in the fields for significant parts of the year. I had my first encounter with the cotton fields at age of 3. My mother and I visited my father on a cotton field, because even the employees of Uzbek Television were sent out to work there!

Shakhimardan

One year we did something different for summer vacation: we went to Shakhimardan for a whole week!

Shakhimardan is a small town in a valley in the Pamiro-Alai mountains in eastern Uzbekistan. Interestingly, it is completely surrounded by Kyrgyzstan. The town is famous as the place where the well-known poet and playwright Hamza Hakim-Zade Niyazi met his fate. An Uzbek version of Maxim Gorky, he wrote about the aspirations of the working class and was the first to write plays about women who had shed the burka full-body covering. In the late 1920s, he was stoned to death by Muslim extremists. We were taught about this in school.

Shakhimardan is also called the Uzbek Switzerland because of its natural beauty; people visit this area to treat all sorts of ailments or just to relax in the clean mountain air.

Soviet people deeply believed in the miraculous healing powers of seawater and mountain air.

I had never seen mountains before. They seemed endless and were so tall, that their tops were always hidden in the clouds. I looked at them dreamily - I wanted to fly over them and view this beauty from above. The rivers were crystal clear, and the locals drank water directly from them.

We had rented a room in a Kyrgyz house. Every morning the lady of the house brought us fresh milk from their cows and fresh flatbread from their clay oven. What a wonderful aroma! I still remember it!

The moment you stepped out onto the street in the village, the neighbors would call you in and offer you something to eat. A bunch of sweet grapes, some apples, some mountain cherry-plums ... a cherry-plum that was so delicious, you could not find anything like it anywhere else in the world! Only in Shakhimardan!

There I also tasted "dzhida" (Russian olives) for the first time. *Dzhida* is an interesting fruit that grows on trees, which reminded me of olive trees. But *dzhida* is smaller and grows on small trees. It tasted dry, like papier-mâché, and felt bristly like velvet.

The house we stayed in was located on a mountain slope and had a big sycamore tree in front of it with swings. Never before in my life had anything taken my breath away like swinging on those swings. I felt like I was flying over the trees and mountains!

When I recall those days in Shakhimardan, I see the giant snow-covered mountains and the deep blue lakes. I recall the feeling of endless flight and a world of overwhelming smells of fruits and flowers!

Isfara

During another summer vacation, my parents took me to the city of Isfara. Isfara is part of Tajikistan and has been the epicenter of religious and ethnic unrest since the region gained independence in 1991. The leaders of the Soviet Union deliberately drew artificial borders mixing several different ethnicities in each republic in the firm belief that by creating ethnic tensions, they would secure their control over the area. Tajikistan's independence was followed by a six-year civil war which resulted in the loss of 50,000 people and the devastation of large parts of the country. It also contributed to Tajikistan ranking among the ten poorest countries in the world today.

But back then, Isfara was a place where Uzbeks, Kyrgyz, and Tajiks would go to relax and escape the heat of low-altitude cities. Isfara was beautiful and green - and famous for its apricot groves. There were ripe apricots all over the place.

My dad had gotten tickets to the resort from Uzbek TV. People would periodically get free tickets to such resorts from their places of work. That summer my father was lucky and got tickets for the whole family.

On our way to Isfara, we visited our family in Kokand. My uncle, an important local official, decided to join us and bring his family, too. When we arrived in Isfara, I found out what it meant to be an important person in Uzbekistan. We had an entire large villa in Isfara to ourselves, complete with a swimming pool, which was a major luxury for everybody. Every morning, breakfast was served on an ottoman under a huge sycamore: freshly baked naan flatbread from a tandoor clay oven, freshly harvested grapes, a bowl of heavy cream, local honey with an unforgettable smell – it seemed like they had just harvested the honey that morning. Everything was fresh and delicious.

We saw peacocks walking in the garden. Finally, my dream to have a peacock feather came true. In fact, I could have as many of them as I wanted!

After breakfast, which usually lasted a couple of hours because a lot of people came to greet my important uncle, we would drive deep into the mountains, which were covered with millions of apricot trees. When we arrived, there would be another gathering, and we would be served lunch. They would slaughter a sheep and make us a very rich soup and *shashlik* ("shish-kebabs"), which we ate sitting in the orchard with a beautiful view of the mountains.

One day, after trying every possible delicacy, I got bored and decided to check out the local area. I saw kids playing among the trees not far from us and decided to join them. They looked exactly like Uzbeks, wearing the same kind of silk dresses and long pants, but their language was different. I couldn't understand a single word! They were speaking Tajik, which I didn't know at all.

This is a weird phenomenon: Tajiks look exactly like Uzbeks, have the same music and dances, eat the same food, but speak a totally different language!

Isfara is located at the border of Tajikistan, Uzbekistan, and Kyrgyzstan. Although we were different peoples with our own languages, cultures, and traditions, something united us.

I was used to having neighbors from different ethnic and religious groups: Greeks, Kazakhs, Koreans, etc. We knew they were different, we knew they spoke their own languages, we knew they ate different food (very spicy food). In Tashkent there were even rumors about Koreans eating dogs. But we grew up tolerating different types of people.

I don't know how, maybe body language helped me, but soon I was climbing trees with the local kids, picking fruit, and running up and down the mountain. I lost track of time altogether.

Suddenly, I realized that I had lost my parents, but I couldn't explain to the kids who I was and how I had come to their village! After a while my family found me, and I was severely punished. The next day I had to stay in my room all day long, while my siblings and the other family's kids were enjoying the swimming pool, running up and down on the hills of Isfara, and climbing fruit trees. Once again, I had been punished unfairly for my curiosity and love of exploration!

Village Kids

Each time I visited the provinces in Uzbekistan, I realized how different the kids in the village were. You could feel the difference in everything: in their dress and in their behavior. Village children are very modest and disciplined, and they have a rather narrow view of life. These poor kids hardly ever travel outside their villages. A visit even to Tashkent was something exceptional for them! We all were Uzbeks, but I was different, not because of my looks, but because I had a better education and I knew more than they did. I was from Tashkent and my school year lasted 9 months, whereas they were in school for barely 6 months because they had to work in the fields. Also, I had opportunities to travel and enjoy Russian and European music and movies. Most of the village kids didn't even speak Russian. These poor kids didn't really have time to play, because they were always helping around the house, in the garden, and in the fields.

Their diet was very poor. I remember how, during arguments, my mom would always say how spoiled I was, and that Uzbek kids from the provinces only have meat once a week!

I told you how hospitality is one of the most important aspects of Uzbek life. Even if someone was poor, as soon as you entered their house, they would ask "Choy ichasisizmi?" and offer you a cup of tea.

Once we were invited over for dinner and *plov*. As a spoiled townsperson and "aristocrat", I asked for a spoon. In surprise, the hosts asked me "Oh, aren't you able to eat *plov* with your hand?" It is customary to eat *plov* with your fingers, and villagers even manage to eat soup without a spoon, using a piece of flatbread instead. The lady of the house felt demeaned, but she said, "Go ahead and eat, my girl, a Muslim hand is clean".

Even if there is not enough time – or the desire – to have a full meal, Uzbeks would at least offer you some flatbread, dried fruit, and nuts. The Uzbek people are very warm and welcoming, very simple and open. They offer guests the very best they have. When we had sweets and delicacies in our house, we would beg our mother to give us some, but she would always say, "This is for our guests!" The best things in the house had to be saved for guests.

When you travel through Uzbekistan, you will see 5- and 6-year-old kids carrying their younger siblings on their backs. Young children take sheep out to graze, carry firewood on their fragile shoulders, and weed the cotton fields.

What does this have to do with socialism, the system which formally prohibits child labor! These kids even didn't have heat in their houses. Their mothers were cooking in an outdoor kitchen on a primitive mud hearth or in a clay oven. Even for me it was painful to see those poor kids, and I realized how spoiled I was growing up in a house with a bathroom, central gas heating, and a gas stove. Plus I attended an elite school and regularly went to the theatre. These kids would probably never see a theatre. The best they would get was the local movie theatre.

Movies

In the villages, movies were shown in wooden sheds or on open-air screens. The most popular movies during my childhood were from India: *The Flower and The Dust*, *Rama and Shama*, *Samgam*, and the world-famous Indian classic, *The Vagabond* with Raj Kapour. The local young people knew all the songs from these Indian movies by heart, and the girls even knew how to dance Indian-style. Indian actresses were their ideal of beauty.

In the 60s and 70s Indian movies were being shown throughout Uzbekistan. Was it the friendship between our peoples, the similarity of our mentality, or just the visit of the Indian Prime

Minister to Tashkent in the 60s which made those movies so incredibly popular with Uzbeks? By the way, after Indira Gandhi's visit to Tashkent, a lot of people started naming their daughters Indira.

Personally, I was not much of a fan of Indian movies; I was more interested in French and Italian films, which were also showing in our movie theatres. It was obvious that the local Uzbek population was crazy about Indian melodramas, whereas the Russian-speaking population was more into European cinema.

In our theatres there were a lot of French films with popular actors like the comedian Louis de Funès in the *Fantomas* series, Jean Marais, Belmondo, Jean Gabin, Annie Girardot, Alain Delon, and Pierre Richard. I remember the very popular actress Simone Signoret who was in a great movie, as well as the greatest blonde of that time, Catherine Deneuve. We probably went to see her in *Les Parapluies de Cherbourg* a dozen times. And I remember a movie with an Yves Montand concert, and TV programs with singers like Gilbert Bécaud, Charles Aznavour, Édith Piaf, Dalida and Joe Dassin. All the girls were in love with Joe Dassin and knew all his songs by heart. Other famous French singers were Sacha Distel and Mireille Mathieu. Her hairstyle was so popular that all girls tried to get Mireille Mathieu haircuts.

Yes, and we grew up with Italian movies like *La Dolce Vita* and *Marriage Italian-Style* with actors like Adriano Celentano, Sophia Loren, and Marcello Mastroianni, who were super-famous in the Soviet Union. The first time I saw Mastroianni was in Fellini's *8½*. This movie was revolutionary, and I remember how my friends and I would discuss it endlessly. It was a cult movie for us. Anyone who considered themselves even a little bit intelligent had to know almost every scene from the movie by heart.

In Tashkent we even had the privilege of live performances by foreign musicians and singers.

When I was a child, the very impressive Peruvian diva and singer Yma Sumac visited our city, along with forty other cities in the Soviet Union.

I remember her as a giant person with the face of a transsexual. Her voice spanned five octaves, and she produced sounds nobody had ever heard before: the thunder of the jungle or a waterfall, an underground groaning, the roar of a leopard, the squealing of a wild boar, and the songs of exotic birds from the equator. Her voice was stunning. She reached extreme heights and crossed sound barriers, which had seemed impenetrable. When her voice pierced through the thunder of applause, she seemed to freeze for a second, and then would produce an even higher final note from her mighty chest.

I was so afraid of her singing. At night when her voice appeared out of nowhere and sounds from the powerful jungle seemed to jump at me, I was afraid to go out into our yard... Where has she gone, where is the legendary Yma Sumac now?

And what happened to another legend of my childhood, Robertino Loretti? The little boy whose song "Jamaica" we children sang with all our heart? Thanks to him, I heard such wonderful classics as "Ava Maria", "O sole mio", "La Paloma", and the famous "Serenata" by Schubert.

And of course, "Besame mucho", the super hit of my childhood, which everybody loved. With its melody, it could easily have been a Russian folk song.

So movies and music were a big part of our "European education". Later in life my French and Italian friends were surprised how much of their cultural heritage I knew inside and out.

Everyday Music

There was another kind of music in Tashkent every morning: Through the clinking and rattling of milk jugs came the heavy voice of the milk lady: "Meelk!", "saua and sveet!"

Just behind her came another voice, a little bit younger - the second milk lady with different varieties. And then, later, came more voices, this time boys shouting, "Do you have dry bread for us?" They collected leftovers for their animals.

And even later came yet another voice - an elderly one shouting "Sharabarah!" That was the voice of the used clothes dealer.

Twice a week an old, old man in a padded jacket drove down our street on a wagon with a little half-dead donkey: the kerosine man, shouting "kerosine!"

Then came the glasscutter or the knife grinder with their mobile machinery.

My favorite Uzbek of all was the corn guy, who rode on a donkey and shouted "roasted cooorn!" All the children would run home to beg their parents for some change for a little bit of roasted corn. When there was no money, we children would exchange empty bottles, i.e. cotton oil containers. Oh, how many bottles I collected just to get some roasted corn!

Yes, roasted corn was a delicacy within our reach: just collect some empty cotton oil bottles around the neighborhood (which usually got thrown out in the trash anyway) and go and exchange them for a serving of corn!

Ice cream and cake were something extraordinary for us. We had to beg our parents for ice cream. My elderly aunt, who lived with us for a while, had a sore back. Once in a while she would ask us kids to walk on her back as a kind of massage. After that treatment, she would give us money for ice cream. I would go to the ice cream shop and buy my favorite ice cream treats, such as "Eskimo" and "Plombir".

But there was another problem: my mom was pretty sure that eating "very cold" ice cream would give us strep throat. So she would take the long-awaited ice cream right out of our hands and put in a pot to warm it up! Every single time she did this we would cry and beg her not to, but instead of enjoying our ice cream, we would end up drinking a sweet milk cocktail; i.e., what remained of the ice cream.

In our "gastronom" ("supermarket"), you could buy unusual cakes decorated beautifully with buttercream. I would look at them in the display case and count the days until my birthday. That was the only time I could get one.

We also got cake when guests brought cakes. We kids would get just one piece each of those dreamy sweets, so we would try to make the delight of eating the most delicious thing in the world last as long as possible. We had to drink hot tea with the cake – that was our tradition, but the tea was hot, and I had to wait till it cooled down before I started eating my cake. First, I would enjoy the decorations on top of the cake, which were made out of heavy cream and biscuits soaked in syrup.

Besides sweet stuff, I also liked pickled cucumbers, tomatoes, and patty pan squash, which my parents preserved in gallon-size glass jars in the summer. They also made eggplant caviar, which we would enjoy spread on black multigrain bread. It was good to have the eggplant caviar in the refrigerator; you could eat it for breakfast or lunch, or have it as an appetizer.

All winter long, our pickled and preserved vegetables replaced fresh ones.

During the winter we couldn't buy vegetables and fruits at the store. You couldn't buy these things all year round. We ate what was in season.

In the spring, summer, and fall we had every possible fruit and vegetable, as they started to ripen in April and grew through November.

In the winter we always had cabbage, different types of radish, and even a lot of greens like dill, cilantro, parsley, garlic, and fresh onions. We ate garlic and onions raw, sometimes between meals, with just bread and salt. Actually, bread with onions and garlic was my favorite snack!

In the winter, when my mom served us food, she would put bunches of dill or cilantro, a couple of heads of garlic, and onions on the table, which we would eat up very quickly, even before the meal was served.

Uzbeks don't usually have dessert after meals; instead, we would always eat fruit. In the wintertime we would eat pomegranates, apples, and grapes. We stored grapes by hanging them in the basement.

Some varieties of honey melons and watermelons could also be stored in our basement well into the new year.

I remember our joy when, after dinner, our dad would squeeze the precious pomegranate juice into our cups, a whole one for each of us!

Summer was paradise for us: there were plenty of fruits!

For breakfast we often had bunches of grapes which we had picked right there in our yard! They were so sweet and fragrant!

We collected the leftover fruits and vegetables by the bucket, and at night the neighbors' kids would come over and take them away to feed their cows or sheep.

Everybody had fruit trees in their courtyards; it is an Uzbek tradition to eat a lot of homegrown fruits and vegetables. Fruit trees were everywhere - not only inside the courtyards, but also along our streets. We had cherries, apricots, peaches, and every kind of apple tree around our house.

Springtime was always beautiful, with fruit trees blossoming in white, pink, or violet and emitting a breathtaking aroma! Wherever I am in the world, I always try to catch that same that aroma in the spring.

We planted all sorts of herbs, tomatoes, paprika, and green onions in the spring.

It was my duty to pick fresh vegetables from our garden for us to cook.

Everything on our table was fresh!

The cherries and strawberries were already ripe in early May. In the markets the first things you could buy were tomatoes and cucumbers. We kids would often chow down even green sour apricots and stuff ourselves.

In June we would pick the first apples and melons. And so on throughout the summer.

Often our favorite way to hang out was just sitting under the fruit trees!

The Uzbek House

As I wrote before, I grew up in Kokcha, one of the old neighborhoods of Tashkent. When I tell people where I am from, they look at me perplexed. Obviously, my looks do not fit with this neighborhood. Kokcha was considered a conservative, traditional area.

Kokcha is associated with a famous mosque, the ancient cemetery with the Sheikh Zayiniddin Mausoleum, and the square where many Uzbek holidays are being celebrated, especially after the "urozah" ("religious fasting").

You could find everything there: schools, doctors' offices, hairdressers, shops. And of course - *chaykhana* teahouses on every corner. Uzbek men cannot live without their teahouses! They are like pubs for the English ...

Wearing their traditional long striped or dark blue "chapan" overcoats, hats and turbans, Uzbeks would lounge there for hours, drinking tea, sweating, and conversing. Sweating in those thick cotton overcoats is quite beneficial: it cools the skin and keeps the body temperature constant throughout the day. This is an age-old technique to fight the heat.

Kokcha seemed like a city within the city. It's sort of like Bagdad, with its endless maze of side streets and dead ends. Displaced Russians, Tatars, Armenians and Jews lived on the neighboring streets. And there were thousands of Uzbek homes surrounded by high walls.

The courtyard of the typical Uzbek house was always neatly swept. The house would have everything necessary for the life of a big family and as such, was a self-sufficient and self-contained unit.

Some houses had additions on top, which were called "bolhana"; they were not exactly balconies, but almost like an upper level which made a one-story house look like a two-story one.

The roofs of many houses were covered with dirt, and grass would often grow on them. Here and there you could even see delicate poppy flowers swaying in the wind ...

98

A small "aryk", or canal (something very typical in Tashkent), usually flows through the courtyard. An *aryk* is also one of the main features of the streets of Tashkent, but the ones out on the streets are pretty wide and sometimes up to a meter deep. To us children, they seemed like wide rivers.

Aryks separate the sidewalks from the road. In the central streets of the city, the canals are mostly lined with concrete; everywhere else they just ran in their clay banks.

The water was used to sprinkle the streets and to water the trees and plants. It was also cool and, of course, a favorite playground for kids.

On hot days we would hike up our skirts or pants and walk in those cool streams for as long as we could. In deeper places, the older boys would swim and dive all day long.

One of my favorite pastimes was to closely study the bottoms of the *aryks*. Beautiful, long, dark green grass was swaying elegantly down there.

Inside the courtyard, many families had an "ayvan" (a wooden platform) built over the *aryk*, which served many different functions. During the day and in the evenings, you could sit on them with your guests, have your tea, and listen to the gentle sound of running water. At night from April through October the entire family could sleep on it, padded with cotton-stuffed blankets. Over time, those "kurpacha" blankets would acquire a specific odor, because you don't wash them, you just dry and air them in the sun. The sound of *aryks* would relax us and lull us to sleep ...

There was an intoxicating softness not only from the sound of water flowing through the *aryks*, but also in the air, in the distant blue mountains, in the trees covering the quiet streets like a rich green vault, and in the white, yellow and pink houses in the city center...

All of the houses were large and had high ceilings, which was a blessing on hot days; some of them even had columns in front and fretwork on the eaves.

Once I saw a paper ruble in the water and caught it! What great luck that was: in those days you could buy the whole world for a Soviet ruble! 10 rooster-shaped lollipops, 5 servings of ice cream, or 10 big white crispy balls of roasted corn, which were sold on every corner by sun-dried, dark-skinned elderly Uzbek women. And how much lemonade one could have just for the change left after one of those purchases! What a fortune it was for me to hold this paper ruble in my hands!

And bountiful sunlight shone in our yards from early morning on, penetrating through the foliage, playing in yellow and green patterns on the sidewalk. It would shine until the very inky-starry night, when the sunlight turned into an afterglow of aromas from the trees, bushes, and grasses. We felt all this vividly, falling asleep out in the open on our family *ayvan*, all the children packed in a row. Because of the tremendous heat, which could go as high as 115°F, it was unbearable inside the house, and only our yard would save us ...

Then there was the sound of Uzbek music, playing for a wedding somewhere on any given day during the summer and fall.

Our little street was very charming with its greenery and the quietly murmuring *aryks*.

Towards the end of summer, we would collect grapes first thing in the morning. I especially loved the ones that had almost turned into raisins.

We always had a "summer kitchen" annex in our yard and a small clay tandoor oven, where we baked our flatbread and our samosas.

You simply can't forget the "spirit" of fresh hot Uzbek flatbread. You dream of it everywhere and always.

In my dreams, I see my aunt poking the breads inside the oven and catching them as they fall off the oven's walls. Fresh bread with slightly burnt spots and cumin seeds. Fresh round flatbread with its crispy center and its soft rim, emanating a hot aroma... It is difficult to convey this aroma, which is somewhat similar to the smell of one's mother, which is deeply embedded in a child's memory. A whole world of emotions is connected to the aroma of fresh bread.

Inside the houses we had a "hontakhta", something like a low coffee table with a sort of fireplace below it, where you put hot ashes. We would sit round the *hontakhta* on thick *kurpacha* blankets and stick our feet underneath the *hontakhta*, where they would stay warm.

Especially in the wintertime, when we came home freezing, it felt ever so good to slip your feet underneath the *hontakhta*, sipping freshly-brewed hot tea and eating dried fruits, while the heat would slowly crawl up your body.

The toilets in Uzbek homes were built on the opposite end of the yard - little outhouses with holes in its floor, where you would do your business squatting. There was also a bucket full of pieces of smooth clay in the outhouse for cleaning yourself afterwards. In Russian outhouses, you would usually see pieces of newspaper or pages from school notebooks stuck on a nail on the wall. Back then there was no such thing as toilet paper. I think it appeared in the 70s or 80s and was always a big "deficit" item in the Soviet Union. When you saw a long line at a store, you could be sure they were selling toilet paper.

In the evenings, when the scorching heat of the Asian day gave way to long shadows from the apple trees and apricot trees playing on the yellow brick pathways, long snake-like rubber hoses would crawl out of their homes. Some of them were made out of several pieces of hose of different diameters and colors which were connected with aluminum wire. Then the dry earth would happily present her dry hot back to the tongues of water from those rubber snakes.

People would bring out tables and chairs and start preparing dinner.

The smell of grilled onions and meat would appear… it was time for family dinners.

The yards would fill like boiling pots with chatter, laughter, cries, shrieks, and shouts. The yards would hum and sing along with the sounds of music from radios and record players.

After dinner, people would go visit family and neighbors for chats over cups of tea, while the children had time to run around and play until dark.

Some families had TV sets, which back then were small with black and white screens, and some even had big magnifying glasses in front of the screen.

If a neighbor invited you in, the room would quickly fill up with people who brought their own chairs and stools, and little kids would sit on somebody's lap or lie right in front of the screen.

Luckily, this kind of "public viewing" at home was enjoyable, and after the program, people would discuss it, arguing and interrupting one another.

These simple get-togethers - watching TV and chatting over tea (discussing the latest news, a new movie, or just gossiping) – has never occurred in my life since then.

The entire street was a quiet, closely-knit network of families and clans. Everybody knew everything about everybody. We shared our joys and sorrows. An upcoming wedding, an illness, a death in the family…there was always somebody there to help and support you. There was no such thing as loneliness. People could not physically stand being alone for one minute. We were always surrounded by big families, relatives, and friends. Three or more generations would live under one roof: grandparents, parents, children…

When a son got married, he would most definitely live with his parents. It would be very shameful if he were to abandon his parents. Society did not tolerate people not honoring their parents. Parents were something holy in Uzbek society. And in any important matter, the elderly – parents and grandparents – always had the last say.

Chapter 6.

High School

I have always been interested in journalism and art, but when I said I wanted to go to college to study cinematography in the art history department, my dad reacted negatively. He knew by experience that it would be hard to find work.

My parents dreamt of me becoming a doctor, and to fulfill their dreams, they hired tutors for me in physics and math. These were the subjects that I hated most of all, but I couldn't disobey my parents. As I said before, in Uzbek families respecting your parents was the most important thing of all.

By age 15 I started having headaches, and my parents decided to switch me to a local school so I wouldn't have to spend two hours a day travelling to and from school. After my first day at my new school on September 1, I returned home with tears in my eyes. The quality of the teachers, the school program, and the other students in no way compared to my previous school, which was considered to be the best in the city academically.

Nothing but gossip interested my new classmates. There were no conversations about politics and art, as in the other school. Compared to the students in the new school, I was a real European. The teachers would separate the students into groups and assign grades according to their parents' positions. The classrooms were poorly equipped.

I told my parents that I wouldn't go to this school. They proposed another school that was also not too far from our house. From day one I was treated well there. The girls surrounded me and were curious to know everything they could about me. The class was mainly made up of Russian-speaking children who lived among

Uzbeks. There were Tatars, Ukrainians, Greeks, Koreans, and Crimean Tatars. There were also a lot of mixed children: i.e., children whose parents were of mixed ethnicities.

Since they lived among Uzbeks, these children had no contempt for the locals as the students had in my last school. They were friendly, and after school they would do things together. After classes were over, it was obvious that no one wanted to go home; instead, everyone would hang around the school and gab and gab. Later they would spend lots of time walking each other home.

I fell in love with everyone right away. I finally felt that people respected me. And then some!

I had gone to a prominent school, I dressed stylishly, and I was the best in most of my classes, so everyone wanted to hang out with me. I always looked forward to the next day. As soon as I got out of bed in the morning, I would fly to school. I had never been as happy in my life as I was during that school year.

For the first time, boys were falling in love with me, and no one cared what my ethnicity was. I had been suddenly transformed from an ugly duckling into an attractive girl. I wanted to look even more stylish and began to sew trendy clothes based on styles I saw in fashion magazines. Later, I began to create my own fashions and knitted trendy vests and sweaters. Once I had an incentive, I immediately discovered that I had hidden talents!

I even cut my own bangs - and was severely punished for this by my parents. In revenge, I decided to cut bangs for all the neighboring girls. I have no idea how I managed to talk them all into it. The girls were from traditional Uzbek families, and our culture strictly forbade cutting women's hair. You can imagine the scandal this caused in our *mahalla* neighborhood. My parents didn't know what to do with me.

Then I decided to shorten my school uniform as much as possible. Miniskirts were all the rage then, but not in our traditional Uzbek neighborhood. In the morning I would leave home in my regular long school uniform, but before I made it to the street, I would shorten it as much as possible. I walked proudly past the harsh glances of my neighbors and completely ignored them. They started complaining to my parents about my outfit, and my parents defended me because I was leaving the house dressed in my regular uniform. Until one day my father caught sight of me!

No punishment, however severe, could make me stop dressing stylishly. I started sewing the widest possible bell-bottom pants and was the first in our city to wear them. It was the 1970s and hippies were in fashion. As I said before, there were shortages of everything, and finding trendy clothes to wear was impossible. If something more or less fashionable from the Eastern Bloc appeared in stores, you would have to stand in line for hours to get it; then you would end up somewhere with another girl who was wearing the exact same outfit purchased at the same store. But people weren't too concerned about that sort of problem; in fact, the opposite was the case - it highlighted the fact that you were the lucky owner of imported clothing!

I never allowed myself to look like anyone else. That's why I came up with different ways to make clothing – through sewing and knitting. In school I was always dressed more fashionably than anyone else. I would ignore the judgmental, sidewise glances of my neighbors. I knew that the Uzbek girls who lived next store were jealous of me, and that if they had had the opportunity to dress like me, they would have. But apparently, I was the only person in our traditional *mahalla* ("neighborhood") who had any courage! I was already sure that no Uzbek man would ever marry me anyway, so I had nothing to lose.

Surprisingly, the degree of internationalism was different in different parts of the same town. The students in my previous school lived in the European part of the city and lived a European way of life. The kids from the new school, who lived among and were friends with Uzbeks, became like them, and that was completely natural. This is because Uzbeks are a very hospitable people who constantly invite their neighbors over and entertain them. It is natural that the Uzbek culture of hospitality would catch on with them. After all, several generations of various ethnic groups lived side by side with the Uzbeks – literally on the other side of a fence, and many of them understood Uzbek, and could even speak it.

105

This was particularly true of the Greeks who lived in our neighborhood. The Greek parents of my friends were former partisans – communists who had fought against the Germans. When there was a reactionary wave in Greece, they ended up in Uzbekistan. Stalin allowed them to immigrate to the USSR as political refugees and settled them around the country. We grew up together, knew Greek music, danced the Greek dance *syrtaki* together, and loved Greek food. You could hear Greek music performed by Michael "Mikis" Theodorakis coming from the windows of their houses. Unfortunately, in the mid-1970s democracy returned to Greece, and the Greeks gradually began to return home. It was hard for us to say goodbye to them. I can't imagine how hard it was for my friends who were born and grew up in Uzbekistan, then had to go to a country they didn't know at all. They didn't even know Greek well.

All the students in my class were friends. We frequently skipped class together, went to the movies together, and walked around town. I was friends with Rakhim (a Dungan), Ramil and Rustam (Tatars), Zyova (an Uzbek), Marina (a Russian), and Sveta (a Ukrainian). We all listened to the same music, Soviet schlagers. Records had just appeared and were pretty expensive, so we would trade them with each other. Then we started getting together for parties to celebrate birthdays and holidays. Since I was an Uzbek girl, I was never allowed to go anywhere, and could only go to events if they took place during the day. Once again, my traditional culture deprived me of the joy of being a teenager. At times I was embarrassed to have to tell my classmates that I wasn't allowed to go to parties in the evening.

Since I really wanted to go to these events, my friends and I would think up ways to make it possible, like saying we were studying for a test or had to meet up in the evening to do homework. My friends would help me out – they would call and ask my parents to let me go out, but I was never allowed to stay out after 9. My friends who weren't Uzbek could go to as many parties as they wanted to and stay out as long as they wanted. Every day after class I was supposed to be home by 3, then gather my things and go see my tutors to study the subjects I hated: physics and chemistry.

That's precisely when I made up my mind to leave Uzbekistan and try to get accepted at a university in Moscow or Leningrad. As I already said, I got in touch with these universities when I was in Leningrad and found out everything I needed to know about getting accepted and how to study for the entrance exams. Incidentally, it didn't hurt at all that I had extra lessons in physics and chemistry. I regularly went to see the tutor, who lived in the European part of the city, the Chilanzar District. My parents chose her because she taught in the medical school that they wanted me to go to. She was very strict; after all, she had to earn the 5 rubles per hour my parents were paying her, which was a lot of money at that time. She gave me a lot of work to do, plus I had to travel a long way to get to her house, which was particularly unpleasant because I had to drag myself across town on public transportation with multiple transfers in the heat. Meanwhile, my girlfriends were going to the movies or on dates.

Highschool Sweetheart

I fell in love with a boy in my new class. His name was Rustam, and it was love at first sight. I remember how good looking he was, and how unique he looked on my first day in the new school. The girls were crazy about him and would whistle at him. When I looked at him, an electric shock ran through my body. I had never felt anything like that before. I had liked boys before, but that was the first time I had ever felt anything like that. He also froze when he saw me, and so we stood, looking at one another for several minutes in front of everyone. He was immediately surrounded by other girls, but I noticed that he was still looking at me.

A few days later he walked up to me and introduced himself. He invited me to sit with him at the same table in class. I agreed, of course – after all, that was exactly what I was dreaming about at that time. Our romance began at that moment. I know that there were some girls who disliked me because they were jealous that I had Rustam, but they knew full well that there was no chance of us having a long-term relationship, because I was Uzbek and he was a Tatar. But I wasn't thinking about that at the time. I wasn't thinking about the future. I was living completely in the present, focusing only on the days, the minutes I spent with him. He was very romantic, with elegant hands and manners, and was quite debonair! He had such beautiful brown eyes and long eyelashes. Oh god! He looked just like Omar Sharif!

I liked how affectionate he was toward me. Every day he gave me poems he had written for me. In the morning before he and his friends skipped out on classes, he would leave me love letters, which he had written for me the night before. He was a talented writer. It was the first time in my life that anyone had written poetry for me or declared their love to me. He even got a tattoo with my name on the thumb of his right hand as a sign of his love for me.

But he was strange. For example, after stopping by school to give me letters, he would disappear with his friends and skip classes. I hoped that he would come back to school at the end of the day and wait for me so he could tell me in person everything he had put in the letter, but alas, he didn't appear.

Sometimes he would call me in the evening and say he was hanging out with his classmates in the park, but he never invited me. Maybe he knew that my parents would never let me out at night. I was so jealous of them all! They were hanging out, talking, kissing, holding each other's hands. But my parents deprived me of that; they deprived me of the joy of being a teenager. All I heard from my parents was "Study! Study! Study!" All that was important for them was that I get into college. My mom never asked about my private life. I really wanted her to be a friend to me, the kind you can talk about everything with. Especially now that I was in love. Finally, one day I couldn't take it anymore, and I told her about Rustam. Her reply was, "Shame on you"!!

I was supposed to feel ashamed of everything - of asking questions about menstruation or how to buy a bra, which was something you couldn't get in stores. As a teenage girl, I never got the support I needed from my mom with things like personal hygiene, her first love, etc. For some reason, thanks to Muslim culture, it was considered inappropriate to talk to girls in Uzbek families about these things. I was jealous of my girlfriends who had extremely close relationships with their mothers and were able to share everything with them. My mom would always say "That's forbidden," "Aren't you ashamed?" or "Focus on your studies instead."

One day she slapped me because I said the word "no" to her, which was forbidden to do to parents in my family. I was so hurt by this injustice! I was also a human being with my own opinions and views on life. I wanted my parents to respect that, but all I would hear is, "That's just not done!" or "We Uzbeks/We older people are right about everything!"

Nevertheless, I love my mom a lot, and I don't hold this against her at all. After all, she was a typical Uzbek mom.

I loved to go see my Russian friend Marina. Her mom was happy to listen to us talk and give us advice. We loved talking to her about the boys that we liked, and there was nothing inappropriate in this. Marina's mom was her close friend. I always wanted my mom to be my friend, but alas!... It's true that she became one later, but when I was a teenager and was having so many problems, I needed her. At that time, I already knew that I was only allowed to marry an Uzbek, but I wasn't thinking about that and continued to see Rustam, even though he was a Tatar. Together we would go to the theater or walk around the downtown. It seemed to me that that was the only place that my friends or relatives wouldn't see us, but I still was very nervous. There weren't any cafes where you could just sit with your beloved one and talk. Sometimes we took walks in parks. But we had to skip classes if we wanted to spend time together; after all, after school I had to be home and study, study, study.

One day the boys from our class were playing basketball with boys from another school, and our whole class went out to cheer for them after school. I knew that my parents wouldn't let me go, but I went anyway to root for our team. We left the building at 5 pm when the game ended. It was already dark, and Rustam offered to accompany me to my house. When we got on the bus, I immediately got nervous – after all, people I knew might see me. When we got off at my stop, I asked Rustam not to go any further, but he said it was dark, and he would feel better if he at least were able to walk me to my street. And, of course, a few of the neighbors saw me. When I came home, my parents didn't want to talk to me. When I cried, "After all, I'm only two hours late. What's the big deal?", my dad slapped me and added, "You take walks with boys. Do you want to bring shame on our entire family?"

In the 20C, in a socialist country which was fighting for women's rights, where they had TV shows about famous women actresses, political figures, and female Uzbek scientists, feudal traditions were flourishing in families. What a hypocritical society! And I was so tired of it!

I was upset that I didn't have the right to fall in love, date, or enjoy life just because I was an Uzbek girl. In the morning, I would go to a Russian school and conduct myself like a progressive European girl until 2 pm, then I would return home to a feudal environment. Everything inside of me protested against this hypocrisy. I hated the hypocrisy of my society, my school, and the adults around me.

I would always ask myself, do Uzbeks need progress? Do they need these comfortable high-rise houses they live in? Maybe they should have been left in their traditional homes with their gardens and their outdoor toilets. After all, that suited the way of life and culture of the local inhabitants better.

I heard that after the earthquake in Tashkent, the Russians, Ukrainians, and people of other Soviet ethnic groups who came to the city were not the best representatives of their respective ethnicities. It seems that professional workers who had their own houses and families wouldn't have left their lives to come to god knows where in 105° weather to help the provincial (as they viewed us) Uzbek people rebuild their city. And when they began to tear down the typical one-story homes in downtown Tashkent, people surrounded the bulldozers and tried to prevent them from destroying the clay houses. They yelled that they didn't need high-rise apartment buildings and that they didn't want to live up in the air. That it was more comfortable in the traditional clay houses and that no one had asked these "Russian brothers" to come here!

In 1917 the Uzbek people were not ready to move from feudalism to socialism. To value progress, you have to fight for it. But it was brought to us by the Bolsheviks, and the Uzbek people

110

never asked them to do this. So for 70 years this hypocritical society existed, and people like me had a hard time living in it.

We had a split personality, and sometimes we didn't know who we really were.

My parents, who at one time were in love themselves and were able to successfully fight for their love, continued to play by the rules of the game. They were convinced that they could control the emotions of their children and get them moving in the right direction. But then they shouldn't have sent us to Russian schools and keep telling us how important an education and a career were. And yet, in spite of all this, my parents were rather progressive. All my girlfriends in that neighborhood were in an even worse situation. They were raised in traditional families, most of them had trouble speaking Russian, and they rarely, if ever, went to theaters or the movies. When they came home from school, they had to do housework for the family - clean, sweep the courtyard, and make dinner for the whole family. They never went beyond the city limits, and to visit the mountains near Tashkent would have been something unusual for them. And yet they all were pioneers, then members of the Komsomol, and in the future, they would become members of the communist party.

If they were smart enough and if their parents let them, after high school they would go to college, then get married after the first or second year there. After the wedding, they would become baby factories, producing, above all, baby boys. A big family is the dream of every Uzbek woman. Happiness is when you have sons ("After all, girls will ultimately get married and go off to live with another family.")

It was believed that sons would help parents in their old age and properly see them off on their last journey. Traditionally men played the main role at funerals; only men were allowed to take the deceased to the cemetery. Thus, everyone in the family wanted sons, and they were treated better than girls. From early childhood on, girls were aware that they were being treated worse than boys. And once a girl was married off, all that was expected of her was to produce sons.

111

As I already said, a girl's parents needed to start saving money as soon as she was born. I remember a trunk in my parents' bedroom where my mom collected various textiles for our dowries. All the money they saved would be spent on the wedding, so there was no chance of vacations or family trips!

Although socialism existed in our country for 70 years, feudal traditions were never rooted out. I was always surprised that the winds of advanced socialism had no impact on the consciousness of the so-called highly educated Uzbeks, even those who had completed their educations in Russia. They, too, sent their daughters from matchmaker to matchmaker and forced their children to marry the person they thought was best. There was also the caste system: children of higher cases couldn't marry anyone from a lower cast. What happened to all that Soviet ideology in all this? What happened to the ideals of equality, progress, higher education, etc.? In short, Uzbekistan continued to live with medieval traditions! And they ignored the things shown on TV day and night and advocated by the government. This double life was the norm in all the former republics.

Friends

Rustam and I continued to date. Nature triumphed, however. One day my mom found my diary and, of course, read it all. She even took Rustam's photographs and the letters and poems he had written for me. But my mom did not feel ashamed about violating my privacy without my permission; instead, thanks to being raised in traditional Uzbek culture, I was the one who felt ashamed. Luckily, I had a bunch of friends I could talk to about this: Luiza the Tatar, Berta the Bukharan Jew, Jamilya, who was mixed (her mom was Tatar and her father Uzbek), and Marina and Sveta, who were Russian. I could count on their support at any time. They really understood my problems. In general, friendship between us girls was something sacred, and all our teenage problems were resolved in this group. All I had to do was call one of them, and immediately they would all be at my side. You only had to pour out your heart to them, and just like that, your problems would disappear!

112

We didn't need psychologists.

In our understanding, psychologists were just for people in psychiatric wards. I could talk with my girlfriends about any problem in the world! And we skipped classes together and watched many, many movies together. In fact, we knew everything about one another.

Uzbek Wedding Traditions

In Uzbekistan, weddings are a complex process consisting of several key events: *Fatiha-tui, Non-Sindirish, Nikokh-Tui,* and *Kelin-Salom.* There are many regional differences in these rites and rituals because Uzbeks are a mix of many different clans scattered throughout the country. Within each clan the traditional ceremonies are very similar, but in different regions, these differences are more distinct.

The "wedding" begins with the parents' search of a suitable girl for their son. An extensive search begins, as the parents get information from relatives, neighbors, friends, and acquaintances about girls of marriageable age. Every detail is taken into account: the social status of family, the girl's education, her character and reputation, etc. Social status is not important in terms of the size of the dowry; rather, families prefer a girl from the same circle and level of income as the groom's family, as it ensure the maximum level of understanding between the bride and groom.

Sometimes a boy already has a certain candidate in mind, so they discuss her at the family council, but the parents have the final word.

Turkic people, including Uzbeks, never send matchmakers to the house if a matchmaker has already been sent by another family, until a decision is made about that match. Otherwise, it would be disrespectful to the family who sent their matchmaker first.

Matchmaker

When the bride is chosen, a matchmaker is sent to her parents. Matchmakers are chosen very carefully, because they are a big part of the first impression the girl's parents get about the young man's family. It is the matchmaker who will mediate between the two sides.

Matchmakers don't have to be women. The tradition does not prohibit the execution of these duties by honorable men, but in most regions and districts, matchmakers are women.

Actually, both male and female matchmakers have their pros and cons, so in some cases, both a man and a woman are sent.

There is a practice called "Beshik Kerti" or "Quloq Tishlatar" ("ear biting"), which is still common today. It is an agreement made by the parents about the marriage of their children at an early age ("in the cradle" - "beshik" is "cradle" in Uzbek). In these cases, which generally occur when, for example, fathers are very close friends from grade school, there is absolutely no need for a matchmaker.

With such arrangements, expensive gifts are often given. For example, in Jizzakh province, the family of the boy sends a few dozen sheep to the girl's family.

The advantage of such customs is that there is a good relationship between the families, but unfortunately, the feelings of the children are not considered. In some cases, these marriages turn out to be very unhappy. Some girls have even run away from the wedding with their true loves, shaming the entire clan.

That's why these practices are less and less common.

By the way, although there was much greater freedom in the selection of a mate in the Soviet Union than before, Soviet surveys show that 88% of urban Uzbeks and 92% percent of those in the villages still insisted on parental consent before marriage.

The Test Phase

If the families do not know each other well, a test is arranged to assist in the proper selection of a bride or the acceptance of the candidacy of a groom. Remember how in fairy tales, the princess would declare a contest for the candidates asking for her hand? Kill the dragon or get a star or the moon from the sky …

114

Modern tests are simpler, but they help reveal the main traits of a person's character.

In some villages near Andijan, the potential groom may be asked to chop firewood. In other places, his manner of eating Lagman (Uzbek pasta) is observed. In the village of Karamurcha, the fiancé is asked to build a tandoor (clay oven). After these "tests", the nature and character of the male candidate becomes immediately obvious.

To make the union of a couple harmonious and strong, the bride should be well vetted, too. In Andijan, the matchmaker checks the kitchen, the bathroom, and even under the carpets in the house of the girl for cleanliness. Karshi matchmakers are interested in the order of shoes on the shelves; they also examine the style and combinations of the materials and colors of the "kurpacha" ("thick stuffed blankets") that the girl made. Girls in Tashkent are asked to set the table for matchmakers, bring them bread, and pour them tea in order to demonstrate the gracefulness of their movements and their ability to receive visitors. So, the matchmaker (or matchmakers) comes to the house of the girl's parents. According to Uzbek customs of hospitality, they are shown a warm welcome, and must be served bread and tea. By the way, matchmakers in the Khorezm region usually say very beautiful words like, "In your garden there is a flower blooming, we have heard a nightingale singing who is worthy of it."

In Kashkadarya, the formula is much simpler: "We have come to marry ..."

There are very different ways to answer the matchmaker:

In Andijan, Karshi, and the communities of the Jizzakh region, when a match is made, bread and sweets are exchanged. In Samarkand and Kamashi Ramitane, they just cook pilaf.

As a sign of agreement in the regions of Karakalpakstan and Khorezm, matchmakers are offered semolina and milk with butter; in Shahrihane, they are given a snow-white piece of cloth as a present. This custom is called "Ok Lik" ("the white thing").

But if the matchmakers find the tips of their shoes pointed to the door, they know that they should not come back to this house.

Breaking the Bread

The rite of "Non-Sindirish" - literally, the breaking of the bread - denotes the final consent of the parents of the bride and groom to marry. "Fatih-Tui" – engagement or mini-wedding – is the event that begins the wedding celebration.

Previously, these two ceremonies were held separately, but more recently they are often combined.

The date of *Non-Sindirish* and *Fatiha-Tui* is determined immediately after the matchmaker gets consent from the girl's parents.

The ritual of "the breaking of the bread" is always performed by people of honor who have achieved success in life, such as grandfathers or respected elders of the clan or the *mahalla*.

During "the breaking of the bread," the following words are stated: "May these young people live peacefully and beautifully until the end of their days! May they be accommodating and yielding." Pieces of the bread are then given to the families of the bride and groom, indicating that they will now share one loaf of bread.

After that, all the neighbors and relatives are given cakes and sweets, which were brought by the groom's family as a sign that the girl has been promised.

In Tashkent, the combined ceremony of *Non-Sindirish* and *Fatiha-Tui* is called "Malum Oshi", ie. "The Announcement Meal". On this day, the bride's mother brings money, milk, and material gifts for the bride, sweets, *patyr, katlamu*, the agreed-upon animal (usually a sheep), and rice flour.

In some areas, it is customary to put markings of flour on the face or shoulders of the groom's parents. They believe this helps prevent the infiltration of something "black " or "bad" into their house.

After this mini-wedding event, in many regions there is a lull before the real wedding. But not everywhere: In some places immediately after the mini-wedding event, even before the groom's side arrives back at their house, the girl's family sends them samosas, 50 boiled eggs, and sweets. On top of this, they send a complete set of new clothing for the groom's parents …

After that, they will receive baskets full of presents from the groom's parents: again, bread and sweets…

Girls' Day

On the eve of the wedding, the girlfriends of the bride gather in her house. Festive foods are cooked, and often the groom's family sends a variety of delicacies and gifts for this occasion.

Musicians are invited to entertain everyone, and the bride dances in holiday attire.

On this day, the bride is bathed, and her hair is plaited into 40 braids.

The girls compete in their ability to apply beautiful henna designs to the hands of the bride and to draw her eyebrows beautifully with antimony. All evening long, the girls entertain and cheer the bride to calm her anxiety before the wedding.

In Urgut, the person who weaves the braids for the bride is picked very carefully. She should be well off in life, have children, and be well respected among her clan. She weaves the braids with the words "Oyga Karich, Erga Karoq" ("the Moon is longing for hands, the Earth is longing for decoration").

At the end of each braid, they weave in some cotton fibers to hold the ends of the braid securely together and give them additional length.

Dowry

Parents start building up a girl's dowry immediately after her birth. This tradition has existed for a very long time.

In ancient Khorezm, for example, the dowry must include a teapot; in Kashkadarya and Surkhandarya a mandatory item is the "Chankovus" - a musical instrument, as well as traditional decorations for the bride's room, embroidered with her own hand, etc. In the dowry of girls from Samarkand, Urgut, Shakhrisabz, and Kitab, there must be scarves for performing ritual bows.

The Wedding

A wedding in Khorezm is a very costly event for the groom's side. The dowry alone amounts to a large sum, and all the other wedding expenses are also borne by his family. In Tashkent, on the other hand, it is complicated to marry a daughter.

In any case, the share borne by each side is negotiated during the engagement talks, including the shopping list for the young couple and gifts for the parents and other relatives.

On the day of the wedding, the groom dresses in a "Sarpo", a new full set of clothing and shoes, which are a present from the bride's family for the event.

Brides dress in different ways. Most modern brides choose European-style dresses. In this outfit, they "shine" during the registration of the marriage in the state registration office and during the photo session. For the ritual portion of the event, they dress in traditional garments.

After the official registration and the photo and video shoots, the young couple returns to the house of the bride's parents. They celebrate throughout the day with a big feast, which includes a festive pilaf. The same type of festive pilaf is cooked in the groom's house for the evening meal.

For the leave-taking from her home, the bride dresses so that no one can see her, so that no evil eyes can look upon her. She wears a white dress with long sleeves and a long skirt, which touches the floor, and fancy boots. Her head is covered with a small white headscarf as well as a larger one, which knotted in the style of a veil. On top of all this she wears a festive "chapan" ("Uzbek overcoat").

The bride is then escorted by friends and relatives, who hold a beautiful embroidered curtain over her head. All the time a "Yangya" will be by her side - an experienced female relative, who helps and supports her during the rituals.

118

The dowry, as agreed to before the wedding, travels along with the bride. It includes all the household items needed for the first period of family life: linens, "kurpachi" ("light mattresses"), pillows, and a complete wardrobe for the young woman.

The Traditional Wedding Ritual

In addition to the civil registration at the registry office, an Uzbek couple must go through the ritual reading of "Nikokh" – the religious wedding ceremony.

The Imam of a nearby mosque reads the "Hutbai Nikokh" ("prayer for the marriage"), after which the young couple is declared husband and wife before God.

During the *nikokh* reading, the imam says to the fiancé: "Do not leave her alone for six months. Do not hit her with six strokes; do not speak rudely to her. Respect her identity. Before nightfall, no matter where you are, come back home."

To the bride he says: "Always respect the groom. When he leaves, put out his shoes for him. If the groom does not allow it, do not go alone to your parents."

In the Groom's House

As the young couple arrives at the groom's house and his family greets her, the bride has to step on a sheep hide, so that only health and wealth will accompany her into the new house.

Both the *yangya* and her protegee must bow to each family member before they go into the house. At the entrance, family and friends throw small coins, sweets, and rice over them, so they will have a good life.

Next they lead the bride into a room specially prepared for the young couple. There she can rest before the evening's celebrations and eat something, as she won't be allowed to eat at the feast.

Post-Wedding Rituals

After the wedding, the young wife is considered a guest in her husband's house from one to three days, depending on the region. She rests in her room, rarely leaving it.

For the "Kelim Salom" ritual, the *yangya* escorts the young wife out in front of all the guests, where she greets the guests, who bring her presents, with a deep bow.

Chapter 7.

Friends

Parades

At seventeen we were maximalists, dreamers, and of course, patriots of our country and our system. I was even thinking of joining the youth brigades that built "BAM", the Baykal-Amur Railway, which would connect two more major areas of Siberia, just as the Trans-Siberian Railway had done long ago. Young people flocked to the big construction site - it was a real adventure!

We loved to participate in the big parades that took place twice a year: on November 7th, the day of the October Revolution, and on May 1st, International Labor Day.

They were great opportunities to dress up and show off, proudly representing our school.

Parades usually started at 10 a.m.

What did they mean to us?

First there was the official part, when government representatives and dignitaries stood on the rostrum and made tributes to the army, the workers, and the peace-loving Soviet system. Their speeches called the workers of the world to unite and, of course, warned against the imperialist and capitalist systems, against Neo-Fascism, against counterrevolutionaries, etc.

The parade itself started with the soldiers' march and military equipment was showcased.

After the soldiers came the athletes. There were endless legions of athletes who looked physically overstrained, malnourished, and very pale.

After the athletes came the Union of Workers (the trade unions), followed by groups and families, who joined in obediently to demonstrate solidarity. People had lots of red banners.

The banners, flags, and slogans were waved and brandished over everyone and everybody. They were all red to represent the spirit of the Soviet State and Soviet society. There was a terrible conformity in every part of Soviet life, even color.

Some people carried photographs on sticks. Some of the photos were of the great men of communism: Marx, Engels, and Lenin. Then there were photos of the members of the Praesidium of the Supreme Soviet.

Then came the representatives of the factories and collective farms - the working-class heroes! And after them, the employees of all kinds of institutions, such as universities, municipalities, etc.

Finally, after those endless masses of "extraordinary" people, after all the portraits, followed the ordinary folks: arm in arm, carrying plastic flowers, and bunches of colored balloons.

We youngsters walked along, shouting the proper slogans.

It was a real holiday for us, especially when there was good weather. After the parades, we would walk around town in a happy, wonderful mood. Everywhere they were selling special sweets, which could not usually be found in our stores.

Families gathered at home to celebrate these holidays, and they prepared especially elaborate and tasty food for the occasion. In my memory, the November 7 holiday is associated with "Olivier" salad (Russian potato salad), because every family prepared it for that day.

......

The next big holiday after the November break was New Year!

Rustam invited me to walk around town with him on New Year's Eve; he said that if you greet the New Year together, you will stay together for the entire New Year.

If we had lived in the European part of the Soviet Union, greeting the New Year outside your home, away from your family, and with a boyfriend would not be a problem at age 17, but in Uzbekistan?!

Although New Year's Eve is mostly a family celebration, there would be a lot of parties where young people would gather and celebrate. My school class – of course – had a party, but I had to stay at home. And when my parents left after midnight to greet and congratulate other family members and friends, I had to sit at home watching TV, instead of walking around with my beloved boy.

In the mornings I would walk to school past the houses in my neighborhood, most of which were one-story buildings built in the traditional way - with clay bricks which been dried in the sun, and some of which had an upper part – a "Bolhona".

As I made my way through the neighborhood, sometimes a boy, a distant relative of mine, would accompany me. He was one year older than I was and called me by a pet name, "jigar". "Jigar" means "liver", which in Uzbek is very significant. If somebody calls you "jigar", it means they are very close to you or are a relative, because you can't live without a liver.

So this boy Alishér was a prominent and charming guy. Everybody considered him an excellent choice for a groom. He came from a rich family and, like me, from an old family. We were related through the female line; he was not from the Sheikh Zayniddin family tree, but his father held an important position at one of the most prestigious departments in the university. At the age of 17, Alishér often drove around our *mahalla* ("neighborhood') in his family's Volga. Only a few people in Tashkent had cars, and even fewer had Volgas, the top brand in the Soviet Union.

Seeing him in that car, the boys around were probably bursting with envy.

And what an impression he must have made on the girls! Many of them were madly in love with him, but I was absolutely indifferent towards him.

He was not handsome and not very tall, but he was charming. He had a slightly hoarse and – for a man – a rather weak voice.

123

He was dating a girl I knew. She was a beauty with big brown eyes and gorgeous long hair, which shone red in the sun. I think the reason for her beauty was that she was a mestizo, i.e. from a mixed family. Her mother was Russian and her father Uzbek - and from a lower caste than him, so I was pretty sure that Alishér would never marry her.

He was a conformist, not a strong personality who would go against traditions and marry someone "unacceptable".

Everything was easy for him; he did not have to fight.

While students like me would spend day and night preparing for college entry exams during high school, Alishér just had to decide what department he wanted to enroll in, and his father would take care of everything else.

He was always dressed in imported, tasteful, fine clothes, and he always smelled like French cologne and cosmetics, which were insanely expensive in Tashkent and could only be obtained through *blat* connections.

OK, so he was one year older than me, and on my 30-minute walk to school, I often walked with him.

I don't remember what we talked about. He tried to play the heartbreaker and talk about high-flatulent stuff, but he was not really an intellectual and generally failed. He tried his best to impress me, but we mostly talked about nothing of any importance.

Later he married another girl in a properly arranged marriage, and his relationship with the girl he loved, which had lasted for 3 years, was forgotten.

Unfortunately, for a young Uzbek, even a rich and "independent" one, his parents' choice of spouse was law; he couldn't make his own choice.

Uzbek Koreans

One of my girlfriends – Lena – was a "mestizo" from a mixed family; her mother was Russian, her father Korean. She was a real cover girl, a model! Through her I became acquainted with Korean culture. Approximately 500,000 ethnic Koreans lived in the former Soviet Union.

The Uzbek Koreans are descendants of Koreans who were forced by Stalin to relocate during World War II from the Russian Far East, where they had been living not far from the Korean border, to Central Asia. They were deported because Stalin feared that they would collaborate with the Japanese.

The Korean minority is quite evident in Uzbekistan. Central Asian Koreans differ from both North and South Koreans in terms of language, mentality, values, ideals, outlook, behavior, customs, and traditions. Their native language is Russian, and they generally spoke Russian and associated with the Russian population, rather than assimilating into the local Central Asian populations. It seems that they live quite comfortably, both culturally and materially, in Central Asia.

We knew the Koreans to be an industrious people. The majority of them were engaged in the agricultural sector. They set up great irrigation systems and were the region's rice farmers.

Not far from Tashkent there was a famous, frequently showcased Korean collective farm named "Politotdel" ("the political department" – how funny that sounds today!). They were famous for their excellent results. Every guest of honor visiting Tashkent would be shown this place.

The "Koryo-saram", as Koreans in Central Asia were originally called, have preserved Korean cuisine extremely well. There are Korean restaurants in all the major cities and the Korean cold noodle dish *naengmyeon* is a common light meal in Tashkent, where it is called by the Russo-Korean name "kuksy," meaning "noodles".

My favorite Korean food was "kimchi" - spicy pickled cabbage and other vegetables. In any bazaar in Uzbekistan you can find several Korean vendors selling pickled foods, rice, and fresh vegetables.

I imagine their cuisine is different from traditional Korean cuisine.

When I visited my Korean friend, I liked to watch how her mom cooked eggplant with garlic. It was really delicious. Even though they were the third- or fourth-generation Koreans in Uzbekistan, they were still cooking their traditional food, which is very different from Uzbek food.

Koreans are the only minority in Uzbekistan able to speak Uzbek. At the bazaar they easily haggle in Uzbek without an accent.

Korean girls were always dressed very well, very elegantly. Compared to Koreans in Korea, they are very tall and always good looking, because their blood is mixed with Russian or Ukrainian blood. Interestingly, they never mix with Uzbeks. They usually marry other Koreans or people of European origin.

Russian Germans

As I said before, I grew up in a modern-day Babylon with friends from all kinds of ethnic groups: Germans, Greeks, Koreans, Tatars, and so on.

Before Stalin deported entire ethnic groups (the Volga Deutsch, Crimean Tatars, Koreans, Poles, Greeks, Chechens, Meskhetian Turks, Ingush, and so on) to Central Asia before and during WWII, only the Koreans and Germans had successfully adapted in Uzbekistan.

When Hitler invaded the Soviet Union, Stalin was worried that the Volga Deutsch might collaborate with the invaders and ordered the immediate relocation of all ethnic Germans, both from the Volga region and from a number of other traditional areas of settlement. Approximately 400,000 Volga Deutsch were stripped of their land and houses and moved east to Uzbekistan in Soviet Central Asia.

In 1943-44, the Crimean Tatars, along with the Balkars, Chechens, Ingush, Karachays and Kalmyks, were all deported to Uzbekistan.

The Germans were forced to assimilate into the new Russo-Uzbek-Soviet culture in Uzbekistan. The Volga Deutsch lived in harsh areas and in harsh conditions.

They were forbidden to speak German, and most of the Volga Deutsch lost the language of their ancestors in only a few generations. The Volga Deutsch were also denied access to higher education. Until 1970, ethnic Germans were not even allowed to study at the University of Moscow, the main institution providing a decent Soviet education and intellectual liberation.

This may be why they were mainly involved in farming. The Volga Deutsch were an extremely agriculturally oriented community and their lives revolved mainly around physical labor, farming, the harvest, and the community.

When you go outside of cities into the countryside where they used to live, you can see pretty, solidly built houses. These German houses were surrounded by manicured, well-maintained gardens.

We all knew that if you wanted to buy the best milk at the bazaar, you should buy from the Germans.

All my Volga Deutsch friends were from the "provinces", and they usually hid the fact that they were German. I was surprised to find out that my good friends Olga and Natasha were German. I never ever heard them speaking German with their family or mentioning that they were Volga Deutsch. Maybe they felt ashamed to be German, because in the Soviet Union, Germans were associated with Nazi Germany. Soviet TV would broadcast movies about the World War II day and night, where fascists were shown doing terrible things.

During *perestroika* in the late 80s, we suddenly found out how many Volga Deutsch lived in Uzbekistan when they applied to move to Germany. Although the restrictions were gradually lifted, many Germans seized the chance to move to Germany as soon as the doors were opened for them.

The vast majority of expelled Germans fled to Germany as part of one of the largest groups of refugees in the 20th century. The German "Law of Return" ("Rückkehrgesetz") allowed displaced people with German blood to return to Germany and receive full citizenship, as well as a subsidy for their journey.

All my Volga Deutsch friends moved to Germany with their entire families, which sometimes numbered as many as 100 people.

Chapter 8.

University Entry Exams

During the month of June, we had to pass ten exit exams in order to receive our high school diplomas.

After passing all those exams, we started preparing for the big event, the Graduation Ball (comparable to the prom in the US)!

Long before that big night, we ordered our tailor-made white dresses, as there was nothing appropriate available in stores.

The big night started in the biggest room at the school, which usually was the gym. We danced to music by popular bands and hits from abroad, like "Deep Purple", "Angie", "The Rolling Stones", and Bob Dylan's "Knocking on Heaven's Door."

You couldn't buy western music in the store; you had to get it from somebody who had records or tapes. In those days, we had reel-to-reel tape recorders; cassette players would only be introduced to our country a couple of years later.

Soviet rock bands had begun to spring up here and there. They had to wear proper attire and have acceptable content, so there would often be an odd mix of excellent music and ridiculous words celebrating life and society in the Soviet Union.

One Uzbek group named "Yalla" made it to the top of the Soviet hit parade, and even toured the Soviet Bloc countries. "Yalla" did an excellent job of combining traditional Uzbek tunes and modern rhythms, but we were young and more drawn to real rock and roll from the West.

So we danced all night after our final exams to the music of our favorite rock stars.

After the school ball, we went to downtown Tashkent to celebrate until dawn. Staying up late enough to "greet the dawn" had a special appeal and significance for us.

Of course, as you probably guessed, my parents wouldn't let me be with my classmates and greet the dawn. I cried for a whole week before that day, begging them to let me go and celebrate all night long. Of course, they thought I would spend the night with my friend Rustam and not with the girls. They finally agreed on a compromise: I could go, but my dad and one of my sisters had to come along with me. How embarrassed I was in front of my classmates!

Rustam calmed me down and said that we would manage to escape from my relatives and greet the dawn on our own, just the two of us.

When I arrived at the central square (Red Square) with my dad and my sister, we were engulfed by crowds of dancing students and numerous stages with musicians.

Here my sister whispered to me that she would cover my back ...

When we found my classmates dancing to the loud music, my sister and I joined them and danced like everyone else. My dad did not like the deafening music and stayed a little ways away. And then...we ran away, Rustam and I, holding our hands and diving into the nearest park. After that, we walked and walked, holding hands, embracing, and kissing. Oh, what a night! I was 17, and these were my first kisses! Oh, what wonderful feelings!

When dawn arrived, we quickly returned to the crowd. I found my sister and my dad, who was angry. But I told him that I had gotten lost in the crowd, and we went home together. I was sad, because I had to leave, but I was proud I had been able to come and spend that special night with Rustam!

After graduation, my whole family talked to me about what school to go to and what to study.

In the Soviet Union, you could submit college applications until the end of June, and then in early August you would take entrance exams. My parents were dreaming of me becoming a doctor, so I had to apply to the Tashkent Pediatric Medical School. The director was one of our many distant relatives, and having connections was an important factor, since medical school was a very elite and prestigious institution. Most parents dreamed of sending their daughters to medical school. Girls had a good chance of finding a good match if they were doctors. Why? Because the medical system in the Soviet Union had a lot of problems. To get in to see a good doctor, you had to have connections and a lot of money. For this reason, every family wanted to have a doctor at home. However, it was a vicious circle, since the students who got into medical school often weren't the best – they just had the right connections, and this meant that they didn't become the best doctors.

I hated blood, and I have never been interested in medicine, but as an obedient daughter, I set off to submit my application. My classmate, who had already been in med school for a year, went with me, and there we met some other acquaintances who were also med students. They decided to play a trick on me and took me to the morgue, where I passed out for a moment from fear. I don't know how they resuscitated me, but I returned home without having submitted the application. For several days I felt bad, I vomited constantly, and my parents, who were really scared by all this, decided not to put pressure on me and let me to decide on my own where I wanted to go to college.

I wrote above that my dream was to study in Moscow or Leningrad. I knew that at the Tashkent University of Economics you could take the entrance exams for one of the most prestigious universities in the Soviet Union. The Plekhanov Academy of Economics had one spot available in its International Economics department. If you passed the exams in Tashkent, you would be accepted and could go study in Moscow. I was just two steps away from my dream. I handed in my application at the end of June and began preparing for the exams day and night.

Traditionally, universities and institutes conducted their own admissions tests regardless of the applicants' school record. You had to pass four exams.

The Soviet government always considered education to be an extremely an important indicator of progress. They believed that

131

literacy, in particular, proved that the new Soviet regime was a modern state and a protector of the proletariat (i.e., the workers). A literate and educated general populace was needed in order to modernize and industrialize the country, which were important goals for the Soviet state. It should come as no surprise, therefore, that educational advances were an important part of state planning and spurred Soviet economic and technological progress.

There were 62 institutions of higher education, including two academies (in Uzbekistan, which was part of the Soviet system, the word "academy" meant a first-rate research and educational institution), 16 universities ("universitet"), and 44 institutes ("institut").

The Soviet-style system of higher education differed greatly from the American model. For example, a five-year university education was equal to a master's degree in the US. Today this causes confusion when Americans try to evaluate Soviet degrees.

Classes generally ran five to six hours a day, every day of the week. Students often went to classes on Saturdays and usually had to study 30 to 36 hours a week. Semester-long courses had one exam at the end. If the course lasted for more than a semester, then there was a "zachyot" (pass/fail test) at the end of the first semester and an exam at the end of the course. The rule was that you could have no more than five exams (two regular exams plus three *zachyots* or three regular exams plus two *zachyots*) per semester. During the last two to three years of study, students also had a written requirement which was like a master's thesis and demonstrated the student's ability to conduct research. Students also had to take one or two State Exams that covered all the material in their area of specialization.

Because higher education in the Soviet system was free and the government provided assistance in the form of stipends, the demand for university seats was always very high. Thousands of people competed for a limited number of spots (there were sometimes over 10 candidates per spot). By using entrance exams, universities and institutes were able to select the best candidates for their programs, but this also meant that millions were deprived of the opportunity to get a higher education. Furthermore, you could only apply to one

132

university a year. Unfortunately, results of these examinations and selections were too often influenced by high-ranking officials and senior leaders trying to help their children. This was an area where nepotism, clannishness, and even corruption were normal, and ultimately resulted in even some of the most talented and gifted high school graduates being rejected.

There were more than 50 candidates for the spot I was applying for. My parents didn't have connections at this particular institution, so I had to do very well on all four exams to compete with the other 49 candidates from all over Uzbekistan. I had already contacted the Plekhanov Academy of Economics in 9th grade, and they had been regularly mailing me the materials I needed to prepare myself for the entrance exams, which I did over the course of 2 years.

Every day I travelled across the whole town in the terrible heat to get to my tutoring sessions, and I would study all night and almost until dawn memorizing tons of material. Some of my friends told me to drink strong coffee with cognac so I could stay awake. My body, which didn't tolerate alcohol, couldn't endure the exhaustion and the cognac. At the end of July, I was so completely exhausted that I had to go see the doctor. Although the doctor told me to take a break and rest for a couple of days, I continued to study tirelessly. I was so exhausted that after I took the exams, I was admitted to the hospital for a week with kidney problems. Most likely they were the result of strong coffee with cognac, but I had had no choice but to study. I knew that this was my only chance to be accepted into this institute and start a completely different life for myself.

While I was preparing for the exams, I met a young man named Iskander who was several years older than me and was a student at this institute. He turned out to be my distant relative. Suddenly he began showing me attention, giving me advice on various things, and walking me home, and constantly invited me to the movies. Once my dad asked me why I refused to go with him to the movies. I was shocked by this question; how did he know about Iskander, and why did my incredibly strict father suddenly suggest that I go to the movies with a young man?

It turned out that Iskander's parents had already gotten in touch with my parents and started making plans for us to get married.

Upon learning of this, I exploded. I hadn't given him the least hint that I was interested in him and had treated him with complete indifference - at best like a relative and nothing more. You need to know Uzbek men: if you pay the slightest attention to them, they think that you are head over heels in love with them. You have to behave around them as our parents taught us: arrogantly and proudly. As my grandmother used to say, "men must win you over". I had been lax and let him walk me home a few times, because we were in fact going in the same direction, and that is how this young man came to presume that he was my fiancé.

My dad was pleased, since Iskander was from our caste and was very rich, so he was a good match. Lord, at this period of my life I had only one goal: to be accepted at the school of my dreams and get as far away as possible. How did my parents not understand this? I made a scene in front of my parents and told this Iskander that I was busy preparing for exams; in other words, I politely told him that he should stay away from me. Iskander decided that I needed to be won over and began to pursue me even more, and his parents sent over the matchmakers.

I was only 17 years old! Marriage? The world was just opening up before me, and my whole life was ahead of me. I wondered how this young man did not see my overwhelming desire to leave this place. All this motivated me to prepare for the exams even more diligently. And after being the only one of 50 people to pass all the exams in higher mathematics, physics, and chemistry and get As on my written essays, I was accepted at the college of my dreams. I became a student of one of the most prestigious institutions of the Soviet Union! Even my parents were proud!

At the end of August, I started preparing for my departure, and my dad decided that he would go with me and help me get set up in Moscow.

Just a few days before our departure, my dad and I were suddenly invited to the Ministry of Higher and Specialized Secondary Education. The minister himself wanted to talk to us; my dad and I came to the meeting with no idea what was going on. The minister was very friendly and polite to us, but said that he was extremely sorry to report that unfortunately, I would not be able to go to Moscow. Seeing the shock on my face, he explained: since it was a very prestigious university, the General Secretary of the Communist Party Rashidov had decided to send his relative instead of me. I still couldn't understand what he was saying, then he said that he could not do anything since he was too low on the totem pole.

He suggested that I choose any institute in Tashkent, or I could pursue a similar specialty at the Odessa Institute, so that after a year there, I could transfer to Plekhanov Academy in Moscow for my second year. I told him that I would go anywhere, the main thing was to leave Tashkent. I came out sobbing from the injustice of it!

This incident showed me once again what an unjust world I was living in. I was sure that in the European part of the Soviet Union life was fairer. I knew many people who had traveled or sent letters to Moscow for help with local officials, and this often helped. Corruption and bribes at all levels were a normal phenomenon in Uzbekistan.

Such ideological affiliations were possible in the Soviet Union, in part because local elites had managed to maintain their positions in society despite the repressions and purges of the Soviet period. The traditional Central Asian elites survived – and even thrived - in the Soviet system.

Chapter 9.

Odessa[2]

My parents tried to convince me to stay in Tashkent and said I could pick any university I wanted there. I told them I would never ever stay in this country and would ultimately live my life outside of Uzbekistan.

When we came to get information about going to Odessa, I was introduced to other young people who also planned to study there. There was Marina from Tashkent, Rima from Andijan, and two

---

[2] Map source: By This image is a copy or a derivative work of http://www.lib.utexas.edu/maps/commonwealth/soviet_union_admin_1989.jpg, from the map collection of the Perry–Castañeda Library (PCL) of the University of Texas at Austin. Public Domain, https://commons.wikimedia.org/w/index.php?curid=1469033

Uzbek Russian boys from the countryside, who could hardly speak Russian. Only my dad accompanied me to Odessa.

I had never before heard of Odessa, nor was I interested in it, because I had imagined myself studying in Moscow or Leningrad.

Odessa was very different from all the cities I had been to before.

Located in southern Ukraine on the northwest shore of the Black Sea, Odessa is a major seaport and the third most important city in the Russian Empire after Moscow and St. Petersburg. It flourished in the 19th century as a duty-free port and was the most important commercial port in the Soviet Union.

Heavily influenced by French and Italian architectural styles, Odessa looks more like a city located on the Mediterranean, than on the Black Sea. Odessa has played an important role in Russian and Soviet culture. Pushkin was exiled here, and it is home to the world-famous "Potemkin Steps", which were featured in the internationally acclaimed and groundbreaking movie by Sergei Eisenstein, *The Battleship Potemkin*. In the climactic scene of the film, hundreds of protesters are shot dead on these steps, while a carriage with an infant rattles headlong down them.

Since the collapse of the Soviet Union, Odessa has lost none of its charm, energy or beauty. Even today it is a green and beautifully planned city with tree-lined boulevards, long beaches, and leafy parks. Its fabulous Opera House was designed by Viennese architects and is considered one of the best in Europe. The great composers Tchaikovsky, Rubenstein, Glazunov, and Rimsky-Korsakov all conducted here, and Enrico Caruso, Fyodor Shalyapin, Nezhdanova, and Plisetskaya performed on this stage.

Odessa has always radiated a spirit of freedom, probably as a result of its location. It is also home to many different peoples, including Russians, Ukrainians, Jews, Frenchmen, Italians, Romanians, Tatars, Turks, Greeks, Armenians, and Bulgarians. Each of these communities has left its mark on different aspects of Odessan life. Odessans were viewed in Russian and Soviet culture as sharp-witted, streetwise, and eternally optimistic. Home to a large Jewish community, Odessa even has its own unique dialect, which is an admixture of Russian, the speech of Odessan Jews, and a multitude of other linguistic influences. "Odessan speech" became the trademark of the typical "Soviet Jew" in numerous jokes and comedy acts. I liked this musical dialect, and later when I was abroad, I could easily identify natives of Odessa by it.

When we flew into Odessa, we went to the dorm, which was considered one of the best in the institute, as it housed foreign students from countries considered to be friendly to the USSR. There were the "friendly" Eastern European countries (E. Germany, Poland, Bulgaria, Hungary, and Czechoslovakia), but also Middle Eastern, Latin American, and African countries who were "building socialism" with the help of the Soviet Union.

Like Tashkent and other cities of Soviet Union, Odessa became an important center for free education and technical training for select young people from all over the world, and this enabled the Soviet government to spread its influence abroad. The foreign students would study everything from astronomy, meteorology, civil engineering, and medicine to painting, music, and ballet. The biggest group of such students was from Asia; very few came from Western Europe.

The Soviet regime offered full scholarships to these foreign students, plus monthly stipends, free room and board, free medical care, and free winter clothing. It spent huge sums of money on these foreign students, especially those from developing countries. Post-colonial Africa was particularly fertile ground for Soviet attempts to spread Lenin's socialist model.

Their stipends were high (90 rubles/month) - much higher than those given to Soviet students (30 rubles/month on average). Their lodging was free, and, even more importantly, they were allowed to travel twice a year to Western Europe, a privilege denied to their Soviet peers.

So, you could say that we were lucky to end up in such good conditions. Marina, Rima, and I had a two-room apartment with a bathroom, which was considered a luxury at that time. In the next room there were four female students from Ukraine who were a year older. My father and I immediately went to see the dean of the faculty.

Traditionally, universities and institutes were divided into "faculties". "Faculties" are like colleges or schools (of business or of education, for example) in American universities. They are structural units reflecting major fields of specialization. "Faculties" are divided into specific departments or programs, representing narrower specialties. For example, the German program and the French program would fall under the "Faculty of Foreign Languages". The latter may be part of the Pedagogical Institute that also has a Faculty of Physics and Math (to prepare physics and math teachers), a Faculty of Geography (to prepare geography teachers), and a Faculty of Biology (to prepare biology teachers). Each institution of higher education is headed by a "rector" (i.e., president); faculties are headed by deans, and departments by chairs.

The dean of the faculty was a Georgian. He and my father immediately hit it off. Incidentally, my faculty was the "Faculty of Engineering and Economics" (which meant that I would have two majors: engineering and economics) and it was part of the Institute of Chemistry and Technology. All this had nothing to do with what I wanted to specialize in, International Economics. But I didn't really pay attention to what my major was. I was too busy getting ready to leave Tashkent and, moreover, the minister himself had promised to transfer me to Moscow in a year, so my first year of gen ed classes wouldn't be a problem.

My dad went in first and asked me to wait a bit. They spoke for a long time, then I met the dean.

My dad spent more than a week with me in Odessa. During that time, we walked around town and went to the incredibly beautiful Opera Theater. My dad also wanted to see a show that was very popular at that time in the Soviet Union. I think it was called "The Steelmakers," and it was about heroes of the Soviet Union. Why did we have to waste time on that? I would rather have walked one more time along Deribasovskaya Street, a famous street lined with restaurants and cafes.

My dorm was located pretty much in the center of the city. You could get anywhere you wanted by foot, and it was only 15 minutes to the beach.

All the famous beaches in Odessa were located nearby: Arkadia, Otrada, Lanzheron, and Chayka. I was more or less indifferent to beaches, since at age 17, I didn't know how to swim. Thanks to my Uzbek upbringing, I had been deprived of the pleasure of swimming in the sea. People from all over the Soviet Union came here to swim, suntan, and relax, but I, who lived only 15 minutes away by foot, couldn't enjoy any of this.

Eventually, I began to develop an interest in this city, and I began to like it.

One day, my father and I went to visit some family friends. One of them was named Aunt Sofa. Both she and my dad thought it was absolutely necessary for me to have people I knew in the city in case I needed help. She and her family lived downtown on Pushkin Street. To get to their house, we passed through a typical Odessa courtyard lined with balconies and apartment windows. In the center was a huge Sycamore tree.

Their apartment was in a very old multi-storied edifice which was apparently built before the Revolution, and perhaps designed as a communal apartment building. It's possible that in the olden days it was some sort of a tenement house, where people rented out rooms. But the fact remains: I had never seen such an unusual layout in my life. Inside there was an incredibly long corridor lined on both sides with doors, doors, and more doors. I can't say exactly how many there were, but probably around 20-25. Naturally, one family lived in each room, as did our friends. The corridor led to a big common kitchen with larger and smaller tables belonging to the 20-25 families who lived there. Not surprisingly, after living in this so-called apartment for many years with no chance of improving their living situation for the better, these Odessa friends of ours were the among the first to petition to leave the Soviet Union when the door leading out cracked open. They went to the States and, naturally, made the right choice in doing so.

I have only seen similar communal apartments in Leningrad, but there they had far fewer rooms – maybe 8-10. So, I guess you can say that in comparison, our Leningrad friends lived in royal style.

When I stopped by to see them, I couldn't believe that three generations of a family lived in these two rooms. The grandchildren of Aunt Sofa were running around; one was 8 and the other - 2. For some reason they were very fat. Later I found out that they were constantly stuffing them with food. For some reason Jews, like Uzbeks, believed that being fat means being healthy. After talking to Aunt Sofa for a few minutes, I understood the point of our visit: my dad needed extra help controlling me. When we were leaving, my dad and Aunt Sofa agreed that I would regularly stop by to see them. Great...I felt like my independence had ended even before it got a chance to start. Later I found out that my father had also convinced the dean and the head of the dorm to regularly report to him about me.

Odessa was a popular vacation destination for citizens of the USSR. Fashionable clothing and foreign goods have always been more plentiful in Odessa than elsewhere in the Slavic world, and this has helped foster something of an 'Odessan' identity among locals.

I also want to mention an Odessa market, the Tolchok, that my dad and I absolutely had to go to. It seemed like you could buy anything at all there (maybe even an atomic bomb, but disassembled, as the police were everywhere).

The name of that market, "Tolchok", comes from the word "tolcheya", or "throng". At one time it was the only such unofficial manufactured goods market in the entire Soviet Union. People from all over our once boundless homeland thronged this market to buy and sell (and even steal!) hot items, like jeans, leather jackets, metallic fabric, etc. At the Tolchok you could find absolutely everything: clothing, electronics, carpets, footwear, hardware... The Tolchok was a flea market! When the atomic bomb appeared, people in Odessa didn't believe it really existed. They said, "What bomb? If you can't buy one at our market, it doesn't exist!"

And there were so many imported things, even jeans! I had never seen real jeans in my life!

Where would I have seen all these foreign things? After all, the simple Soviet citizen could only get items not produced by our advanced socialist economy on the black market. And they managed

142

to do so for many years, even after one of the most powerful secret police agencies in the world, the KGB, had declared war on it.

And then there was the Soviet black market, an important part of the Soviet economy, albeit illegal. "Fartsa," the Russian word for the black market, is believed to be based on Odessan jargon, where a "forets" is someone who buys things cheap and sells them for many times what he paid. In the Soviet era, Odessa was known for its incredible black market. Thanks to its status as a port, black marketeers were able to buy all sorts of hard-to-find goods from people on foreign ships, then resell them at a profit. Black marketeers also bought scarce commodities from international students, people who had traveled abroad, factory workers, store employees, tourists, and even hotel workers and stewardesses. And if anything in high demand did in fact appear in stores, the black marketeers would buy them up immediately and then sell them for more on the black market.

Foreign students who came to Odessa could easily make enough money to live comfortably for a semester just by selling some of their clothes. And Soviet students could make much more than their meagre stipend by selling a few high-demand items, like jeans, on the black market. They would often barter for or buy the jeans from unwitting international students (mainly from Eastern Europe, the Middle East, and Africa), then sell them for as much as 200 rubles, which was about the same as the average monthly salary at that time in the Soviet Union!

So when I saw jeans, T-shirts, and other trendy items, things I had never even dreamt of back in Tashkent, I knew that no matter what, going forward, I had to save up money.

With great difficulty my dad and I managed to crawl out of the market's thousand-people vortex. Finally, I saw my dad off and enthusiastically started living independently, hoping that people wouldn't constantly be reminding me that I was a "modest Uzbek girl".

By the beginning of the school year, which started on September 1st, more students from Uzbekistan had arrived. And we realized that we weren't the only Uzbek students studying at the institute; there were even more from all over Uzbekistan in the upper level classes.

Our dorm was filled with students of every nationality. Besides people from around the Soviet Union, there were students from African countries, Mongolia, Poland, Czechoslovakia, Palestine, Syria, Algeria, Egypt, and Venezuela. In other words, it was a real "Friendship of the Peoples"!

Odessa was very challenging for me in every way. My classes were hard, and I had a lot of science classes – after all, I was in the Engineering Faculty. I wasn't ready for this. I hadn't planned to study Physics, Projectional Geometry, Chemistry, or Mechanics. In fact, I didn't like these subjects at all, and I was bad at science. Then another problem arose: it turned out that my teachers, most of whom were Ukrainian, were prejudiced against other ethnicities. I experienced this a lot myself. For example, I had trouble with instructor Deyneko, who taught Scientific Communism – a required course in every university of the Soviet Union, which was hastily spun from the quotes of Marx, Engels, and Lenin.

Deyneko looked down on anyone who wasn't Ukrainian. No matter what the quality of my work was, she always gave me Cs. So the next time I did excellent work and she gave me a C, I asked her in front of the 100-student class why she always gives me Cs. She clearly didn't expect such bravery and insolence from a female student from somewhere in Central Asia. She shocked everyone when she rudely responded, "What do you expect? We know you people have no understanding of communism. You guys probably still ride donkeys and use kerosene lamps!" I responded rudely as well, saying that if she considers the peoples of Central Asia second-class citizens, then I would write a petition to the president of the university demanding she be fired. She was totally shocked – after all, in her entire teaching career she had never had a student dare to contradict her, not to mention write a petition. The Soviet educational system was authoritarian in nature. Students had to show unconditional respect to their teachers; it was out of the question to contradict them or speak one's mind during class. The teacher was everything! But I could no longer be silent. I didn't come from Uzbekistan to Ukraine to be belittled here as well. And I

144

had problems not only with Deyneko, but with some of the other instructors. They were all convinced that all of us students from Central Asia were insufficiently educated simply because of our ancestry. So that's what our equal rights and the "friendship of the peoples" of the Soviet republics really looked like!

I knew that I was in for trouble, and I was. I was called in to see the dean and asked to explain my behavior. Thankfully the dean was, as I said, a Georgian, so he knew what I was talking about and didn't make me apologize to Deyneko. When I took my exam with another instructor, I received a B.

The assistant dean of the faculty was a Jew. He told me that if I had any problems relating to my ethnicity in the future, I should come to him, rather than arguing in front of the entire class. He understood what I was going through as he was a Jew living in Ukraine and was quite familiar with anti-Semitism.

We Uzbek students were not only held in contempt by the teachers, but by the local students as well. The other Uzbek students tried to calm me down and told me to ignore them, because I couldn't change anything anyway. I said no, I will never let myself be denigrated and will prove to them all that I am better than they are. My first step was to use the money my father had left me to get new clothes, but since I didn't have enough to go the Tolchok and buy imported clothes, I decided to design and sew a few things myself in the dressmaking shop. At that time there were a lot of such shops in the country. Since there was a shortage of clothing in stores, women sewed clothes in these shops; they just had to get hold of good fabric to do so. The fabric was usually purchased privately – from black marketeers, friends, or under the table.

I knew that our friend Aunt Sofa was receiving care packages from relatives in America. I went to visit them, and she offered me some fabric that was in style at the time. I told them that I would have a coat made from it. Aunt Sofa tried to tell me that you could only use such fabric for a dress; I said I could make a coat with raspberry-colored backing. I didn't want to look like everyone else. I wanted to have my own style and stand out so much that the local Odessa girls would notice me. They had a few articles of imported

145

Western clothing; I decided to have more clothing which may not be from the West, but would be designed by me.

By that time, some of the male students who sold Western goods had taken a liking to me and sold me some super-stylish shirts and T-shirts for very little. I combined them with the sleeveless shirts I had knitted myself. I knitted the sleeveless shirts in different colors, so they would look good combined with the blouses I bought from on the black market, and that would give people the impression that I had a lot of clothes.

When I wore the coat I had designed myself, everyone wanted to know which Western country I got it from. To match the coat, I ordered bell-bottom pants.

I was apparently looking pretty good because suddenly a large number of young men were interested in me. My admirers included a somewhat heavy Czech, who was ready to carry me off to Czechoslovakia, an African from Cameroon who was always dressed really stylishly, but for some reason always in white (classy white jeans and white T-shirts), and an Armenian, who could sell you anything you wanted from the West. He lived across the way from me in the dorm and was always waiting for me by the entrance.

All this began to irritate the local Odessa girls in my class, who wouldn't even talk to me because I was not from Odessa, and who were ecstatic that I had had a conflict with my teacher. I made a firm decision to show them that I was in no way worse than them.

Most of the girls were in love with an athlete named Seryozha. He was the local college champion in swimming and the best-looking guy at our institute. I constantly heard the girls sighing about Seryozha. When I heard the girls in our dorm talking about how to get his attention, I told them we should have a contest, and that I could win him over in 48 hours. I had already seen him looking at me and knew that he liked me. If only you could have seen the smirks of those girls! Literally on the next day he smiled at me as he was walking by and we started talking. He suggested we take a stroll that evening, and I told him to meet me near the dorm, but that I might be a bit late. I wanted him to wait in front of the dorm so everyone would see. I was purposely late, and while he was waiting,

146

he was surrounded by those girls. When I came out, he said, "Dildora, you have no idea how long I have been waiting for you. I have never waited so long for anyone, not to mention a girl!" Hurray! It was my first victory over the local girls.

But I wasn't actually interested in Seryozha at all. Sure, he was good looking – tall, built, and well-dressed, but he was rather dumb...after all, he was an athlete. At that moment I couldn't have imagined that he would fall madly in love with me. I had only needed him to demonstrate my superiority over the local Odessa girls. After that, they started to respect me. But then I started having problems with Seryozha. He was so in love with me that he soon proposed. This was a pretty serious thing; when one of the girls in our dorm heard about it, she almost committed suicide. It was only then that I realized what I had gotten myself into and that you have to pay for everything you get in this life.

I continued to enjoy my freedom and my popularity with the guys and my classmates. I also showed my fellow Uzbeks that you don't have to feel like you are second-class to the Odessans. We weren't any worse, and sometimes we were better than them. My experiences with instructor Deyneko and Seryozha proved it.

I gradually fell in love with the city of Odessa and its international atmosphere. There were so many new things to discover: new people and a new culture.

Some male students from Arab countries started flirting with me. And by that time, I had become friends with a student from Palestine named Valekh. He was a lot older than me and told me a lot about Palestine. I knew he had had to leave his country, but thanks to the Soviet Union, he was able to get a higher education. Students from Syria would come by to visit him. An Armenian girl from our dorm was in love with a Syrian and the two were very serious about one another, but we all understood that they could never marry. The system wouldn't allow it. Every time he went home to his country, she would have a meltdown and couldn't stop crying. When I asked her how she imagined her future with Salekh, she said that she didn't think about that: the main thing was that she was liked being with him. Salekh would bring her a bunch of beautiful things every time he returned. Nona was always dressed beautifully. And stylishly.

Students from Iraq who were studying at the Odessa Military Academy would also visit Valekh. God, what handsome uniforms they had! Valekh was a great cook, and every time he had guests over, he would invite me, too. He told me that he loved me like a sister, and that I was his sunshine girl. One day Valekh told me that one of the Iraqi students, Khasan, was in love with me. He said that Khasan's father was the military mayor of Baghdad, that he was very rich, and that they had apartments in Paris and New York. And that if I were to marry him, I would get to decide where we were going to live.

What! Get married? Go to Baghdad?

At some point Valekh and my Iraqi admirer came over to drink tea. It was on the day that they were giving out stipends, and they brought me the 40 rubles that I received once a month. When Khasan saw how much I received, he asked if they gave us stipends every week. I said no, the 40 rubles was for the whole month. You really had to see the expression on his face!

He immediately offered me part of his stipend, which was 800 rubles a month – plus he got part of it in Western currency. He said that he wasn't even able to spend all the money he was receiving and would be happy to share it with me. At that moment my Soviet pride kicked in! I categorically refused his help. Every time he would come visit us he would bring American gum and, for some reason, Western cigarettes (I didn't smoke). As soon as he left, the girls in my room would attack the cigarettes and happily start smoking them. They would also pressure me, saying it was time for me to learn to smoke. When I said that I can't smoke and don't know how, they immediately decided to teach me– they also, it seems, wanted to make fun of me. They gave me the strongest possible cigarettes, called "papirosy" (filterless tubes with coarse, strong tobacco) and showed me how to inhale the smoke. Copying them inhaling, I almost passed out. My head was spinning, and I felt nauseous from that horrible stuff. But the girls wouldn't give up and kept insisting that every girl should be able to smoke because it impresses men. Plus it was just plain cool. So gradually I overcame the nausea and inhaled a cigarette (still not enjoying it all all) in front of the girls. I don't know if it could actually be called smoking, but it looked good. And I kept the cigarettes, menthols, originally meant for me.

At the same time another admirer – a med student from Kuwait – would always hang out under my window. He came to study the famous methods of Filatov, who cured eye diseases. He also wanted to marry me and carry me off to Kuwait, promising I would live just like in the tale "1001 Nights"!

I gradually became aware of the fact that I was actually lucky that I didn't look like a typical Uzbek woman. My family members always told me that because of my looks and character, no Uzbek man would ever marry me. But in Odessa my looks did nothing but help me. The entire world (with the exception of Uzbek men) was ready to marry me! It turned out that I was really good looking! For the first time in my 17 years of life, I was respected by everyone in the world – except Uzbeks. Hurrah!

My parents were always worried about me and called regularly. Mobile phones didn't exist in the mid-1970s, so they would call the front desk of the dorm, and one of the students would come up and get me. On top of that, every week they would send me care packages by plane. The care packages contained fruits, fresh vegetables, and a lot of prepared food. Apparently, my parents couldn't forget their own hungry student years and were afraid that I would spend all my money on all sorts of entertainment and clothes – on anything, but food, so they tried to take care of me this way. There was one flight from Tashkent to Odessa a week, and all my friends knew that. They would all offer to go with me to the airport and help me bring the heavy care package back. By the time we got back to the dorm room, around 10 people would be sitting there to help celebrate the arrival of my care package. Everything edible in the care package would be consumed that very night, which meant that I would walk around hungry until the next care package came.

Unlike the Ukrainians, we Uzbeks were hospitable and never ate alone. When someone walked into our room, we would always offer them tea, at the very least. And naturally, my whole care package would be shared by all the hungry students. However,

149

whenever I visited my fellow students from Ukraine and they were eating, they never invited me to join them at the table. For me, in the context of my culture, this was a sign of very poor upbringing. After all, weren't they the same people who, just a few days ago, had been sitting in my room and happily partaking of the food in my care package? And I didn't begrudge them food from my care package; I just couldn't understand how you can eat yourself and not offer some to the person sitting next to you. After all, things are better together! So this is one way our cultures were different. And there were a lot of such cultural differences. Even though people of a variety of different ethnicities lived in Tashkent, they adopted our eastern culture – maybe because we were all friends. I couldn't understand why Ukrainians were so greedy. I could understand that they were poor students – they were as poor as I was, but you can always offer someone a cup of tea.

Anyway, the 40-ruble stipend would disappear immediately: you would pay off debts or buy some trendy item of clothing from foreigners.

On the first floor of our dorm there was a cafeteria, where you could buy cheap food subsidized by the state. The food was inedible, half of it was stolen by the cooks, and part of the meat was always replaced with bread. Thanks to the filth, the pharmacy smell, and the cockroaches running all over, I had no desire to eat there.

The grocery stores were half empty, and there was nothing to buy besides canned goods. In the produce stores the vegetables were rotten. That's why we were always half-starving. The only thing that was very cheap was wine, which is probably why all the students drank it. The girls from the next room really shocked me: sometimes they would get up in the morning, light a cigarette, and drink the wine left over from the night before, then run off to their classes. These were Ukrainian girls – was there any reason to emulate them?

We called the 1970s the period of the "Brezhnev Stagnation". Under Soviet leader Leonid Brezhnev, the economy had slowed down and beginning to stagnate. It was still heavily dependent on agriculture, and since Stalin's collectivization of agriculture had effectively destroyed the nation's independent peasantry, agricultural productivity remained low despite massive state

150

investment. Soviet agriculture was increasingly unable to feed the urban population, let alone support industrial productivity and provide for the rise in the standard of living the regime had promised as the fruits of "mature socialism". Additionally, Soviet production of industrial and consumer goods had stagnated and failed to keep pace with demand. The enormous expenditure on the armed forces and on prestigious projects like the space program and the Baikal Amur Railroad, further aggravated by the need to import grain at high market prices, reduced the possibility of putting funds toward modernizing factories or improving the standard of living. Growth of public housing and the state health and educational systems had stagnated, reducing morale and productivity in the urban population. The response was the huge "informal economy" (i.e., the Black Market) which, as I described above, provided consumer goods and services that were in short supply. You could buy anything on the black market, but everything was much more expensive than in state-run stores.

Whenever we had some extra money or the girls and I just wanted to eat some fried potatoes, we would put our money together and go to the famous Odessa Privoz Market. Of course, the Odessa Privoz Market was an amazing sight. It wasn't a market like the one in Tashkent – a market and a show (as they say today). But it was huge, both in terms of size and the quantity of things available. And like the Tolchok, it was filled with throngs of people, as well as a variety of aromas and sounds, which gave it a vibrant energy.

It is here, at the Odessa market, that you really got to experience the local flavor. The dairy section evoked a myriad of smells, as did the honey and smoked sausage, and there was a cloud of spices hanging in the air.

A huge amount of fish was sold at the Privoz Market. Of course, there wasn't any fish for sale in regular stores in Odessa (just like in Tashkent, but of course, Tashkent has no access to water); but at the Privoz everything was available.

And naturally there was fresh-caught shrimp and the famous Odessa crayfish wriggling in plastic tubs; boiled crayfish was also available. And every starving student knew that there was a way to eat for free: go to the Privoz Market and get samples of the sausage, the smoked meat, and the feta.

When I had just arrived in Odessa, I was surprised to see shrimp being sold on the street the way sunflower seeds are sold back in Tashkent: in cones made out of old newspapers. The shrimp looked like ugly bugs to me, and at first, I couldn't even look at them, not to mention eat them. The girls in my room always bought them by the cup and cracked them in their teeth like sunflower seeds while drinking wine. Gradually I developed a passion for them – after all, they weren't expensive. Later on in Europe, I was horrified at how much they cost in restaurants.

Fish in the Soviet Union wasn't expensive. It was cheaper than meat, so people ate more fish than meat. Frozen fish and salted herring were always available in stores. Herring was one of the most popular foods in the Soviet Union. You couldn't have a dinner party without herring served with some freshly cut onion.

At the end of December, our semester ended and in January, after we passed all our exams, we went to Tashkent for vacation. The vacation was short – I just barely managed to see my former classmates. All my friends in Tashkent were students at the university now, except Rustam, who didn't get in and was about to go into the army. If you couldn't get into college after high school, you were sent to serve in the army for 2-3 years, but if you were going to college, you would be left alone. Moreover, every university had military programs, where young men received professional military educations and didn't have to go into the army.

I later found out that Rustam had been sent to serve at a place in Kazakhstan not far from where they were testing nuclear weapons. Later, as a result of this, he had a son who had disabilities. Of course, no one warned him that this could happen, and I don't think the soldiers serving in that area even suspected that they were testing nuclear weapons nearby. I saw Rustam for the last time after he had been shaved to go serve in the army. He asked me to wait for him to come back, but I already knew that we were very different people, and I doubted we would get together in the future.

I returned from warm Tashkent to cold Odessa. That year there were major storms and an unusual amount of snow in Odessa. I remember how, on one occasion, all the wires and trees were covered with ice after a wet snow. For several days the city was completely dark. Classes were cancelled, and we were thrilled to stay in the dorm and spend our days drinking tea with friends.

At that time, I acquired a new admirer from East Germany named Dieter. He was older than me, had already graduated from the Polytechnical Institute, and was working on his PhD. I wasn't serious about him, but he was always inviting me out. Once Dieter invited me to a party at his dorm where the German students were putting on a slide show, and he was going to show pictures of Dresden, his hometown.

It was a Saturday, the day my girlfriends and I would go to discos. We had a plan to hit every disco in every single institute in Odessa, and there were a lot of them. The best part was getting ready to go: trying on clothes, putting on makeup, and meeting other young people. I felt like a bird that had been locked in a cage for a long time and had finally been set free and allowed to fly. I wanted to do everything; after all, I had just started developing some self-confidence. At last, no one was constantly harping on the fact that I was an Uzbek or putting me down because I was different. In fact, it was just the opposite! I had managed to get to the point where the teachers didn't put me down, and I was really popular among the other students. My parents were far away, and I was completely independent. What else could you want at 17?

Tanya, a close friend of mine from Ukraine, was a professional gymnast. She regularly took part in competitions and made our institute proud. There were a lot of athletes in our institute, including my admirer Seryozha, who did a good job defending the honor of our institute. Tanya and I had hit it off and would go to discos together on Saturdays. That Saturday, the Food Technologies Institute was on our list of destinations. As with many of the institutes in Odessa, most of the students there were young men. Tanya and I had already been to the Maritime Academy, where future sailors were trained, as well as the Military Academy, where future officers were trained. When Dieter invited me and Tanya to a

153

party that night, it was hard to decide whether or not to go. After all, we were planning to go the Food Technologies Institute, but then there were these Germans. After spending two hours discussing the issue, getting dressed, and putting on make-up, we decided to drop in on the Germans briefly on our way to the Food Technologies Institute. It would have been awkward to turn Dieter down.

It was the end of February, snowy, and cold out. The Polytechnical Institute and the dorm for foreign students were just across the way. Dressed up in mini-skirts and thin stockings, we popped into the dorm. It was kind of awkward, since slutty girls would hang out at the dorm for foreign students - and even prostitutes, according to the rumors. But of course they wouldn't be there on such a cold night.

When we walked into the lobby, we didn't see anyone. Clearly Dieter had gotten tired of waiting – we were really late, but then we saw two young men standing by the door to the hall. When I looked at one of them something happened to me - I can't even explain what.

I really liked him; I had never liked anyone so much from the start. I didn't know him at all, but I immediately wanted him to come talk to me and invite me in. When I told this to Tanya, all she had to say is that she liked the other one better. We didn't have the faintest idea that they were Germans. They were both tall blonds with fair eyes. The color of Juergen's eyes was so light that it was hard to tell if they were gray or light blue. In terms of looks, he was the exact opposite of the type I usually liked. I, of course, liked dark-eyed brunettes. I would never have imagined that I would like a blond. In the context of my life, blonds simple didn't exist, especially not in Uzbekistan. It was nearly impossible to find a blond in Tashkent.

The young men approached us. We asked where Dieter was, and they said he had been waiting for us for a long time, and had finally gone to show his slides of Dresden in the hall. They invited us in and helped us take off our coats; then they led us inside. In the hall Dieter was showing slides of Dresden and saying something about them, but I was looking for the blond. I wanted to be near him; I was all excited and couldn't understand what was happening to me. When they turned the lights back on, he wasn't in the hall, and I got

154

scared that I would never see him again. When Dieter approached, I asked him about the young man who met us by the door. He said his name was Juergen and his job was to stand by the door and greet guests.

The music started to play, and everyone began to dance. People invited me and Tanya to dance, but I said "no" to everyone, all the while praying to god that Juergen would come in and ask me to dance. I even said no to Dieter, which really upset him, but I thought that if Juergen were to walk in and see me dancing with Dieter, he would leave. As it turned out, the second young man who had been standing by the door was named Frank. He invited Tanya to dance, but I stood there all alone, saying "no" to everyone who asked me. And then Juergen appeared. He walked up to me and Dieter and asked me to dance. I liked dancing with him: I could tell he knew how to dance, and he was very musically inclined. He did a good job leading me to the beat of the music. I never wanted the music to end. Song after song played, and the two of us kept dancing. Tanya also kept dancing with Frank; clearly she liked him, too.

Dieter wasn't very happy; after all, it was he who had invited me, and he clearly wanted to introduce me to his fellow countrymen, but I had completely forgotten about him and kept dancing with this other German. Juergen and I talked a lot. I am sure that when I told him I was from Uzbekistan, he had no idea what that was. For some reason I bragged about knowing English and tried to say a few sentences to him in English. I wanted to look as good as possible. I had never tried so hard to look good in front of a young man before. In the past I hadn't cared whether or not someone liked me, but this time I really wanted him to like me.

Later, Frank and Juergen walked us out. Wow! What a gentleman Juergen turned out to be! He took the purse from my shoulder and carried it for me, led me around the puddles on the ground, and gently held me by the hand. What attentiveness! When we got to my dorm, he gently kissed me on the forehead in parting. He had none of the gruffness so typical of Soviet men.

Tanya and I flew into the dorm and shared our impressions. I confessed to Tanya that I had fallen in love, that it was love at first sight - something that had never happened to me before. She replied that he was a blond and that I had never liked blonds, and moreover, he wasn't my type. And on top of all that, he was German. The word "German" made me burn inside. He was German. A foreigner. We were forbidden from having close relationships with foreigners, even if they were from countries the USSR was officially friendly with. I knew some girls in our dorm who had dated foreigners, and that had caused a lot of problems for them. I told Tanya, "Whatever happens, happens, but for now, I really like him." Just think, I didn't even know if he would come visit again. I only knew his first name, not even his last name. I didn't have the faintest idea what faculty he was studying in.

For some reason, Tanya and I decided we would never see them again. A day passed, then the following evening I was told that a certain young man was waiting for me downstairs in the dorm. When I got downstairs, I saw Juergen. I was super surprised, of course! I honestly didn't think he would ever visit - and certainly not so soon! He gently kissed me on the forehead and told me to get ready to go out, since he had two tickets to the movies. He said that he had bought the tickets in advance so I couldn't refuse. I naturally flew up to my room and started to gussy myself up as quickly as possible. When we were walking to the theater, he gently held my hand. At the movie theater we watched a love story about two not-so-young people who had lived their entire lives in love. The film was called *Anna and the Commodore*. When we were leaving the theater, Juergen said that he wanted to have a relationship like that and be with one partner his whole life. He also told me about his family and his grandparents, who he dearly loved and who lived in the village. It was so interesting to listen to him – after all, I didn't know anything about Germany. All I knew about Germans was what they showed in WWII movies, which were always playing in our theaters.

After I got home from the theater, I ran over to see Tanya. I told her that I thought I had really fallen in love, and that this was a catastrophe, since he was German! If my parents were to find out about this, they would kill me for shaming them like this. It might even kill them. I said that I didn't see any future with him: in my wildest dreams I couldn't imagine a future with a Russian or Tatar, or anyone else besides an Uzbek…and not just any Uzbek, but one from our clan. So how could I have a future with a German?

I decided not to think about it and just date him. Later I looked at Tanya and said with envy, "Tanya, I so wish I were you and not an Uzbek! My life would probably be much easier. I would be completely free; instead, I'm terrified of falling in love with the wrong person." Even when I was over 600 miles from Uzbekistan, I wasn't free from the burden of my ethnicity.

I decided to see how things went and not think about it; the main thing was that I liked being with him. When Juergen came over a third time, I invited him to my room. If guests wanted to visit us in our dorm, they had to leave their ID with the receptionist and leave by 10 pm. When Juergen gave his ID to the receptionist, she looked at it and realized he was a foreigner. In a whisper, she warned me that this would cause problems. But I didn't care. I was in love.

I introduced Juergen to my roommate from Uzbekistan. Tanya arrived and we started drinking tea. Juergen wanted to learn more about Uzbekistan, and we naturally spoke lovingly of our country. Then, when he was leaving, he said in front of everyone that he was going to take me away to Germany, and he was sure I would like his country.

Juergen and I first met at the end of February. Rumors that I was dating a German spread quickly through the entire institute, eliciting a variety of different reactions. Juergen started coming over almost every day. He noticed I was walking around half-starved and began taking care of me. He would bring me food from the market or dishes he had made from packages sent from Germany. Since it was impossible to rely on the Soviet food system, foreign students would bring prepackaged food from their home countries. Plus, they had more money than us and could frequently buy expensive items from farmers markets or eat out at restaurants. Juergen occasionally invited me to the restaurant by the train station. The food wasn't bad and going to a restaurant was a huge luxury for me.

He seemed to be the most intelligent person in the world. He knew everything. I was also astonished by his phenomenal knowledge of Russian.

In mid-March, "Yalla", an Uzbek musical group that was popular throughout the Soviet Union, came to Odessa. They sang in Uzbek. I bought tickets and invited Juergen. In the concert hall I ran into some young people I knew from Tashkent. When they saw me with Juergen, they made rude comments, and I was convinced that news of my relationship with Juergen would immediately reach Tashkent. This event left me feeling uneasy. I was upset, but I couldn't tell Juergen what was up. He simply wouldn't have understood. After all, he was a civilized European living in the 20C, whereas my traditional clansmen were still stuck in the feudal ages.

I was having trouble in some of my classes, like Projective Geometry, where I was getting Cs and Ds; I was also having issues with my Physics teacher. Juergen decided to help me and was surprised that I didn't pick things up right away. He also couldn't understand how someone who hated Projective Geometry and Physics could be studying to become an engineer. He was a straight A student. Imagine a young German man who studied Russian in grade school – and we all know how foreign languages are taught in grade school - then comes to the Soviet Union and from day one is getting As. I can understand how he was acing Math and Physics, but classes in the Humanities where you need to really know the language!??

Even my fellow Uzbek students looked down upon my relationship with Juergen and started avoiding me. It was fine when the male Uzbek students dated, had affairs with, and even slept with local Russian and Ukrainian girls, but in their opinion an Uzbek girl was supposed to do nothing but be serious and study.

One day the person in charge of the Uzbek students approached me. He was just a few years older than me. He said that we need to have a serious conversation, and told me that by dating a foreigner, I was disgracing not only Uzbeks, but the entire Soviet people. I asked him if it's acceptable for him to date one girl after another, going from Ukrainians to Russians. He said it was completely fine, since he's a man!

I ignored all of this until I received a telegram from Tashkent in late March saying that my mother, my religious aunt, and my sister would be in Odessa in a few days. I couldn't understand why they were suddenly coming for a visit to Odessa and why such a big delegation. Aunt Sofa, our family friend in Odessa, called me out of the blue and asked me to come over and see them right away. When I arrived, they criticized me for not visiting them regularly, as had been agreed upon with my father. They also said that my dad had called and had heard I was dating a German, and that my relatives were on their way to deal with this serious problem.

When I met my relatives in the airport, my mom laid into me: "How dare you date a foreigner! Don't you know what this means for our family? Your father will kill you and our family won't survive the shame of it." That's how my mom, who I hadn't seen for several months, greeted me. I brazenly decided to introduce my mom to Juergen. I was sure that she would like him. She was polite to him, but categorically forbade me to date him anymore. I learned that my dad had found out about me dating a German not only from the young people I met at the concert, but from the dean of our faculty and the superintendent of our dorm. It turned out that when my father brought me to Odessa, he had asked the dean to tell him if I was ever behaving inappropriately. It also turned out that my father had been regularly calling the superintendent of the dorm, who told him what I was doing. And here I never suspected and had thought I was a free person.

My relatives left after a week, but I wouldn't promise to stop seeing Juergen.

At the end of March, Juergen invited me to a party at his dorm organized by the German students. When I arrived, they were all dressed up in costumes to celebrate German Carnival. In the Soviet Union we didn't celebrate Carnival and adults didn't wear costumes; therefore, it was really interesting for me to see young Germans in costumes. There were musical instruments on stage. Wow, I thought, there will be live music! Juergen told me that he had to leave for a short while, but I didn't want to stay there alone. I was uncomfortable, and I didn't know the language. Suddenly Juergen and some other young men appeared on stage and started to perform. Juergen played the guitar and sang beautifully in English. What a surprise! Later I found out that he played the keyboard, the piano, and percussion instruments just as well. Now that was talent!

I decided to take advantage of his musical talent. My other friend Tanya, a singer, was preparing for a party in our faculty. The organizer of the party was the physics teacher who, as I wrote above, I didn't get along with. They didn't have enough musicians, so I proposed a vocal-instrumental group of German students. The physics teacher was thrilled about my idea, and Juergen and his friends performed at our faculty's party. He accompanied my friend Tanya, who sang Russian songs, and a Hungarian student who sang in Hungarian. The concert was a hit. My relationship with the physics teacher improved, and once again I had cause to be proud of my boyfriend.

Our two dorm rooms became friends. Juergen would come visit us with his roommates, and we would drink tea and take walks on Deribasovskaya St. It was already spring, it was sunny out, and everything was in bloom. May 1 was a holiday, International Workers Day, in the Soviet Union. We decided to go to the beach for a picnic on the sea. The water was still cold, but the beach was nice. We brought a bunch of food and wine and set off. It was wonderful: we sat on the beach, Juergen grabbed his guitar, and we sang songs.

May 6 was my birthday, and I decided to have a party so I could show off my culinary abilities to Juergen. After all, I had been cooking for my whole family since I was 10. I sold some of my things and went to the Privoz Market to get supplies and cook some gourmet dishes. I mainly prepared Eastern dishes, and Juergen told me how much he liked my cooking.

Meanwhile, my dad had stopped talking to me. Only my mom would call. At the end of June, the semester ended, and we went home for the summer. I was supposed to leave for Tashkent, and Juergen was supposed to go to Germany. Right before I left, the dean summoned me and told me that my father had asked him to transfer me back to Tashkent, where I would be studying from then on out. I was in shock, but there was nothing I could do, as the paperwork had already gone through. I knew Juergen and I couldn't stay together forever, but I didn't think we would have to part so soon.

By then I had already told Juergen about our traditional way of life and that there was little chance I could plan a future with him, but we weren't ready to be separated so soon. We decided that we could extend our time together by taking the train to Moscow and spending a little time together there. My parents said I could go home via Moscow if I stayed at with my Aunt Sasha, my mom's friend, and then immediately bought a ticket from there to Tashkent. So, I had a place to stay in Moscow, but Juergen didn't. Foreign students couldn't stay in hotels without special permission from the head of their institute. Hotel rooms were expensive, and it was impossible to find a vacancy in Moscow in the summer. There weren't very many hotels in general, anyway, and people traveling around the country would stay with friends and relatives. For some reason hotels were for people on business trips and foreigners, and the prices were high. When my friends found out that we were going to Moscow and that we needed a place to stay, they gave us some names of people in Moscow to contact, but no one could help.

We bought train tickets and set off for Moscow. When we arrived, both Juergen and I went to Aunt Sasha's. When I called to warn her that I was coming with my boyfriend Juergen, she fell silent and didn't invite him over. We didn't have any other options, so we went to her house. She lived far from the downtown. I had never been to her house and really didn't know her. Juergen and I were both really nervous, as we didn't know how she would greet us and if she would actually let us both spend the night there.

It turned out that Aunt Sasha lived in a one-bedroom apartment with a tiny kitchen. Even though I was brazen enough to bring a foreigner to her house, she wasn't rude when we arrived. She was a professor and had a good job at the university. I think that she, like the majority of Soviet citizens, didn't want problems with the authorities. Moreover, at the time she had a relative from the countryside staying with her for a few days. After him, some other relative was supposed to visit. Everyone who was travelling would go through Moscow, and poor Muscovites constantly had to put up an endless number of relatives, friends, and friends of friends. As I said already, people had nowhere else to stay and took advantage of any opportunity to spend the night at someone's house. Eventually people got used to this, but I think that when my mom asked Aunt Sasha to put me up for the night, she didn't imagine that I wouldn't come alone.

161

I left Juergen in the room with Aunt Sasha's other guest and went into the kitchen with Aunt Sasha. I started to tell her an emotional story about my problems with my relatives. I tried to present Juergen in the best possible light, told her that he was from a friendly country, and wondered why it was so hard for us to be together... I told her that I had been transferred back to Tashkent without my permission, and I didn't know if I would ever see Juergen again, so we wanted to spend a few days together in Moscow. I also asked her not to tell my parents that Juergen was in Moscow with me. I don't think Aunt Sasha was very happy about this and didn't want the responsibility, but she showed compassion toward me and made dinner while we talked.

Guests were received well in every republic of the Soviet Union. Aunt Sasha made a good dinner, and I tried to help her.

Before inviting the men to the table to eat, she told me that Juergen couldn't stay at her house. She said that a few years ago she had lived as an expat in Mongolia, and even though the USSR and Mongolia were on friendly terms, she was warned not to get involved with anyone there. I sighed deeply and told her that Juergen couldn't stay in a hotel because he didn't have special permission from the dean. She left the room and called someone. Then she invited everyone to dinner. During dinner, she told us that she had friends who worked at a hotel for foreigners and that she had arranged for Juergen to go there after dinner. On the one hand, we both sighed with relief, but on the other, we didn't want to be separated.

Aunt Sasha and her guest were both amazed at how well Juergen spoke Russian. And in fact, unlike his compatriots who had studied in the Soviet Union, Juergen spoke very well. He barely had an accent and was often taken for someone from the Baltics.

The next morning Juergen and I met in town. I had to buy a plane ticket to Tashkent, and there were usually long lines to buy tickets for distant travel. But after spending a long time in line, I found out that there were no plane tickets to Tashkent in the near future. It wasn't surprising, as it was high season; moreover, I didn't have any friends at the ticket office who could help. I called my parents to tell them what was going on, and they said I had to come home immediately, and since there were no plane tickets, I should take the train. After standing in line for a train ticket for a long time, I finally got one. I had no desire whatsoever to spend over 3 days on a train in the heat, but what could I do?

Juergen and I still had two more whole days together in Moscow. One the one hand, that was great, but on the other, we knew we would be parting soon, and we didn't know for how long, or if we would ever see each other again. We spent a lot of time walking around town, and in the evening Juergen would walk me back to Aunt Sasha's house. She would invite us in for dinner, and it seemed that she had taken a liking to us. On the last night we were there, she even told us to fight for our love and not to give up. She said she would help us in any way she could, and we realized that in Aunt Sasha we had found a true friend. She really did in fact help us later on.

The final day of our trip arrived. Juergen left first, and I went to the airport to see him off. We spent a long time saying goodbye. Juergen made it clear that he would visit me as soon as possible. I didn't believe it, because there were so many things standing in our way: countries, cultures, systems, traditions, and even religions. Although officially there was no religion in our country, Muslim culture was very strong in my community.

When Juergen disappeared into the airport, I burst into tears and cried all the way back on the bus. At that moment, I was the most unhappy person in the world. I had always found a way to solve every problem, but this time I was completely powerless.

I left for Tashkent. You can imagine the mood I was in for those three days on the train. Thankfully, I shared a cabin with an intelligent young man. A scholar, he tried to engage me in various conversations and discussions. When I finally told him why I was in such a bad way, he whistled and shrugged, saying it was a complicated issue. He said he didn't know of anyone who had married a foreigner. And it was still the era called the "Brezhnev Stagnation".

In the 1970s, during the "Brezhnev Stagnation," a lot of dissidents were arrested for criticizing the Soviet system. At that time, any serious criticism of communism, communist leaders, Soviet literature, or even everyday Soviet life was seen as anti-Soviet propaganda.

Although the dissidents were small in number and had little popular support, they were treated harshly by the government. Many were sentenced to prison or forced into exile and, while they were abroad, their Soviet citizenship would be suddenly and unlawfully revoked. During this period, the writer Solzhenitsyn, the poet Brodsky, the bard Galich, the musician Rostropovich, the sculptor Neizvestny, and the director Lubimov were all kicked out of the country. It was also during this time that Academician Sakharov was arrested and exiled from Moscow. A nuclear physicist, the "father of the Soviet hydrogen bomb," and an ethnic Russian, Sakharov was one of the foremost moral and intellectual leaders of the Soviet dissident movement. Furthermore, a number of prominent cultural figures defected, including the dancers Rudolf Nureyev and Mikhail Baryshnikov, and the film director Andrey Tarkovsky.

One of the cruelest ways the regime had devised to punish dissidents was to put them in psychiatric wards. Between 1962 and 1983, around 500 citizens, including many human rights activists, were incarcerated in psychiatric hospitals.

Everybody was afraid to talk about dissidents and foreign countries. The Soviet people's fear of the regime was genetic.

Anyway, this young man warned me about the problems I would face if I were to stay in touch with my foreign boyfriend. He said: "Foreigners are foreigners." The Soviet government didn't distinguish between people from "friendly" countries and the West: they were all foreigners. Everyone who left the country was considered a traitor and a cosmopolitan. And that's kind of strange, since "cosmopolitan" is actually a positive word.

Clearly, the young man I was traveling with understood the system we lived in better than I. After all, I was only 18!

I was back in Tashkent in three days. My two sisters met me at the train station; my parents didn't even deign to come. I excitedly began to tell my sisters that I was in love with Juergen and that I was going to marry him no matter what. They stared at me; apparently, they were completely unable to fathom what I was saying. What German? What marriage?

When I arrived home by taxi, I was greeted coldly by my parents. My father told me in front of the whole family, "If you continue dating the German, I will kill you and marry you off to another man as soon as possible!" The word "kill" didn't mean he would literally kill me. It was normal for hotheaded peoples like us to yell things like "I will kill you," "I will stab you," or "I will kick you out of this house." But his words were nonetheless pretty serious. My mother told me which institute I was going to attend now. No one had asked me whether I wanted to study there or in general what I wanted to do.

It was typically hot during this time of year in Tashkent - around 115°F. The heat was unbearable in the house, and there were no air conditioners. I decided to visit my girlfriends – I had a lot to tell them. They all listened to me with curiosity: after all, it's not every day that an Uzbek girl falls in love with a German. But when I declared that I was going to marry Juergen, they all started looking at me as if I were crazy.

However, my only Russian girlfriends, Marina and Sveta, were in awe of me and said, "It's so cool that you are in love with a foreigner, and a German to boot!" However, I think it was just a matter of curiosity for them. They would not have wanted to be in my shoes. Unlike me, a person madly in love, they had no illusions about things. They knew that there was no way to get out of this country, and they knew the consequences of such behavior…

I didn't even say a word about Juergen to my Uzbek girlfriends. Even girls of my generation would judge me and gossip about me. And this would have been some juicy gossip! My parents, their colleagues, my relatives, neighbors, and friends would hear about it - there was no way to prevent that. But I wanted so badly to tell everyone that I was in love!

Exactly a week after my return, I received a letter from Juergen in Germany. The postman handed the letter to my sister, and she slipped it to me in secret. The envelope was foreign and thin; the letter in it was written on blue paper that was as thin as papyrus. My hands shook from excitement, and I probably reread the letter 10 times, as I realized, "He really, really loves me!"

He had written the letter as soon as he got home, and it had taken a week to get to me. After that, I received letters from him each week. Luckily, the letters would arrive during the daytime, so my parents had no idea I was getting them until one day when, out of the blue, the postman asked my father who was regularly sending us letters from Germany. That led to another serious conversation with my father; this time I was silent. I didn't justify myself or defend myself. I just decided that whatever will be, will be, and time will tell.

At the end of August, I got a telegram from Juergen. He said he was planning on coming to Tashkent in September with his brother. Juergen was in his last year of studies in the Soviet Union and would finish school in a year; then he would have to go back to Germany. He had been planning for a long time to tour the Caucasus and the Black Sea with his brother before he left, so it made sense for him to bring his brother to Tashkent. And since we met, he had been dying to see the republic where I was born and grew up.

The news of his plans to visit simultaneously shocked, terrified, and thrilled me. I had a million thoughts in my head: Where will they stay? How can I keep my parents from finding out? How will his brother react to everything? I couldn't even invite them over. I would be so embarrassed, so ashamed. Lord, it was the twentieth century, but we had to behave like it was the Middle Ages with our Uzbek traditionalism.

I had to tell my mom that Juergen and his brother were coming; she didn't take it well.

In September I started studying at the institute that my father had chosen. My major was, once again, "Economic Engineering", but in a different industry. There were mostly Uzbeks with me in my group, but one Russian girl named Irina was very friendly and asked me a bunch of questions about Odessa. She couldn't understand how I could come back to Tashkent from Odessa. I soon understood why she was so curious: she, too, wanted to leave Tashkent and study somewhere in Russia. We quickly became friends, and I told her

166

about Juergen. Her response was, "What!?!? Did you forget you are Uzbek? How can you talk about a German? He's a foreigner!" She didn't believe me when I told her that he soon was planning to visit with his brother, and that I had a million problems to solve. She promised to help me as much as she could – at the very least by telling my parents that I was studying at her place when I was with him.

So I met them at the airport. His brother was very tall and didn't speak Russian at all. They decided to stay at a hotel. When we got there, they wouldn't even let me in because it was a hotel for foreigners, and local people were forbidden from entering.

That was the first time I experienced discrimination against Soviet citizens in my own country. I learned that foreigners in my country got special privileges that citizens didn't. I don't think there is another country in the world which discriminates against its own citizens like they did in the Soviet Union. All the special services for foreigners like the Intourist Travel Agency, special restaurants, and special stores automatically made Soviets second-class citizens in their own country.

I waited for them on the street; after a little while Juergen and Dietmar came out very upset because they had been told the hotel room cost an insane amount. The letter from the dean saying that Juergen was a student didn't work this time. They couldn't afford to stay at the hotel for the time they were supposed to be in Tashkent, and I had no one to go to for help. I realized then that in a city where I had tons of relatives and friends, there was no one I could turn to for help because Juergen was a foreigner!

I didn't have any other choice than to go to my mother. I explained that Juergen had come with his brother, and it would be un-Uzbek of us (i.e., inhospitable) if no one were to help them. My mom immediately called some people she barely knew on the outskirts of town and asked if they could put up our guests from Germany. She presented them as our friends from Moscow. My mom took Juergen and his brother there and forbade me to go with her. No one could know that Juergen had any sort of relationship to me. I had to warn Juergen about this and explain that this was our traditional way of life.

167

Luckily, although the people they stayed with were not well off, they received them well – with lots of food and vodka. The next day, Juergen and Dietmar complained of headaches from the amount of vodka they had consumed. Thank god someone received them in proper Uzbek fashion! All day I walked around town with them; in the evening we returned to our friends' house; they didn't even suspect that Juergen and I were in love with one another. I don't know whether or not Juergen managed to explain my situation to his brother Dietmar, but I was very ashamed that I couldn't invite them over to my house.

One day they were waiting for me in front of our institute after my class. I wanted to introduce them to Ira. Seeing me and Ira with foreigners, my classmates began to ask stupid questions. I think it was at that moment that I became an outsider in my group, and that was only because I hung out with foreigners.

For the entire time that Juergen and his brother were in town, I had to be careful that none of my relatives, friends, or friends' friends saw me with them. I tried to show them as much of the city as possible. Even when we were sitting together in a downtown tearoom, I kept looking around to make sure no one I knew would see us.

On the last evening, Juergen wanted us all three of us to eat together in a restaurant. My first thought was that I had to bring a friend because I, an Uzbek girl, couldn't be seen sitting alone in a restaurant with two foreigners. I invited my Russian friend Sveta, and then my sister Gulnoza decided to come with me. Incidentally, it was easier to get out of the house with my sister.

The Tashkent Hotel in downtown Tashkent had a restaurant on its roof with a great view of the city. We decided to go there, but when we sat down the people (mainly men) sitting at the other tables looked at us unpleasantly. Thanks to our appearance, no one took me and Sveta for Uzbek girls, but my sister was clearly a local girl. The waiter tried to ask us a few times how we know the young men; we said they were friends of friends. I was more than sure that the waiters were working for the KGB. At that time, KGB agents worked in the guise of waiters and hotel administrators in places where foreigners might go.

After dinner Juergen and Dietmar decided to walk us home. I tried to dissuade Juergen from doing that, but he insisted. As we rode the tram, I was completely stressed out and kept looking around to make sure none of our friends or neighbors were there to see us with foreigners. When we got off the tram, I was barely able to convince them not to walk us home, and instead, we sent them off with my sister in a taxi. As soon as they had left, I felt relieved that no one had seen us. At that moment, my sense of terror was greater than the thought that Juergen had left and I wouldn't see him again for a long time.

Ira was fascinated by Juergen, and she understood why I was in love with him. But now, my days were once again full of sadness. The people in my group weren't interesting; all they talked about was local gossip. I missed the atmosphere of Odessa and my freedom. After all, wherever you were in Tashkent, everything you did was always being watched by everyone else, so you would fall into certain behavioral norms from which it was impossible to escape and be yourself.

As I said before, at the end of September, when the cotton-picking season began, students from kindergarten through college were taken to the cotton fields. The conditions were hellacious; students had to bring everything with them, even mattresses and blankets to sleep on. The hygiene situation was terrible, there were no showers, the toilets were outside on the street, and we slept in barracks on quickly built bunks. I told my parents I wasn't going to go pick cotton and that I didn't intend to be a slave of the government, but it was impossible not to go – you could be kicked out of the institute for that.

Luckily and unluckily, I had started having health problems, and that got me an exemption from cotton-picking. The doctors said I needed to go to Moscow for a consult. We didn't go to Moscow, but they put me in a hospital for observation. I was happy that I didn't have to spend all day bent over picking cotton on pesticide-laden fields.

When we went to visit my sister, who had been sent by her institute to pick cotton, I was shocked by the conditions. All the students were bloated from being fed macaroni and bread day and night. They were only saved by regular care packages from home. And they were only able to wash once a week at the public *banya*.

Luckily, they were having fun. After all, they were far from their parents, and it was a fun group of students. It was thanks to that, I think, that they survived in these conditions. They only returned toward the end of November, when the first snow was falling and there was nothing left to gather from the fields. By that time Uzbekistan had already managed to report to Moscow that they had successfully picked a million tons of cotton. The cotton was sent to Russia; in Uzbekistan it was hard to find even a cotton dress.

My classes were boring. I hated math and many of my other subjects; after all, the engineering major wasn't my choice. I lived on letters from Juergen, which I got every other day, and once a week we managed to speak by phone. After talking to him I would again liven up for a bit, until the next phone call.

His letters were full of words of love. He really missed me, and we wrote poems to each other. Since Juergen drew well, he depicted a lot in pictures. He had long ago decided that we would get married, but he had no idea when and how that would happen.

I wasn't so sure, especially when I looked around and saw how traditional my society was. All the marriages were arranged by parents, and girls of my age were married off without being asked if they wanted to or not.

One unpleasant story unraveled right before my eyes. A girl in my class named Gulya was not very attractive and not particularly special in any way. Her parents arranged a match for her with a student at our institute who had already been dating someone else for a few years. We all knew that he and the other girl were in love with one another; even Gulya did. After all, the love affair of these two took place right in front of us. You couldn't have separated them if you wanted to. They were always together. And then there was this rumor… We asked Gulya if she would actually agree to marry him. She could see how he and this other girl loved one another! She replied coldly that she would do as her parents said. We were in shock; I couldn't understand her at all. Everyone said that this was clearly the only chance this homely girl Gulya had to get married, but how hard it was for the couple that was madly in love? The young man was being married off to Gulya because her father held an important position in one of the government ministries, and being married to her meant a bright future for him. And what do you know – exactly a month later Gulya and this young man were married, because they couldn't go against the wishes of their parents. I would never have lowered myself so and built my happiness on the unhappiness of others.

And there were a million cases like this. Young Uzbeks who were in love were unable to just go out and get married.

So what did that mean for me? In such conditions, could I even think about marrying a foreigner? On the other hand, I was self-confident, and I knew I could achieve what I wanted.

At the end of November my family began to arrange a marriage for me with a young man who I had never met before. My parents wanted me to meet him and told me that if I didn't like him, I could refuse to marry him. I categorically refused to meet him.

This happened several times. The third time I refused to meet with a potential husband, my father had a serious conversation with me. He said that he knew that Juergen and I were corresponding with each other, and that that was just a waste of time, as they would never let me marry someone who wasn't Uzbek. When I started to say, "What about the Soviet system, where everyone is equal irrespective of nationality, etc., and that they work for this system," he smirked and said, "Who cares about the system. Tradition is more important than anything else!"

In January our winter vacation began, and Juergen sent me a telegram from Odessa saying that he was planning to come to Tashkent for 10 days. I jumped for joy and decided that I would no longer hide the fact I was in a relationship with a foreigner - at least not from my fellow classmates.

That winter was unusually cold; the temperature reached -22° F, which rarely happens in Tashkent. After I met Juergen at the airport, we went to the hotel foreigners usually stayed at. As a student, he had managed to reserve an inexpensive room for 10 days. We were happy, but our happiness didn't last long. They wouldn't let me into the hotel with him, saying that it was only for foreigners. The small foyer was located across from the reception area, and we had to sit across from the receptionist, who was probably KGB. It was freezing outside, so what could we do? It was impossible to be alone with the man I loved and who I hadn't seen for several months. O God, what could I do?!? In our huge city there was nowhere to go.

I called Ira, and she invited us over for tea. We went all the way across town to her house. Ira couldn't help us with anything except sympathy. We sat for a while and drank tea together, then it was time for us to go. The next day I managed to get into his hotel room, as there was no one in the corridor, but as soon as I entered his room, a hotel attendant called and said that I had to leave his room immediately. Juergen told them that I was his fiancée, that he had come just to visit me, that it was cold outside, and that we had nowhere to go. Nothing helped. We were young and inexperienced and didn't know that if we had paid a bribe or given someone a present, they might not have bothered us.

Because of this incident, Juergen was told he had to leave the hotel and could not stay there again in the future. So there we were, standing together on the street, in the snow and freezing cold, with nowhere to go. I decided to call a fellow student. I knew that he was renting an apartment with his friends. I told him the situation over the phone and asked if he couldn't maybe let Juergen stay with him for a few days. He told us to come over; we went. A few guys from our region lived there. I told my classmate that Juergen was my friend, and he said it was no problem for him to stay there. It was late and I had to go. Then Uzbek hospitality kicked in! These guys had never interacted with foreigners before, but they decided to receive him properly, and made *plov* and drank vodka with him. When dinner was ending, some girls appeared. When Juergen said he was tired and wanted to go to bed, they told him that he could choose whichever girl he wanted and that as a guest, he would get first pick. Juergen, who didn't understand what was going on, asked why. They immediately explained that these were prostitutes and that they had paid them to come over. They did this as a special treat for an important guest. Juergen was in shock and said that he was

172

engaged, but that didn't stop them, and they kept pushing him to go off with a prostitute.

The next day when Juergen was telling me this story, he said he barely managed to escape from their hospitality!

On the day I took him to the airport, there was another earthquake in Tashkent. Although it was not as strong as the one in 1966, the lamps in the room started swaying a lot. I was happy that Juergen didn't have to live through an earthquake, although we had basically gotten used to them. From 1966 on, there were regular earthquakes in Tashkent.

Because of bad weather in Odessa, Juergen had to land in the Ukrainian city of Dnepropetrovsk. At that time it was a closed city, and foreigners weren't allowed there. Poor Juergen had to sit in the airport for 6 days straight and couldn't go out into the city once. They simply wouldn't let him. There were a lot of such closed cities in the Soviet Union. Usually they housed military facilities and heavy industry.

My health problems continued, and the doctors in Tashkent said that I needed to go to Moscow for an operation. In Moscow everything was better, even medical care, and that's where the best specialists were. But it wasn't so easy to get in to see a good specialist: you had to have connections, just as with everything else. My mom had a friend there named Aunt Inna, who she had studied with in grad school. Aunt Inna had connections everywhere because she had a high-level job.

At the beginning of February Aunt Anna called said that there was a long wait to get into the clinic, but that if we were to come in a week, we might be able to get into see a well-known specialist, and he might even put me in the hospital and do the operation right away.

My dad and I immediately packed our things and set off for Moscow. We stayed with Aunt Sasha, and the first thing I did was to ask her not to say anything about Juergen in front of my dad. I told her that my dad had no idea about our relationship. She was a tactful person and understood me.

The doctor looked at me and immediately put me in the hospital. He said they would do the operation in a matter of days and that I would be in the hospital for a week. He also told my dad that he didn't have to stay in Moscow and that he could go back to Tashkent. My dad needed to go to work, and anyway, Aunt Sasha promised to look after me. So I immediately sent a telegraph to Juergen saying that I would be in Moscow for 2 weeks, and that if he could come, we could see one another. I had no expectation that this would work because vacation was already over and classes were well under way. No "Dean of Foreign Affairs" would let him come. But he wanted to see me so badly, especially because Aunt Sasha said he could stay with her if he came, so he wouldn't have to deal with hotels or getting a letter from the dean to get a room.

Juergen sent me a telegram saying he was coming to see me outside the hospital. Hurrah! There was no one in the world happier than me at that moment. The operation had gone well, and in the US they would let you go home the day after that type of operation, but in the Soviet Union, where there was free medical care, they kept you there as long as possible.

In the bed next to me there was a nice woman from Estonia. She was Estonian, and we hit it off. In general, Soviet people made friends with one another quickly and easily. In a few minutes you would already know the entire life's story of a person you had never met before. I, of course, told her about my affair with Juergen and that we were definitely going to get married. She replied that she couldn't imagine how someone would go about marrying a foreigner. Even in progressive Estonia she had never met anyone who had actually married a foreigner.

I told her how traditional my culture was, how marriages were arranged for girls by their parents, and how girls would obediently marry men they didn't love. She was in shock and couldn't believe such things were still going on. She knew that Uzbekistan was a conservative place, but not to that extreme! What about educated women? After all, your women study in universities, and they should be emancipated from such slavery. I couldn't explain why, after 70 years of socialism, women in Central Asia still had no rights. When I was released from the hospital, I decided to go to

174

Moscow State University before Juergen arrived. I was on the student council at my university, and before I left Tashkent, I promised my colleagues that I would visit Moscow State University and ask them to share their experience.

After the meeting with my Moscow colleagues, I peeked into the University Bookstore. There someone called me by name. I turned around and saw a young man from Tashkent. The previous fall his parents had tried to get us to marry. They really wanted us to be together. The young man was a promising scientist pursuing a PhD at the best university in the Soviet Union. Honestly, I never expected to see him there, especially as we didn't know each other well. Maybe we had seen one another a couple times, but we had never talked. He was pleasantly surprised to see me and immediately invited me to have a cup of coffee with him. But there was no way I could do it because in 2 hours I was supposed to meet Juergen at the airport, and I was counting the minutes to our meeting. And then, as bad luck would have it, he was there and as an Uzbek woman, I had to be polite. I could tell he had a lot to say to me, and I knew he liked me. He would have been happy to marry me the next day. And a thousand Uzbek girls would have been happy to marry such a promising young man. When I rejected his parents' offer, my parents were really upset. After all, he would have been an ideal match: he was the youngest scientist – before he was 20, he had made scientific discoveries. He was also good looking and the child of professors. In other words, he was an ideal candidate in every way.

I knew one thing: I would never marry an educated, progressive Uzbek because I would immediately become the family servant. I would have to live with the parents of my husband, and cook, clean, and wait on everyone. I respected myself too much to get married just to become a servant and, moreover, a servant to a man I didn't love. In response to these arguments, everyone told me that in Uzbekistan millions of girls do this. Let them do it, but not I!

I profoundly apologized to this young man, saying I was in a hurry; he responded that he would be expecting me that evening for dinner at his place, and that he wanted to have a serious conversation with me. I had to promise to come – otherwise he wouldn't have let me go. Later we met in Tashkent on the eve of his wedding. He was being married to a girl who was a good catch. He told me I was the only girl who he had ever liked, and that that evening in Moscow he had waited for me for a long time. I later heard that he had an unhappy marriage, and that his parents wouldn't let him get divorced. How terrible to have one life and to live it in misery just to make one's parents happy and not break thousand-year old traditions. He went on to occupy important posts and made a lot of scientific discoveries, but what did all this do for him when he wasn't strong enough to fight against those traditions and live a happy life? Well, perhaps it's just easier to live like that – to live like everyone, go with the flow, not stand out, not be different. Not everyone can be the odd man out.

Even though it was winter in Moscow, Juergen and I had a great time walking around the city for the few days we had. We didn't care; all that mattered was that we were together. We were really hoping that Juergen would be able to stay on for the PhD program, since he was the best student from the GDR. That summer – i.e., in a few months, he would finish his studies and go back to Germany. After graduating, he didn't have the legal right to remain in the Soviet Union, and his student visa would expire. We really hoped that he would be able stay, and he tried to talk to his professors about this, but the decision had to be made in Germany, and that was difficult.

Dietmar, the person thanks to whom I met Juergen, was in the PhD program, but I remember him saying that it took two years to convince officials in Germany that he needed to complete this program. We didn't have two years, so I had trouble believing there was any chance Juergen would be able to stay.

As always, Juergen and I parted not knowing how long it would be until we saw one another again. We set off in different directions very upset.

I had a new excuse to keep my parents off my back. After the operation, the doctors said to keep me from getting excited or worried for a while.

Luckily, I had a bunch of girlfriends I could see every day and talk to about my concerns. They were always nearby and really helped me, especially my Russian friends Sveta and Ira. I could go on and on with them about Juergen without worrying that my relatives would find out about my feelings for him. At that point, we all felt that there was no good way out of my situation. There was no way we could get married at that time, and leaving the country didn't even enter my mind. I couldn't imagine life without Tashkent, my big family, or my girlfriends, so I didn't think about leaving for even a second. The only real option was for Juergen to move to the Soviet Union.

Unfortunately, as it turned out, Juergen was not allowed to continue his work on his PhD in Odessa, so when he graduated in June, he had to go back to the GDR, where a job was already waiting for him. He was supposed to work for Carl Zeiss Jena and live in the city of Jena. In communist countries you were generally guaranteed a job after graduating from the university. In other words, the university would send its graduates to different places to work. You couldn't choose where you wanted to go, and you had to work for 3 years at the place you were sent. If you were lucky, you would get to stay in the city you were from, but often you would be sent to a village. I know girls who tried to get married during the last year of their studies to avoid being sent to the countryside.

After a year in Odessa, I couldn't get used to life in Tashkent. Life there was completely different. It wasn't boring, but it lacked the intense interaction with people of different cultures, and I wasn't utterly and completely free, as I had been in Odessa. There were no parties or discos, and I was once again living at home under the strict control of my Uzbek parents. In June, Juergen wrote to tell me that he had gotten permission to come to Tashkent and stay here until the end of July. I jumped for joy – my vacation also started at the end of June. But once again, my joy was clouded by problems: how and where would we spend a whole month without anyone in my Uzbek community finding out?

There was a big chance people would see us together in the city. My mom, who knew about my continuing relationship with Juergen, wasn't too pleased with this news, but she suggested setting us up in her institute's student camp in the mountains. But then there was another problem: my institute's camp was right next to hers, and I knew that many of my classmates would be at that camp at the same time, and would probably find out about my relationship with Juergen. Some of my classmates were Uzbeks who would never condone my relationship. For them it was unacceptable for an Uzbek girl to be with a German. But I tried not to think about that at the time, and I was surprised at my mom's suggestion. I couldn't understand how my mother herself had offered to help me stay alone with Juergen for two weeks in a camp. Later I realized that she only did this to keep us as far away from the city as possible, so that at least no one in the city would see us.

When we arrived at the camp, the head of the camp, an Armenian, told us that we were going to stay together in one tent. I didn't expect this; usually unmarried young people didn't dare stay together. Juergen and I were the only ones in the whole camp who were together in one tent. Understand that it was 1977 and Soviet citizens could only live together if they were married. Apparently, that is why people got married so young in the Soviet Union. After all, there was no concept of sex in the Soviet Union.

I remember how, in the 1980s, the first "Citizens' Summit" telecast (Leningrad-Seattle) was broadcast on Soviet TV and, for the first time, Soviets and Americans were talking openly and directly on live TV. The moderators were a Russian, Vladimir Pozner, and an American, Phil Donahue. During the live broadcasting a Russian woman proudly told the American audience that in Soviet Union, sex doesn't exist!

After that show, "there is no sex in our country" became a popular expression. At that moment, the word "sex" didn't even exist, and co-habitation by two unmarried young people was completely unacceptable and contrary to Soviet morals.

Maybe the camp director thought we were married? But everyone around us knew that wasn't so. My younger sister, who was studying at that institute, was with us; she tried to tell her classmates, who were asking about us, that we were just about to get married. So, on the one hand, Juergen and I were happy, but on the other, I was still uncomfortable.

Moreover, my classmates, who knew that I was from a solid Uzbek family, showed up at the neighboring camp, which belonged to the institute where I studied, but they didn't suspect that I was living in a tent with a foreigner. You can't imagine how this simply didn't fit into the notions of morality in that society. When I saw them, I was horrified. Some of their parents knew my parents, and one was the son of our dean, who was friends with our neighbor. A rumor momentarily circulated, and that was disgraceful for my whole family. You have to understand Uzbek society, where in certain circles, everyone knows everyone. People live in communes, and it's impossible to be an outsider, or you end up isolating yourself completely from society. To be isolated from your circle, your acquaintances, your friends, colleagues, and relatives is the most awful thing that could happen. It's not even possible to imagine.

When someone dies in this commune, hundreds of people come to the funeral to support and help the family, and as many as 500 people attend weddings. Imagine being excluded from all that. In times of trouble, they wouldn't reach out to help you. And I, an Uzbek girl, behaving in such a shameful way – that was disgraceful for my whole family. Although I criticized these vestiges of traditional society at times, I would never have allowed my family to suffer and be outcasts in their own society. That is why I never spoke of my love for Juergen and hid him when he was in Tashkent. Luckily, my classmates never came onto our territory, and I tried not to run into them, but it wasn't easy.

The camp was located in the Chimgan Mountains, and Juergen and I would take off in the morning to hike in the mountains.

Located in the Western Tien Shan mountain range, Chimgan is 85 km (52. 8 mi) from Tashkent. The Chimgan range is very high, and its highest peak, Greater Chimgan, is 3,309 m (10,856 ft) above sea level. Chimgan is a "green" mountain; i.e., a wonderful place for skiing, travel, or just relaxation.

Every day we explored different parts of the mountains. Some days we would walk upstream and have lunch on the banks of river. We enjoyed the coolness of the water. The next day we would climb up the peaks of different mountains. We would always spend time enjoying the beautiful view of the valley. On other days, we would enjoy the magnificent view of the Beldersay River Valley, then we would walk to the Gulkam and Novotasha waterfalls. Our daily walks gave us a chance to be alone together.

Uzbek people are not very active, and we were the only ones who tried to take a walk every day. The locals never even go to the Tien Shan mountains, even though they are located near Tashkent. It never enters people's minds to escape the heat in the cool mountains, even in the summer, when the heat in Tashkent becomes unbearable. In the mountains in summer it is 15-25 degrees cooler than in the city. There are all sorts of summer homes you can rent near cool mountain rivers and in the clean mountain air. But since Uzbeks don't know how to relax and enjoy life, what can you do? Even the young people in this camp were too lazy to go on hikes, but for Juergen and me it was a help, since no one would catch us alone together.

On one of the days right before we left, Shukhrat, the son of our dean, unexpectedly came to see me. We were on good terms, and he said he wanted to meet Juergen. O God – was our whole conspiracy in vain? How did he know? But it no longer mattered, and I introduced him to Juergen. After that he came to see us every evening. We would sit by the campfire and talk about everything. He seemed to be understanding about my affair with Juergen. But later when I saw him at the beginning of the school year, he said to me, "Dildora, you're a good-looking girl. Are you really not able to find yourself an Uzbek man? Why do you need to date a Fritz?" He said this to me even though he was my age and had been so understanding and spent evenings having interesting conversations with us in camp. Of course, it was easy to be like everyone else, go with the flow, listen to and obey your parents because it's an Uzbek tradition, and marry whoever your parents pick, even if you like – or love – someone else. It's easier to live that way, and it's easy to belong. It's always hard to be an outsider. There nothing primitive man fears more than separation from his community. All virtue is collective, all evil is individual. What holds everything together is good, what divides it is bad.

But ever since childhood I have been different, and I chose a more difficult path for myself, one which made me an outsider. It wasn't even my choice; the community I grew up in made me strong and different than the other people around me. I didn't belong to any community. I never felt comfortable either among Muslim Uzbeks or European Russians. But ever since I was young, I knew how to behave wherever I was. With the Uzbeks I was an Uzbek; in Russian-speaking society, I was a progressive young woman. But anyway, I never wanted to be like everyone else. Being like everyone else irritated me and made me want to protest. I am not like everyone else. I have my own personality, and I don't want to suppress it, nor will I allow anyone else to.

In this particular situation with Juergen, I didn't give a crap about ancient feudal traditions. I wouldn't let anyone decide how I should live or what my fate would be. Therefore, I told this young man that he had no right to butt into my affairs. If he had told my classmates about my relationship with Juergen, they would have stopped talking to me. I would have ended up all alone – except, of course, for my friend Ira, because she was Russian. For Russians it is normal to marry the person you love, irrespective of nationality. Maybe 100 years ago parents arranged marriages in Russia, but today that was impossible to imagine, although Russian parents would probably not have approved of their children marrying foreigners, either. I was always amazed at how these two cultures were able to exist alongside one another. The first – an Uzbek one based on feudal principles, and the second – a Russian one based on contemporary norms. Unfortunately, I was not a representative of the more progressive of the two.

Since Juergen was supposed to leave the country forever after graduating from the university, he decided to meet with my father and ask for my hand. My mother, who was well acquainted with my obstinate character, had to fulfill the role of diplomat between my dad, Juergen, and me. Now I understand how hard this role was for my mother. At first, my dad categorically refused to talk to Juergen, and when he found out that Juergen was in town, he stopped talking to me altogether. But after long conversations with my mom, and when he realized that no matter what, Juergen had to leave the country, he decided to see him.

Juergen came over in the evening. My dad forbade my mom and me to be part of the conversation. It was customary for us to feed guests, but guests were supposed to be humble and refuse the food offered. Juergen, however, happily accepted the food and chowed it all down right in front of my dad. After all, Europeans have a completely different culture, and they show respect to the host by eating a lot of food. But with us it is completely the opposite. Only poorly brought up people brazenly eat a lot of food in front of their hosts. My dad later said it was funny to watch Juergen, who quickly ate the first helping of food and didn't refuse the second one. When Juergen asked my father for my hand, my father said, "In Germany there are a lot of pretty young girls. You will go home and meet a young German girl." But Juergen was insistent and said that he loved only me, that there were no girls like me in Germany, that he was ready to move to the Soviet Union to be with me, and that he would do everything to make that happen in the near future.

After he had exhausted all his arguments, my dad suddenly announced that in our culture you have to pay a dowry for the bride, and for some reason named a sum that was astronomical at that time. Juergen hesitated for a moment – he was apparently figuring out how many years it would take him to get that much money. Then he asked my dad, "Do you take credit?" At that point my dad couldn't hold back and started laughing, then stood up and made it clear to Juergen that the meeting was over. He wished him success in Germany and walked him out to the street. I was watching the whole time through the window – they were sitting in the courtyard. I couldn't hear anything, but when my dad walked back in, he said that I should forget about him and that he was going to marry me off as soon as possible without asking my opinion. It's true that he told my mom that Juergen was a pleasant, intelligent young man, but there was nothing to be done about it, since he was a German!

That evening they wouldn't let me out of the house, no matter what excuse I came up with. I didn't sleep all night worrying about Juergen; after all, I didn't know the details of the conversation and had no idea what my dad said to him as he was leaving. With my mom's help, he was able to stay at the home of my former nanny, Aunt Nina, who lived near us. I already mentioned that in the Soviet Union everyone avoided any sort of contact with foreigners, so Aunt

Nina only agreed to take him in because she loved me so much. She knew about our love for one another and was very concerned about us. To help ease the situation a bit, she made some really good food and spoiled Juergen. She was a professional chef. I will never forget the Napoleon pastry that she made; I have never had a better pastry in my life.

In the morning I had barely opened my eyes, when, after making sure my dad wasn't home, I ran off to Aunt Nina's. Juergen was depressed and said that he couldn't keep fighting, after all, my dad had categorically refused to let us get married. At that moment I realized that our fight to be together had been an illusion, and that the two of us couldn't beat a centuries-old tradition. If 70 years of Communism couldn't beat it, how could we? And it wasn't a matter of just fighting against tradition, it was a matter of fighting against the entire system. It would have been very difficult for me to get an exit visa from the Soviet government. Even though Juergen was from a friendly socialist country, the procedure for getting permission to leave was the same as for someone going to the West. We both cried about the situation which neither of us could fix. I said, "What can we do? That means we can't be together." And so on the next day when Juergen was leaving, I wished him happiness in Germany and said that maybe he would really find happiness there. Juergen, who had been ready to give up a minute before, suddenly hugged me tight and said, "I will never have anyone but you in my life!" He said he would do everything he could to come back and that we would most definitely get married. I knew that he was afraid for me; he was afraid that I wouldn't be able to hold out against the pressure of my relatives and would allow myself to be married off.

At that moment, Juergen was underestimating me. No power on earth could make me marry someone against my will. Especially a man who I didn't love. I couldn't even imagine living with someone I didn't love, submitting to the authority of a mother-in-law, and being a servant for my husband's entire family. I valued and respected myself too much to do that. I would rather live alone, even though being an old maid in Soviet society is not a position anyone would envy.

Saying goodbye was hard. I spent a whole month in misery thinking about our uncertain future. I barely spoke to my parents; at that point they were my worst enemies. At 18 years old I had been blinded by love and couldn't put myself in their shoes. For them it was twice as hard, as there were already rumors going around about my affair with a German.

My relatives found out the truth, which meant that there was a blemish on the reputation of our family.

When I returned to school in the fall, I didn't care about my studies. I was already sick and tired of my engineering major, and my classmates irritated me. Some of my female classmates had gotten married over the summer and came back all happy that they were married. After all, in our society girls were terrified of ending up as old maids. If you didn't get married by 23, no one would want you. There were more women in the population than men. Many of the girls in Tashkent were gorgeous – the mixture of ethnicities had done its job. Therefore, the less attractive girls who managed to get married (even if the marriage was an arranged one) were happy simply because they were married.

Time passed slowly; the only thing that kept me afloat was letters from Juergen, which he wrote every day. I knew that he loved me, was suffering, and was doing everything he could to make it possible to meet soon. Since he had graduated with honors from a Soviet institute, he got a good position at Carl Zeiss Jena as an assistant director. Graduates of Soviet institutions of higher education generally got good positions. It was prestigious for high school graduates from Eastern European countries to study in the Soviet Union. It was well-known that the Soviet academic education was solid, and only gifted students were sent here to study. After graduating from a Soviet institution of higher education, a good position and a promising career were waiting for you at home!

Juergen wrote me that it was a big help knowing Russian in his country, that he was in demand, and that he would have no problem getting into the communist party if he wanted to, which would give him even more opportunities in his career.

184

He told me about his classmate, who had married a Ukrainian, apparently in order to show me that things weren't so bad in Germany. After finishing their studies, they came back to the GDR together. He often got together with them for lunch. He said that Nella liked everything there, and although she didn't know German, she had started working and her coworkers were nice to her.

Famous Grandfather Asatullo, ca. 1927

Father (far left on my grandpa's arms) with his family

Grandfather's brother, famous poet Hislat (center)

My aunt Muhtabar

My beautiful mom, Dinara

Mother at the time when she met my father

Mother on her wedding day

Mother's PhD graduation picture

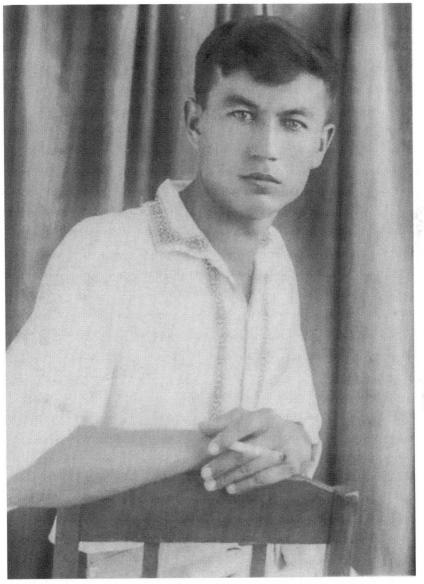

Father on his 30th birthday

My good-looking father

Father on a cotton plantation (far left)

Myself, 1 year old

My parents and I, age 3

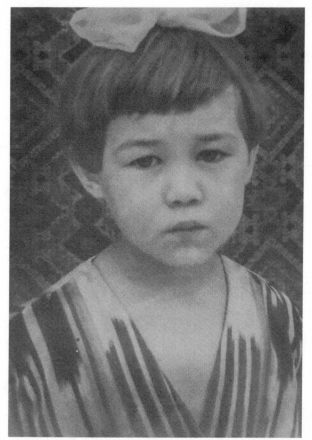

Dildora in national dress

In kindergarden (4th from left front row)

194

The house I grew up in

My cousins and I (far right)

195

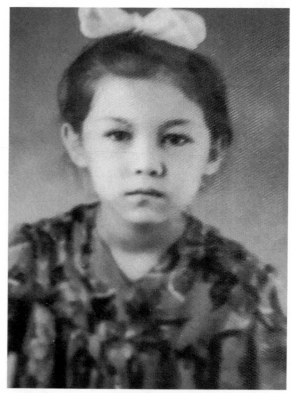

Myself, age 6

Sister Gulnoza (l.) and I (r.)

My favorite Aunt Muharam and I

On family vacation in Yalta

197

Family Portrait (far right)

With relatives (front row right)

On family vacation (front center with little brother)

My Grandma

My Bashkir family

My first love Rustam (second from right)

With my father at the Odessa Opera

First year at Odessa University

Juergen in Taskhent

Happy student time

My dad with my aunt Mattar

With siblings

With my brother

My grandma's brother Myfakar 1979

My father with grand- and great grandchildren

My father with his grandchildren

My son, center, in Tashkent with cousins

My father in traditional dress

Just married. 1978

My daughter Indira

My son Alisher

With my friend Janyl from Radio Liberty

My German family

My parents and I, 2003

My mom in America

My parents in America

Just became an American citizen

My friends Barb and Kathleen

A happy family

My favorite destination, Italy

My dear friends in America

With best friends in America

Happy Couple

In traditional Uzbek attire

On Fox News Detroit

My Love, Detroit

My love, Detroit

On Tour in Detroit

Eminem mural in Detroit

With my grandson

Enjoying Glühwein

My favorite season, spring

Enjoying Michigan summer

Chapter 10.

The GDR

Suddenly in December of 1977, I received an official invitation to go to Germany over winter vacation. It was a surprise; Juergen wrote that he had found out how to make it happen, and that on a guest visa I could come to visit him for a couple weeks. Immediately a million problems came to mind: what would I tell my parents, how would I manage to file the huge number of documents, etc. In February I had a two-week vacation, and in principle I was supposed to go to Moscow for a check-up a year after my surgery. If I had an exit visa, I could easily go from Moscow to Germany. Hurrah!

I took the invitation to OVIR, the organization that gave permission to leave the country. OVIR was "The Division of Visas and Registration". It was formed in 1935 in the USSR and continued to exist in post-Soviet Russia until 2005. It was responsible for registering foreigners in the USSR, as well as processing exit visas for Soviet citizens.

I was met there by an official who was a female Uzbek lieutenant. She was curious about where I was going and why. I said I wanted to visit friends, but suddenly she looked at me with a penetrating gaze and asked, "Do you love him a lot?" I became flustered and didn't know what to say, so I asked what made her think there was a guy involved. She said that she figured it out by the way I said Juergen's name. I thought, well, that's it. They won't let me go. But suddenly she said, "Don't worry. You can go see him. Aren't I a woman, too? How could I not understand? After all, this is the first time I've encountered a romance between an Uzbek girl and a German. It's so cool!" I couldn't believe my ears. For the first time I heard words of support – and this was from someone in an official capacity! I thought maybe this was some sort of game – after all, the KGB (the Committee for State Security) was such a sophisticated organization that it could get all sorts of information out of you, and then lock you up.

The official gave me a list of documents to fill out. The most difficult thing to get was a letter from the dean of my college, but I decided to lie and say that I was going with a tour group to a friendly country. The dean was out, and the secretary was taking his place. I was surprised to get the signed form back the next day.

So I managed to quickly get all the documents I needed and take them to OVIR. Then I had to wait. I had a few weeks before the trip, and during that time I told my mom what I was doing. She was very worried about me. I knew how hard it was for her to be between me, my dad, our traditions, and our society. After all, she had fought for my dad back in the day. She said that she would talk to Aunt Sasha so if needed, I could say I was at her place during my vacation. Papa had no idea I was planning to see Juergen. Moreover, matchmakers kept coming over, and I behaved impolitely and refused to go meet my prospective husbands. I could tell my dad had already gotten tired of me.

The tickets were clearly going to be expensive. My parents would of course pay for my flight to Moscow, but not to Germany. At that time, I knew how to earn money if I wanted to. When I was in school, I would design and sew trendy clothes; now I was knitting stylish sweaters. The most popular item was the wide cowl-neck sweater. When I knitted myself one, my friends went crazy over it and asked me to knit some for them. Eventually I had a list of orders, and I got to work. I used every free moment to knit, because I needed money for the plane. I would knit on the way to the institute, on breaks between classes, while watching tv, and while talking on the phone. Finally, I filled my last order and bought a round-trip ticket from Moscow to Berlin.

By mid-January I had my documents and tickets in hand and set off - ostensibly for Moscow. No one but my mom and my sisters had any idea I was going to visit Juergen. Without stopping for a minute in Moscow, I transferred from one airport to the next and flew on to Berlin. This was, of course, my first trip abroad. Although I had already been in Russia and Ukraine, where the languages and cultures were very different from in Uzbekistan, I was ready to discover a new world. I flew as if I had wings to see my beloved man.

A bunch of Russian military men and their families flew with me on the plane. I spoke to the woman sitting next to me, and she told me how wonderful Germany was. They had been living there for a few years in a military garrison. When she found out I was going to see my German fiancé, she started praising Germans non-stop and urged me to marry my German without hesitation.

Juergen was waiting for me in the airport. I still couldn't believe I had been able to leave. It turns out that when you wish for something, you can achieve anything! We had to travel a few hours by train to the city where his parents lived. The famous German trains, which connect the whole country and run like clockwork! I was surprised by how clean everything was. I could hear everyone speaking German, a language I didn't understand. For some reason I suddenly remembered WWII movies about German soldiers and officers, which were constantly running on TV. I apparently remembered those movies because everyone around me was speaking German, a language I usually heard only in movies.

We boarded a clean, orderly train, which was designed completely differently than our Soviet trains. Our trains were generally designed for long trips, and you would have to spend at least one night sleeping on the train to get where you were going. But in the small country of Germany, trains were regularly used for short distances between cities, and train cars were built for comfort on short trips of just a few hours.

I really wished there was no one in the train car but me and Juergen, but unfortunately there were a lot of passengers, and the people sitting across from us kept changing.

First two young men who kept chowing down sweets sat across from us. One of them was holding a whole pack of Haribo gummy bear-type candies, and the other was taking bites of a whole bar of chocolate as if it were bread. I had never seen two healthy young men chow down candy like that. In my country it was mainly women who ate sweets; men, as I understood it, were supposed to eat hearty food like meat. If our men chowed down sweets in public like that, they would stop looking manly! And anyway, how can you eat a whole bar of chocolate in one sitting? I probably wouldn't have let myself do that over the course of an entire year. So thus began my encounter with a completely different culture.

Juergen's mom met us at the train station with a bouquet of flowers. She made a good impression on me; we walked on foot to her house, and I told her about my trip.

At the very least I had expected to be welcomed with a table full of fancy food, so imagine my surprise when there was no meal waiting, and even the lights weren't turned on. In the living room where Juergen's dad was sitting, only the floor lamp was on. After saying "hi", his parents sat me and Juergen on the couch and started asking us questions about unimportant matters.

Suddenly his mother asked if I would like some pudding. I asked Juergen what that was, and he said it was a dessert. I said I would love some after dinner. Then his parents got up, wished us a good night, and went to bed. I had no idea what was happening; after all, it was only 9:30 pm, and in my country we might just be sitting down to dinner at that time. And what about dinner? Juergen explained to me that they didn't eat late and that his parents assumed that we had had sandwiches on the train. But at least they could have offered me some hot tea! I didn't know then that after 18 years in Germany, I would never accept German culture.

The cold reception shocked me. When Uzbeks receive guests, they cover the table with food and serve them everything they have in the house. Even when a neighbor just stops by out of sheer boredom, we at least offer him some tea. So I thought maybe the problem was that his parents didn't like me.

While I was in Germany, we traveled to a number of different cities, such as Dresden, Gera, Halle, and Jena, where we visited Juergen's relatives. They were very friendly toward me and treated me to German dishes. I was crazy about German baked goods like bread, pies, and cakes. Juergen's grandparents lived in the village. All their food was homemade, even the sausage. Unfortunately, I couldn't eat it because it contained pork. I had grown up with

Muslim traditions, and we Uzbeks didn't eat pork even though we didn't believe in God. It was apparently a cultural thing. But I happily chowed down the cakes and pies his grandmother made. They were the best pies that I have ever eaten in my life.

The entire time the only problems I had were with food and table etiquette. The first time various utensils appeared around my plate, and I had to eat sandwiches with a fork and knife, I panicked. I had never used a knife before. In the whole Soviet Union, no one ate with a fork and knife, and we didn't even know that there were special knives for fish and so on. The Germans ate a lot of dry food, whereas we ate soup every day. The peoples of the former Soviet Union had made a cult out of soup. They believed it was healthy to eat soup every day. In Germany, they ate a lot of sandwiches; for breakfast and sometimes even for dinner they ate bread with sausage and cheese. It's not accidental that they are called the sandwich nation! In Russian the word "sandwich" comes from the German word ("buterbrod"). While I was in Germany, I discovered that a lot of Russian words came from German. This is because Peter the Great brought a lot of German craftsmen to Russia, and they left behind a lot of German words.

When I was walking around town, I had the feeling that I knew these buildings and stone streets from the war movies that were always playing on Soviet TV. Apparently, they were filmed in the GDR. There was a lot of smoke in the air, as a lot of houses were still heated with coal, whereas in the Soviet Union we had already had central heating for a long time. Because of the coal smoke, everything seemed gray or as if it were winter. Incidentally, the sun never came out for the whole time I was there.

Knowing I came from a country where there was a shortage of everything, Juergen took me shopping. My eyes were spinning from the abundance. Although the GDR was a communist country, in comparison to the Soviet Union, its stores were full of food and merchandise. I had a list of orders from my friends to fill. And on top of that, I had to buy gifts for the family members and friends who knew I had gone abroad. Shopping gave me enormous pleasure. Since Juergen had to work, I had fun spending the time he was at work going shopping. My suitcases were full, and I couldn't believe that I had managed to buy everything I wanted without standing in long lines. In principle they had everything imaginable in their stores, whereas in the Soviet Union the shelves were absolutely empty!

And what a selection of food, sausage, and cheese! After I returned home, I would describe the shop windows to my friends, and they couldn't believe it. You can only imagine the shortages we dealt with in our lives!

On the last day of my visit, Juergen decided to take me to Buchenwald in Thuringia, Germany.

Created in 1937, Buchenwald was the first concentration camp in Germany and one of the largest. By 1945, over 280,000 people, including Jews, Slavs, and Roma, were held there, as well as criminals, homosexuals, Jehovah's Witnesses, thousands of Soviet POWs, and 350 Western POWs. Nearly a quarter of those prisoners perished. Besides succumbing to hunger, disease, and torture, many (including 6,000 Soviet POWs) were shot outright, and others died after being forced to participate in human experiments. When I was at the camp, there were exhibits chronicling the stories of both the victims and their tormenters, as well as cases displaying soap and purses made out of human flesh, and gold fillings, which the Nazis had removed from corpses. How could mankind sink to such a level? And in particular, a nation with such culture… How did this happen? How could people be treated so horribly just for being different? This was the first time that I had my doubts about Germans: would they accept me as one of their own, or would I remain an outsider?

We left the camp. While we were walking to the bus stop, I had a million questions and doubts, and I was filled with hatred for the people who had treated the innocent so terribly. My mind was spinning. It was a good thing that we visited this site at the end of my visit. Should Juergen even have taken me there? To be honest, at that moment I hated all Germans! Even Juergen. I was shocked, and my entire body was shaking. I didn't want talk to Juergen. I knew he had nothing to do with this, but the impression it made on me was so strong that I cried all afternoon.

I was sad all day and didn't even want to talk to Juergen. I saw Juergen, an innocent man, as one of the perpetrators. I was clearly in serious shock. It was one thing to watch a film about the war on TV, and another to see the scale of what had happened. To see photos of the people who lived through it. To think about their families, who didn't know what had happened to their loved ones for years after the war and probably kept waiting for them to return, and the children who were so mercilessly murdered in gas chambers. I felt sick about all this.

It's a good thing that by this time we had already visited all of Juergen's relatives. After visiting Buchenwald, I would probably not have been able to greet them with a smile and be nice to them. I know that even today Germans have a guilt complex about what their ancestors did – that's a given.

When I was flying home, I knew for sure that I didn't want to live in another country. Even if Juergen and I were to get married and live in Germany, it would only be temporary. I wanted to live in a place where I understood the people – not only in terms of the language, but in terms of the mentality as well. I realized that if you don't know a language from childhood, even if you learn it over time, nevertheless you are never going to speak like a native. And that automatically makes you inferior. If you can't argue on the necessary level or express your feelings and emotions?!

No, no, no, I wanted to live in my homeland. I was proud that I lived in the Soviet Union. I was proud to be like all other Soviet citizens; I never even thought of being different. We were all equal in the Soviet Union! I was proud, because the Soviet Union fostered and expanded quality education. It cultivated respect for higher education and culture, particularly literature. It subsidized the performing arts and increased official support of science. It broadened access to sports and leisure activities, and all this was free. It eradicated the worst excesses of popular culture, especially the backward and violent aspects of life in the Russian countryside. It built towns. It defeated Europe's most vicious right-wing military power, Nazi Germany. In subsequent decades, it finally managed to meet the basic needs of nearly all its citizens: food, shelter, clothing,

227

healthcare, and employment. It offered a peaceful, predictable framework for people to live their lives in.

At 18, I was a real Soviet patriot. Although I saw that it was possible to live a little better on my trip to the GDR, we were so brainwashed by Soviet propaganda, that we couldn't even imagine that people lived better somewhere else. We had no information about other countries or cultures. I understood that I had to do something.

I don't know whether or not my father suspected that I had taken a trip to Germany; to this day I don't know. Juergen and I continued to write letters to each other every day, missed one another, and suffered. Our letters weren't only about our feelings for each other; we also shared our impressions of the books we read and philosophical ideas about the problems of life and the future. Juergen always cited song lyrics to express his feelings – mainly from songs by singers like Albert Hammond, Cat Stevens, Uriah Heep, and Suzi Quatro.

From Demis Roussos:" A dream is something we create, deep down, inside of our soul."

From a song by Albert Hammond: "I love you! Everything I do, I do because I love you" or "All I need is the air that I breathe and to love you!"

Or: "It is evening of the day, I sit and watch the children play. Doing things I used to do, thinking of you! I sit and watch as tears goes by..."

And from the group Slade: "How does it feel " and "Far away".

And from Rod Stewart "The first cut is the deepest...."

Juergen began working on an application requesting a transfer to the Soviet Union for work; he was exploring all possibilities. But he was refused everywhere he applied. He was told that he was still too young, that he didn't have the proper experience, and that he needed to work a few more years before he would be ready. There was one interesting opportunity to work for 5 years for a company in Moscow as an expatriate, but during the negotiations it became clear that the candidate had to be married! In short, nothing was working out for him.

There was only one option left: I would transfer to the correspondence course division of the university and go live with him temporarily. I was in my third year at the institute, and had two years left before graduation, which we would barely have been able to survive if we were apart. Juergen was lonely in a new city where he had practically no family or friends, and my family continued to try to marry me off. Each one of my refusals led to a scandal.

In March, Juergen wrote that there was an opportunity for him to come to Odessa for a week for a conference. He received permission to go, and they even said that they would pay for his airfare. He begged me to come and said that if I didn't have the money, he would pay for me. I was not to worry and just get busy organizing the trip.

And so at the end of May, under the pretext of going to Moscow for a medical checkup, I set off for Odessa. The semester had just ended, and I had 10 days between exams. Juergen met me in Odessa, and there was probably no one in the whole world happier than us! We found out that I could stay with Juergen in his room if he got special permission from the conference organizers. Fortunately, he managed to get permission for this without difficulty. We spent our time meeting with friends nonstop and strolling by the sea. Everyone wanted to see us, and it was nice how concerned everyone was about our future. My friends unanimously advised me not to torture myself and Juergen, and to transfer to the correspondence course division and get married. This time, Juergen and I were already seriously discussing marriage. He had brought all the necessary documents for this. We decided that I would transfer to the correspondence course division and would move to Germany, and we would get married as soon as the papers were ready.

We could only get married in Germany. In order to get married in the Soviet Union, Juergen would have needed so many documents that it would have taken him another year to collect them. I named my conditions: I would come to Germany temporarily, and he would do everything possible so that we could return to the Soviet Union in the near future. I definitely didn't want to leave the Soviet Union

- I was clear on that from the very beginning. But I had to do something, because the situation at home was very tense due to my constant refusal to marry potential candidates who had been chosen by everyone but me. We were constantly quarrelling, and my parents were at their breaking point. There were already rumors that I was having a serious relationship with a German. Even the teachers at the institute looked at me askance. Once, when I was taking a test, the teacher said: "Couldn't you find yourself anyone besides a German fascist?" Another teacher said: "What a shame that you are disgracing such a respectable family!"

When I went to the dean to apply for a transfer to the correspondence course division, the dean asked why I was doing this. I said it was related to my health. He looked at me closely and said: "If you marry a German, then everyone will turn away from you, do you understand that?" At that moment all I could think was, "God forbid he should tell my parents anything, because they didn't even suspect that I was transferring to the correspondence course division and planning to leave." And indeed, my parents didn't suspect anything; if they had found out, I would not have been able to leave the country.

I went to Office of Visas and Registration (OVIR) to apply for permission to leave the country. The same female lieutenant who had helped me so easily draw up the documents before was there. I told her everything and said that I needed my parents to sign my documents. She reassured me by saying that she would help in any way that she could. She explained what documents I needed to get. One of the documents I needed was a certificate stating that I was not married. I went to our local Vital Records Office and asked for a certificate. They confirmed that I had not gotten married in their section of town, but said that there was no guarantee that I had not gotten married in another section of town. In the terrible heat - it was July and 105°F outside - I had to go around to all the Vital Records Offices of the city. They all said the same thing, and no one would give me the necessary certificate. In the last Vital Records Office in the city, they scared me by saying that I would never get the certificate I needed because the Soviet Union was large, and I couldn't prove that I hadn't gotten married somewhere in Siberia. When I left the building, I sat down and burst into tears of desperation. I knew that they were simply trying to humiliate me. They were low-level bureaucrats using their power to abuse people. Such mistreatment of Soviet citizens was normal. But the certificate was just the first of many documents that I needed. In such cases, bribes and connections worked well, but I had no one to ask for help. After all, I had to hide my departure from everyone. I couldn't ask anyone, because no one from my community had any idea that I was planning on leaving.

I went to see the woman at OVIR and started crying, saying that there was no way I could get all the necessary documents. She called the Vital Records Office related to my place of residence, and they gave me the certificate right away. So this big unresolvable problem could be resolved by just one phone call!

But I had to collect a huge amount of paperwork! Another big problem was getting my parents' consent so I could go abroad. Nobody would give this to me, but the Uzbek lieutenant advised me to talk to my mother, saying her signature alone would be enough. Oh my God, I thought, if my mom finds out she will tell my dad, and I'll never be able leave. They did not even suspect that I had transferred to the correspondence course division. I decided to first collect all the other documents I needed, and then at the very end ask my mother for her signature.

It took me three months to gather all the documents, and it was a nightmare. When I brought them to the lieutenant, she said that after I brought her the letter with my mother's signature, I would have to wait 5-8 weeks to get permission to leave, if I got it at all. I asked why it was so complicated - after all, I wasn't going to West Germany, and I was marrying a man from a country we were friendly with. She smiled and said, "Don't worry, I will help you. I am really rooting for you. After all, Uzbek women don't usually marry non-Uzbeks, especially not foreigners. I understand how hard it is for you." It seemed to me that god had sent her in the form of an angel to help me. But in my heart, I didn't believe that she would actually help me. We had gotten used to the fact that you couldn't trust the authorities.

It was September. Juergen was constantly calling to see how things were going. He needed to set a date for our wedding. The first date he set was in mid-October, but my documents still weren't in order. At that time my parents were trying to marry me off to a promising up-and-coming young man, and had even begun to tentatively set a date for the wedding in November. So I told my mom, "Ok, I will marry the person you want me to, but I will leave him and come home the next day. You can imagine what an embarrassment that will be." The girls who came home right after the wedding night were the ones who weren't virgins. They were kicked out and shamed when it was revealed that they weren't virgins. And there was no greater shame among Uzbeks than not being a virgin! The first night after the wedding is the night when newlyweds consummate their marriage, and the girl's virginity is checked. On the next day a sheet with spots of blood was hung out for all to see. It was the 20C, and we lived in a progressive socialist country, where women were equal to men. But apparently that didn't apply to Uzbeks.

It's total hypocrisy to force the bride to lose her virginity the night after the wedding. It basically means that the wedding night is what, legal rape? Publicly sanctioned rape? Socially acceptable rape?

Later I met up with a girlfriend who had just gotten married, and I was shocked to hear her story. She got married to a young man who was a PhD student like her.

She had written a thesis on progressive and atheist topics: the Bolshevik movement in Uzbekistan and the vengeful policies of the Basmachi Movement. Her husband was writing his doctoral thesis on the history of the Communist Party of Uzbekistan. When I met her a couple days after the wedding night, she had all sorts of bruises and other injuries. When I asked what had happened, she told me that her husband had brutally raped her on their wedding night. When she said she wanted them to get to know each other better before starting a sexual relationship, he refused and raped her. "He HAD to behave like this. How he would have looked in the eyes of his friends and family? Like a weak man!"

This is what happened with an educated young couple, that was, on the one hand, doing academic work on the science of atheism, and, on the other hand, was unable to resist basic Muslim traditions.

232

Another friend I had from school told me her story when I met her a couple years after she got married. She was forced into an arranged marriage, just as her husband was. They didn't know each other before the wedding.

Her husband did not touch her on the wedding night, nor did he do so for several weeks after. He turned out to be homosexual. When she returned home to her family, it was she they blamed for the unsuccessful marriage attempt and for bringing shame on the entire clan. Since they hadn't consummated the marriage on their wedding night, the clan was sure that her husband had sent her back because she wasn't a virgin.

The poor girl had been dating another young man since fifth grade, and the two of them loved one another, but her parents were against the marriage, because he was Tatar, not Uzbek. After she returned home, her family quickly agreed to let her marry the guy she loved, and they were happily married. But her family strictly forbade her from telling the truth and saying that her first husband was a homosexual.

In Muslim society, truth and righteousness are always on the side of men.

My mom had to think hard, because I had told her everything: that I was now in the correspondence course division at school, that I was getting the paperwork together to leave the country, and that all I needed now was her signature. My mom suddenly started crying and shed bitter tears. A thought flashed through my mind, "What am I doing? I'm creating so many problems for my parents." At that moment I wanted to hug her and say, "To hell with it all! I will stay here and marry the man you want; the main thing is that I don't want to hurt you and dad."

But no, I couldn't do that. The mere thought of marrying a man I didn't know was too much. Maybe he was also in love with someone else, and I would be forcing him to marry me. I could only imagine our life together...no, I didn't want that. I couldn't betray Juergen's love!

Suddenly my mom told me to bring her the paperwork, and she signed it. I wanted to hug and kiss her, but she turned away and walked out.

Later, when I was a mother myself, I understood what it had cost my mom to sign that document. And how I had hurt my parents then. How grateful I am to her for what she did for me. She allowed me to be happy and preserve my dignity and self-esteem. If I hadn't married Juergen, I would never have forgiven myself for my weakness!

And that was it! All my documents were in order. The lieutenant told me that I could order the tickets, and when she handed me my passport, she said she was genuinely happy for me. She said that I had done a good job, that I had stood my ground and not given in, as she had done in her time. Consequently, she was alone and unhappy. She said that she realized too late that you must fight for happiness.

Yet the most difficult step still remained: telling my father. I decided to tell him the day I was leaving, because I was afraid he wouldn't let me go. On the morning of my departure - literally a couple of hours before my flight - I told him. My dad suddenly got weak and fell to his knees. I got scared and thought that he had fallen ill. Suddenly tears started pouring out of his eyes. It was the first time in my life that I saw my dad cry. I immediately said that I would stay. My dad replied, "If you end up unhappy, you will have no one to blame but yourself! You have no idea how lonely it will be living in a foreign country among strangers."

His words have stayed with me my entire life, and I have asked myself many times how he knew, since he had never lived among strangers. I so want to be able to tell him, "You were so right!". Children rarely admit that their parents were right.

He didn't even hug me. I left my house in tears. My mom, sisters, and two close friends, Marina and Sveta, went with me. When I was sitting in the plane, I wept so hard, that at that moment I was not even excited about my future. In Moscow I was met by Ira, a girlfriend I had studied with in Tashkent and who had always dreamt of going off to study in Moscow. Now she was doing just that. When she met me, and I was all red-eyed and tear-stained, she was surprised. When I told her how I had said goodbye to my dad, mom, sisters, and friends, she started to cry with me. Ira said that she could never have gone through all that. She said that she was in awe of me. Since I wasn't flying to Germany until the next morning, we talked all night and didn't sleep a wink.

At the airport she hugged me and said that in fact, I should be the happiest person around. After all, I was going to be with the man I loved. We had been fighting for this for so long. She admitted that when I first told her that I was in love with a foreigner and would marry him, she was convinced it would never actually happen because she knew the reality of the world we lived in. Now she was amazed by my decisiveness and willpower. She said, "As a Russian, it would have been hard enough to convince my family, but to go through fire and water to get all the necessary paperwork and get permission from OVIR, no, I wouldn't have had the strength to do that!!!"

I didn't tell anyone how I terribly I was treated by the City Komsomol Committee when I came to get a character reference from them for OVIR. When I told them why I needed the character reference, a young Uzbek man and several other members of the committee said I was a traitor to our country and a cosmopolitan. I don't know why they called me a cosmopolitan. I later found out the meaning of this word, and it was positive. But in the Soviet Union this word was used to attack traitors and dissidents. When I objected, they rudely replied that they should kick me out of the Komsomol for this. When I asked why, the replied, "For having a serious relationship with a foreigner!" I wonder if the relationship had been casual, would that have counted as acceptable behavior, worthy of a Komsomol member?

In short, I was called a traitor because I was leaving the country because I loved a foreigner. The only thing that made me feel better was that I knew I was only leaving for two months. After all, I had to come back and take my exams in February.

The correspondence course division of educational institutions was introduced in the Soviet Union in the 1930s, when the country needed to train a huge number of specialists in a very short period of time. It allowed students to attend school while still working. Students would send their tests in by mail and only had to come to the school twice for exams - in the summer and winter.

In order to get a diploma, I still had two years of school left; that meant that I would have to come back to take exams in the summer and winter – a minimum of twice a year.

Chapter 11.

The Wedding

Juergen met me at the airport. The wedding date had already been changed three times – this time to November 18. We immediately went to his parents' house where the wedding was supposed to take place. When I asked how many people would be there, he replied modestly, "15." 15? Why just close family members? What about friends and colleagues? It was yet another culture shock. As I have already said, a minimum of several hundred people would be invited to a wedding in Tashkent. With relatives alone there would be over 100 people.

I didn't get a solid answer from Juergen, and there wasn't one to be had. After all, in Germany it was normal to have 15 guests attend a wedding. And I wasn't really looking to have a solemn wedding with a white dress. My family and friends weren't there; for me, the wedding was purely symbolic – and mainly for the legal status.

The wedding took place on November 18, 1978. Fortunately, it was sunny from morning on. I had on a modest light blue dress. His relatives went with us to the city council where weddings were registered in East Germany. We entered the ceremonial hall of the old 19C city hall. The walls were wood, the windows were stained glass with lead frames. In the center of the room a cheap Japanese stereo was emitting sad, solemn classical music. The dark room and the sad music created what the Germans understood as solemnity, but for Uzbeks, it was a very depressing atmosphere. Weddings in Uzbekistan were accompanied with loud dance music, lots of noise, and other sounds of joyful celebration. Here in Germany everything was quiet. You could barely hear the woman who was officiating over the marriage.

At first the woman spoke about me and Juergen, then about the significance of marriage, the role of the family in society, and the laws relating to families. As Juergen had requested, she spoke slowly, and Juergen easily managed to translate everything for me. When the official part was over, she told us to stand and asked us if we were ready to enter into this marriage. First Juergen answered "yes", then I, in turn, repeated the word "yes" in German. Immediately Mendelson's wedding waltz started to play, we exchanged rings, and kissed, and that was it. The entire ceremony lasted half-an-hour.

Juergen's relatives congratulated us, then, we when came outside, they threw rice and coins at us. We went out to eat in a restaurant, then walked around town and put flowers at the memorial to the Soviet soldiers who died liberating Europe from fascism during WWII. Putting flowers at memorials to soldiers who died during WWII was a popular Soviet tradition.

We spent the rest of the day at Juergen's parents' house. I enjoyed myself, but for me, this wasn't really a wedding. And I was sad that my family couldn't be there.

After the wedding, we immediately left for Jena, where Juergen worked. His company gave us a studio apartment. It was small room with a kitchen in the corner and separate bath and shower rooms. By socialist standards, it was a luxury to get our own place right away. In socialist countries, people didn't buy their housing; instead, they would rent from the government, which was responsible for assigning people to living quarters. In the Soviet Union many people waited years – or even decades – to get apartments. In many cases, three generations would live together in small apartments. In East Germany, the housing situation was better than in the Soviet Union. Our apartment was satisfactory for the time being.

I couldn't go to work right away since I didn't have my degree yet. I also had trouble meeting people. At first, I didn't pay a lot of attention to that, and decided it was because I didn't know the language yet - although there were a few other international marriages in our house. For example, Juergen knew the girls from Ukraine from his time in Odessa. I tried to get along with them, but they behaved strangely. They would either call me "Frau Damisch"

238

or, when I stopped by to chat, they were not too welcoming. Later I realized that they wanted to become Germans as quickly as possible, but no matter how hard they tried, they still had strong Slavic accents which gave them away. I spent all my time studying and preparing for my exams, as well as writing letters to my friends.

Every other weekend we would go to see Juergen's grandparents. They were very friendly old people. They lived in the village and had their own small farm with all sorts of livestock: rabbits, pigs, and hens. In the fall, they would slaughter a pig and make sausage out of it. In the summer, they made preserves and compotes. They were curious about me and wanted to know more about me and my culture.

Getting along with Juergen's parents was harder than with the old folks. We were clearly from different worlds. Our first conflict occurred when I saved up my money and bought some boots which I had had my eye on for an entire month. They were brown leather and had high heels – and not at all cheap. I had never in my life seen western goods being sold openly, so I loved to go shopping there. And I saved up my money and bought these coveted boots.

In spite of the deep snow, I wore these boots when I went to the village. When Juergen's family met us in the hallway, I ecstatically showed them my soaking wet boots, but I was the only one who was ecstatic. My mother-in-law started saying something sternly to Juergen, and I insisted that he translate. In the first place, his mom was upset because I had bought something from the West. Secondly, she couldn't understand how I could buy such impractical footwear when there was so much snow in the winter: "Who walks on heels in such snow?" She couldn't understand my impracticality; I couldn't understand her complete lack of femininity. Thirdly, we were just starting out. How could I spend so much money on such impractical clothes when we had a million other problems to resolve? But who cared about being practical; for me the most important thing was that they were pretty.

In my eyes, German girls didn't know how to dress. They were always wearing gray clothing and masculine style shoes (with low heels), they didn't wear make-up, and they were absolutely not feminine. I remember how my dad, when he came to visit, would constantly ask the question, "Why are German girls so unfeminine – they can't even wear make-up or dress elegantly." For Soviet women, your looks were everything. We had no problem walking on the ice in the winter on high heels. I can't remember women falling down left and right and breaking their legs in the winter in Russia. Everyone tried to dress nicely, elegantly. Even if you were just running over to a nearby store, you still had to put on make-up. So I continued to dress up, but the women of Germany did not understand me!

However, it didn't bother me. Of course, I didn't want conflicts with people, but I couldn't put on practical, coarse men's footwear and always wear pants – it just wasn't my thing.

The second conflict I had with my mother-in-law occurred when I categorically refused to eat pork. She couldn't understand that I grew up with Muslim traditions and that we didn't eat pork. At the time, I didn't realize that my mother-in-law didn't have any concept of different cultural rituals. East Germany was a closed country, and East Germans couldn't freely visit other countries (except the nearby "friendly" socialist countries). Moreover, she wasn't interested in different cultural rituals! And of course, she couldn't possibly understand that people could have a different way of life and different values.

She was constantly repeating her favorite phrase, "Alles was auf dem Tisch steht wird gegessen!" ("You must eat everything on your plate!"). Germans tried to spend as little money as possible and save money whenever possible. When we went to visit Juergen's grandparents in the village after the wedding in cold, snowy weather, I noticed that the windows in the bedroom were wide open. In surprise, I asked Juergen, "So where are we going to sleep?" He responded calmly, "Here." "What do you mean, here?" The temperature in the room was the same as it was outside, but he said it was no big deal – it was fresh air. There is such fresh air outside in the winter! I had to get used to this new reality and sleep in the freezing cold. Only one room in the entire house was heated. All the rest, the ones we weren't in all day, weren't heated because it wasn't economical. It wasn't economical to leave the lights throughout the house, to buy extra food, or to heat the whole house.

They kept separate containers in the kitchen for the various types of trash, turned down the heat when they opened the windows in winter, and didn't leave the water running when they were brushing their teeth.

I came from a country where electricity, water, and gas were almost free – although people there did leave small windows open in the winter because Soviet apartments were centrally heated, and it would get really hot. I came from a country where water was always leaking from the faucet, the pilot light on the stove was never turned off, and the lights were on in the whole house. It was hard for me to get used to this new, harsh reality.

I could probably adapt to anything, but I would never stop being a woman. I continued to wear heels and make-up, and care about how I looked. I often noticed how German girls on the street would give me nasty looks because of my outfits. And I couldn't understand why men in Germany didn't look at me. In Tashkent there was not a single young woman who could walk down the street without men giving her compliments or making exclamations as she walked by. And when they did, I would really feel like a woman!

In Germany, people ignored one another. With time I also started to dress in a more masculine way and wear comfortable clothes, like the Germans. I stopped wearing make-up – but even so, my mother-in-law would always make comments about how important looks were for me, and how could it be otherwise? After all, I am a woman. She dreamt of me looking masculine, like a German girl. I knew that I was attractive and feminine, like all the women in my country. Later men even started approaching me and asking if I was a Slav. When they saw my questioning look, they would say, "Slavic girls always stand out because of their beauty and charm." I took this as a compliment – even German men liked femininity.

The weather was constantly gray, and I was chronically deprived of sunshine. There was a very poor selection of fruits and vegetables. People here mainly ate sausages and meat products; they only ate salads when they were in season. In the winter they ate canned fruits and vegetables. When they ate apples, they would eat the entire fruit, including the seeds, and leave only the stem. I realized how spoiled we were in Central Asia, with all the bountiful fruits and vegetables. We would often taste a fruit, and, if we didn't like how it tasted, throw it away. Meanwhile, people in the GDR were dreaming of eating fruits and vegetables even when they were in season. There were no imported foods from around the world. In the winter, there were very few fruits or vegetables on store shelves. In terms of fruits – there were only apples, but in Berlin, the capital of the country, you could buy imported delicacies such as bananas and oranges.

December arrived, and it was the time when the pleasant work of getting ready for Christmas began. Nowhere is Christmas celebrated in such a scrumptious and joyful way as in Germany. There were carousels twirling everywhere, and in the square, they put up a huge Christmas tree that was as tall as the city hall. Everywhere people were selling things at stalls and booths built to look like houses straight out of fairytales. Crowds of people hurried to the square to have fun and indulge in Christmas festivities. There were enchanting aromas everywhere: roasted hotdogs of all types and sizes, and the wonderful smells of roasted almonds, hazelnuts, and peanuts. And above everything the aura of gingerbread and chocolate lingered in the air. You could choose any fruit you wanted: strawberries, bananas, or plums, and right before your eyes they would dip them into melted chocolate and give you a giant sweet treat. There were tents with Gluchwein, hot apple wine, beer, and local wines. Depending on who was in what mood and what they had a hankering for, people would Gluchwein or beer. In the booths, you could buy things made out of leather, clay, stone, and wood. Shiny Christmas ornaments silently twirled in the booths. At the table where they were selling scented candles, you could smell lavender, jasmine, mint, and cloves. At another table, they were selling aromatic soaps with the same scents. The kids would ride on carousels playing traditional Christmas music. And during the holiday season, it was impossible to even get through the crowds. In the shop windows you could see gingerbread houses, which you would want to bite into right there on the spot. Further down, you could hear the jumbo shrimp sizzling on huge grills and see pies swelling in ovens.

Houses everywhere were nicely decorated and lit up, and in the windows colored candles were burning. I went to the Christmas Market almost every day to pick out presents for my relatives and try different holiday foods. All this was new for me. I was sad that my sisters and parents couldn't be there with me. How I wanted them to see all this and enjoy it as I was. Knowing that I was going to Tashkent in January, I began buying presents for everyone. It was a pleasant way to spend time.

I missed Tashkent and my family. I often dreamt of Tashkent: the sycamore trees, elms, and the linden trees. The air of the city and its aroma. And I would always dream about the rustle of the water in the dikes and the delicate silk ripple of plants in the water. Even now, wherever I am in the world, whenever I see a small stream, I try to find the water creatures and water plants I remembered from the dikes of my childhood.

I was counting the days to my departure, but the Christmas holidays had not yet arrived. For Christmas we went to see the grandparents. Juergen's cousins and aunt and uncle also came. At that time, the extended family would still gather on major holidays. Everyone was in a festive mood. Grandma baked her famous cheese stollen for everyone, and for Christmas she cooked carp according to her own special recipe, which was very tasty. Later I tried a few times to cook carp using her recipe, but it wasn't as good. I realized that she had cooked it in a wood-burning oven, which she also used for pies and bread. Since it burned wood, it gave a special fragrance to the food. And they made fruit punch in a huge bowl.

In Germany the main part of the holiday takes place on the evening of December 24, when presents are opened after dinner. Everyone was animated, and there were exclamations and emotions when the presents were handed out. I had never received so many presents before in my entire life. Uzbeks don't even celebrate their children's birthdays or give them presents!

We stayed there on New Year's, and for the first time I drank the "Little Red Riding Hood" champagne that was famous in the GDR, with canned mandarins and mandarin juice added in. This was considered a delicacy, since these cans of mandarins could only be purchased at the "Intershop" – a store where food was sold for hard currency. Apparently one of the relatives had received one of these cans of mandarins as a present or managed to buy one in that store.

After greeting the New Year at midnight, everyone was suddenly ready to go to bed. In Uzbekistan that was when the New Year's really began: after midnight we would set off to visit relatives and neighbors and say Happy New Years to everyone. We would only go to bed in the early morning.

At some point in mid-January I realized that I had skipped two periods. I'm ashamed to admit that I had no idea about the first signs of pregnancy. But how would I have known? After all, in the Soviet Union – and furthermore in an Uzbek family – it was taboo to talk about sex or women's health. Many girls didn't even know how women got pregnant before they were married.

Juergen said that we needed to go see a doctor and make sure everything was going okay before I left for Tashkent. For the first time in my life I went to a female doctor; I insisted that on it. She examined me and said that I was more than two months pregnant. Juergen and I were ecstatic. We wanted a child very much, and at the time we were not concerned about the fact that we didn't have a decent apartment, that I hadn't finished my studies, and that we had no idea whatsoever where we were going to live in the future. But that was normal! Our generation had children young, and in the Soviet Union people thought you should have your first child before age 25; otherwise there might be problems. When you look at new parents of small children today, you can't tell if they are grandmothers or mothers.

I remember having an endless argument with an American friend, who would try to convince me that you can still give birth at 40. With my cultural background, I couldn't even imagine that; after all, in my country many women were already grandmothers at 40. In Uzbekistan, if you hadn't gotten married by 23, you were considered an old maid.

I was 20 when I got pregnant, and Juergen and I considered this to be normal. In East Germany women would get married and have children young. As a rule, in the former communist countries, you would graduate from high school at 17 and from college at 21-22. I believe the reason for early marriage was that at 22 you would already start working, and since there was no sex in our country, young people would start having sex only after getting married.

Chapter 12.

Baby Indira

At the end of January, I went via Moscow to Tashkent to take my exams. I had no idea how long I would be there, because they didn't announce the exam schedule in advance. I had bought presents for everyone, and I knew that everyone was expecting me, but I was worried about how my dad would react when I arrived, and whether or not he would even talk to me.

When I disembarked from the plane, I felt so comfortable and relaxed because I was at home and in a place where everyone spoke my language, behaved like me – including being loud outside on the street and on public transportation. And just like me, they loved the smell of onions and garlic. Incidentally, the entire town smelled like fried onions and fried dumplings. That is the typical smell of Tashkent.

The same people who had seen me off met me when I returned: my mom, my sisters, and my girlfriends. No one said a word about my dad, and when we got home, he wasn't there yet. I don't think anyone in our family knew what his reaction would be. But then, in the evening, he came home from work with a bouquet of flowers, which he had handed to me, and then he hugged me really, really tight. I think that that was the happiest moment of my life. I never wanted anything as much as I wanted to be accepted by my father. I realized how much I loved him in spite of everything that had happened. To this day I remember the words he spoke before my departure to Germany: "If this turns out badly for you, you will only have yourself to blame." He had also said that one day I would realize I am all alone. I'm not even sure what he meant: alone without my big Uzbek family or alone in a distant, foreign land. How often I remember his words today!

All happy from my father's warm reception, I told everyone that I was expecting a baby in August. Mom looked at me sternly, because in our Muslim Uzbek culture, it was not customary to speak about such matters in the presence of men. But my dad and all my sisters were very happy. After dinner, my parents asked us not to let our relatives and friends know that I was married to a German. No one knew. People had been told that I transferred to Moscow for school and was studying there, but I had a hard time believing that no one knew I had married a German. After all, gossip spreads really quickly, especially in our culture, where everyone knows everything. I was right; later one of my relatives asked - apparently in passing - how things were with the Germans. I said I didn't know, as I had never been there; she looked at me and smiled. It was then that I realized that everyone knew. When I told my mom about this incident, she said that the woman was trying to provoke me, and that no one really knew anything. My parents wanted to keep it all a secret for the time being, but alas, they forgot what kind of society they lived in! The thing is, my marriage to a German would undermine the prestige of our family and threaten the chances of good matches for my two sisters.

I suddenly started having problems with my Uzbek teachers, who guessed, based on my last name, that I had married someone who wasn't Uzbek. In Germany, it is traditional for women to take their husbands' last names. My last name was clearly not Uzbek and even sounded exotic in Uzbekistan. The instructors started making stupid comments and didn't want to pass me in my classes. One instructor even said, "You are such a beautiful and sunny girl. You could have married the best Uzbek man. Why did you have to marry a foreigner?" And right there he gave me a grade lower than I deserved. This was difficult; after all, I wanted to pass all my classes quickly and leave the country. Instead, everything was long and drawn out; plus, at that time it was completely normal to give bribes for exams and grades. I would never do that – I didn't even know how.

After spending a month in Tashkent, I went back to East Germany. Once again, I had to get used to life in a foreign land. It turns out that Germans don't see their families much, not to mention their friends, which they have almost none of. I could have made friends at work or at school, but I was always at home. Juergen didn't have any friends, and it turned out that he wasn't a very social person. After work, he was happy just being at home with me. And we couldn't go to the movies because I didn't understand German very well.

There were no clubs to interact with people at, and we didn't see our neighbors very much. At first, I didn't mind this too much and just got ready to have the baby. Then I started having problems because of a vitamin deficiency. As I wrote above, Germans don't eat as many fruits or vegetables as Uzbeks, especially in the winter. I was dying to eat big bunches of dill, cilantro, parsley, and green onions, but there weren't any in the stores.

We lived in a hilly part of the city, and when Juergen came home from work, we would spend two hours a day walking up the hill and back. It was good exercise for me. Since there was a shortage of literature in the Soviet Union, I loved to go to the Russian bookstore in downtown Jena. For me, the selection of books they had there was fantastic. I was always buying and reading new books. During my pregnancy I read a huge number of world classics.

Juergen and I couldn't decide on a name for the baby. At that time, they couldn't determine the sex of the baby in advance, and we didn't know if we were having a girl or a boy. I had two names in mind: "Anora," an Uzbek name, and "Indira" (like Indira Gandhi), a typical Indian name. I liked "Indira" because Uzbekistan had close cultural contacts with India. Indira Gandhi was very popular in Uzbekistan, and a lot of people named their daughters after her. I liked the name, and I identified with this remarkable woman. Juergen said that it would be better to name her Indira, since it was the better-known of the two names in East Germany, as everyone in the GDR knew who Indira Gandhi was. Furthermore, Germans wouldn't pronounce "Anora" properly.

And so, in August our daughter Indira was born. This is a big event in an Uzbek family. After the delivery, a woman stays in the hospital for a week, and all her relatives and friends visit, but in Germany, I was all alone. No one came and visited during that time, not even Juergen's parents and relatives, who only lived an hour's drive away.

I was very sad. I missed my big family and my huge group of friends. In Uzbek society, when the new mother comes home from the hospital with the baby, everyone helps her out, especially the experienced grandmas. They make food, clean diapers, and give the young mother some time to sleep. But what awaited me was books instead of experienced grandmothers. No one gave me any advice, and Juergen and I couldn't find time to cook. During the first 10 days we were so exhausted that I was admitted to the hospital, and Juergen lost a lot of weight. Juergen took a leave of absence from work so I could feed the baby several times a day. He brought her to me three times a day. Later they put me on antibiotics. I got upset when the doctors said I couldn't breastfeed the baby while taking them and that she had to be put on formula. From my relatives and friends, I knew that breastfeeding was the best thing for the baby and that if you don't breastfeed, the baby's immune system is weakened. I cried for several days because I couldn't breastfeed. When I returned home, still weak, a pile of diapers and a crying baby were waiting for me.

I remember how Indira started hiccupping nonstop when we first returned home from the hospital, and I feared the worst. I didn't have anyone nearby to ask for help, and we didn't know the neighbors. I sought help in three books: we had the popular American book by Dr. Spock, a German book, and a book by famous pedagogues in Russia. According to the books we had done everything we should have, but the baby continued to cry, and I thought she would die. Even Juergen was crying. The poor man didn't know which of us to attend to first. In Uzbekistan this never would have happened. There would have been someone nearby to help, most likely my mother.

Juergen has never been able to explain why his parents didn't come and help us – after all, they could have taken a leave of absence from work. I was only told that that isn't done here. How many times while living in Germany did I hear that expression, "It just isn't done." One day I couldn't stand it and started crying while I was talking to my mom on the phone and told her I couldn't take care of the baby. My family had a meeting and decided that my sister Gulnoza would come right away to help me. When the baby was a month old, my sister arrived to help.

She was crazy about her niece. She helped with everything: cooking, taking the baby on walks in the stroller, and washing the diapers; she even managed to have a hot dinner ready for me and Juergen when he got home from work. She was able to stay with us for two months, while her fellow students picked cotton, but in November she had to go back to school. I saw her off with tears in my eyes and cried for a long time afterwards. I understood what loneliness I had doomed myself to in this country.

While Indira was little, I took a leave of absence from my studies and didn't have to go to Tashkent to work on my degree. In the spring, I unexpectedly received a telegram from my father. He said he wanted to come and visit us and see the baby. Juergen and I couldn't believe it and were overjoyed. After all, that meant complete reconciliation.

He came in May, when everything in Germany was in bloom. Juergen and I had just moved into a big three-room apartment a couple months before. Juergen met him at the airport and was very anxious. He had to go to Berlin to get him, and I decided to wait at home with the baby. When they arrived, I opened the door. Without even giving me a hug, my dad asked, "Where is my granddaughter?" He took Indira from my hands, gently pressed her to his chest, and kissed her. Indira brought our family back together.

We took him around and showed him the local sites. He liked everything and was in awe of how clean and orderly everything was. I remember the first night when, before going to bed, he asked if there was a cemetery for Muslims. In response to my look of surprise at this question, he said that he wanted to know where I would be buried if something were to happen to me. Juergen calmed him down, saying that we were communists, and there were many cemeteries for communists.

Another interesting thing happened in Berlin, when he and Juergen were walking around town waiting for the train to Jena. It was Sunday and the stores were closed. My dad saw all sorts of different kinds of sausages in the window of a meat store. In shock, he asked, "Can you really buy all of that?" My dad had come from a country where there were food shortages and couldn't believe that such an assortment of sausages alone was possible. When Soviet

251

citizens went to supermarkets abroad, they were shocked by the quantity of products. People were even warned not to take Soviet citizens to supermarkets right away. And it made sense. After all, in the 70s and 80s the Soviet people lived in a half-starved country. In a country where the military and space industries were cutting-edge, there was nothing to eat. This paradox is hard to grasp.

When my dad realized that Germans eat a lot of pork, wherever we ate, he asked them not to give him pork. When Juergen's relatives invited him over, we warned them in advance not to give him pork. The get-togethers with the relatives were warm. Juergen's parents tried to speak to him in Russian. Russian was taught in the GDR as the first foreign language. People could read the Cyrillic alphabet and were able to say a few things.

My dad really liked Juergen's grandparents for their simplicity and hospitality. His grandfather talked about the war, which he was forced to take part in. This was a sensitive topic – after all, he fought on the side of the Nazis. My dad lost a lot of relatives in the war. His grandfather fought in Poland and told us how painful it was to see the hungry children, and how he and the other soldiers shared their rations with them. Fortunately - and unfortunately - after being conscripted, his grandfather was wounded and returned home. He lived the rest of his life without a leg. I tried to distract them from this topic, which was painful for both sides.

In general, my dad's visit went well. Juergen and I showed him that we were happy. I did everything I could to keep him from realizing how lonely I was in this country.

A year later, Indira and I went to Tashkent in the summer. It was a long flight with a layover in Moscow. I was eager to arrive in Tashkent as soon as possible to show my daughter to them. My parents had already managed to tell everyone that I had gotten married in Moscow and had had a daughter.

I was met at the airport by everyone – an entire delegation of all my family and friends. It was so nice to feel this warmth and attention after being constantly lonely in Germany. My soul was already full at the airport. Lord, why couldn't I have such warm loving people around me all the time? Why did I have to live among the cold Germans?

My family basically tore Indira from my hands and hugged and kissed her.

For the entire time I was taking my exams, I almost never saw my baby. Everyone wanted to take care of her, play with her, and babysit. Uzbeks really love children – they are the center of their universe.

Indira had already begun saying some words in Uzbek and repeated almost everything. At 8 months she had already started speaking – and in three languages. We would introduce each new thing to her in three languages, and she had no problem remembering everything. In Tashkent, people spoke to her in both Russian and Uzbek.

She felt comfortable with my family. In Germany, she wasn't treating with such warmth. She rarely saw her German grandparents, and when she did, it was on the weekend. When we got together, they would shake everyone's hand, even Indira's – there were no passionate hugs or kisses. My family would kiss her and kiss her - and didn't leave a single spot on her body unkissed. And you could tell she liked it!

Chapter 13.

"Gosekzameny" or "State Exams"

I passed my exams. It was particularly important to pass the State Exams on the History of the Communist Party of the Soviet Union and Atheism. If you didn't pass these exams, you couldn't write your thesis. And since that was when the 26th Congress of the Communist Part was taking place, I had to pay attention to that too, because questions about any part of the Congress could show up on the exam. Most of all, you had to be on top of the speech of General Secretary Brezhnev who, by that time, was already suffering from dementia.

As I already stated, WWII was a sacred theme in the Soviet Union, and hundreds of books, films, and shows were dedicated to it. WWII was used to foster Soviet military patriotism. Unlike in the US, the concept of patriotism in the Soviet Union and Europe is directly tied to war. Only during wartime do the people of these countries feel a sense of unity and feel protected by their homelands.

By the way, with respect to war, it was painful to observe the constant funerals of young Uzbeks from our neighborhood. Every day someone was being buried. That was during the pointless war in Afghanistan.

In 1979, the Soviet invasion of Afghanistan shook the Soviet Central Asian communities. Not only did this take place near their borders; a significant percentage of the Soviet soldiers sent to fight in Afghanistan were from Central Asia. The Soviet regime thought that by sending in soldiers who were culturally similar to the Afghanis, they would have a greater chance of success. But it turned out to have the opposite effect: thousands of corpses of young,

255

inexperienced boys from Tadzhikistan and Uzbekistan came back from the war. The kids didn't even understand where they were being sent and ended up being the innocent victims of a meaningless war. A war which was started by the Brezhnev regime. How sad for the mothers who lost their sons. The worst thing was that tens of thousands died for no reason. They weren't even defending their homeland. Nothing was even said about these victims. The press and the media remained silent about the war. People didn't even know that their sons were being sent to Afghanistan, and they weren't allowed to open the zinc coffins their children were brought home in. Apparently, the bodies were so mutilated that the authorities took pity on the parents and didn't let them see the bodies of their children.

Films were hastily made based on Brezhnev's memoirs, plays were written, and oratories composed. Dmitry Nalbandyan, a Soviet court painter from the Stalin era, created a large painting entitled "Small Land." Housed at the Tretyakov Gallery, the finest museum of Russian art, this painting depicts Brezhnev as one of the main heroes of WWII. Even back in school we had to read all of the books written by Brezhnev and watch the movies based on his books. We also wrote essays on the themes explored in his books. Besides being mandatory reading for the public and especially Party members, his works were praised as unsurpassed masterpieces in numerous reviews by leading writers, and were awarded the Lenin Prize for Literature. Brezhnev, their author, was even accepted into the Writers' Union and given Membership Card No 1.

The culmination of Brezhnev's artistic ambitions was the publication of his memoir trilogy in 1978, *Small Land*, *Rebirth*, and *Virgin Soil*. Naturally, Brezhnev's books were written by ghost writers and paid for by state funds. There is nothing unusual about that or the fact that despite their less-than-stellar literary qualities, the memoirs of the leader of a superpower were printed by the millions!

There was a famous joke circulating at that time about Brezhnev:

Brezhnev asks Suslov (a high-level Soviet functionary), "Have you read *Small Land?*"

"Yes, I read it. Twice. I really liked it."

"Maybe I should read it."

It had already reached the point where Brezhnev elicited nothing but laughter from the entire nation. Millions of jokes were circulating about him.

After sitting in front of the TV evening after evening and learning almost all of Brezhnev's speech by heart, I couldn't watch his addresses without laughing when he mixed up words, stuttered, and repeated himself. And it turned out that I hadn't sat in front of the TV set all that time in vain. On the exam the instructor, who was sure that I followed the Congress of the CPSU like everyone else, asked me to retell the important parts of Brezhnev's speech. I recited in detail his speech from the night before. The instructor was thrilled with my answer and gave me an A. To get an A on the State Examination on the CPSU was like a green light to a successful thesis defense. I also got a good grade on the Atheism exam.

After passing my exams successfully, I only had a year left in college, and it was time to return to Germany. Indira and I so didn't want to leave the warm circle of family and friends, which I missed so much in cold Germany. The only thing that kept me going was the knowledge that Juergen would do everything he could to make it possible for us to return. He had submitted applications to every office that sent specialists to work in the Soviet Union, but so far, he had gotten nothing but promises.

My next visit was supposed to be during the following summer, and the thought of not seeing my family for an entire year was very painful. To cheer me up, my mom suggested that my younger sister Shakhnoza come visit us on winter vacation. I only had to wait a few months, and then my sister came for Christmas and New Year's.

Shakhnoza loved taking walks around the Christmas Market and sitting with Indira. My family really loved Indira and absolutely adored her. But the time flew by quickly and she left.

After her departure, I was so sad, and felt even more lonely. We still didn't have any friends. How would I meet people when I was sitting at home all the time, and Juergen, for some reason, didn't make friends. When I asked why we didn't spend time with his colleagues, he said it wasn't customary to be friends with colleagues and that in Germany, business is business, and private life is private. I had a couple of girlfriends from Ukraine who, like me, were married to Germans, but they behaved rather strangely, and it seemed to me that they wanted to turn into Germans as quickly as possible. However, they didn't understand that they would never learn to speak German without an accent, and that the Germans would never accept them as one of their own. I thought it better to hold on to my culture and not be ashamed of my background.

I had had unpleasant incidents due to my ethnicity. Even though the Soviet Union was officially a close friend – and brother – of East Germany, East Germans didn't like Russians. I often heard people me yell at my back, "Go home, Russian occupiers". As they say, the truth comes from the mouths of the people. Once Juergen had to go away on a business trip for a whole week. On the third day, I thought I would go crazy from loneliness, but then I remembered that one of his colleagues lived nearby, and his wife was often at home in the afternoon. So I went with Indira to see her. I rang the bell; she opened the door a bit and coldly asked what had happened. I started to explain that Juergen had gone away for a whole week and that I was very lonely. She told me to be glad that my husband was away, and that I should have a vacation. Then she slammed the door. It was just the most recent of many culture shocks. I came home and cried really hard.

I really needed someone to talk to. Then I remembered that there was a Soviet military garrison in the city, and so I set off to visit it with the baby. Since I had a Soviet passport, they let me right in, even though garrisons are usually closed to the public. Behind the fence there was a whole little city of Russian military personnel with stores and even schools. I went into a store and started talking with some women. Two of them immediately invited me over for tea, and thus I made some friends. Until Juergen got back I would spend the entire day at the garrison with my new girlfriends. So that is what it is like when you have the same mentality. All I had to do is say that I was living among Germans and was lonely, and they said, "No problem! Stop by any time! It's always fun here." I stayed friends with my Russian girlfriends and their families for a long time.

They liked to come to our house to visit, because they didn't get to go to German neighborhoods. I would go shopping with them, as well as to German doctors. They didn't know German well, so I would translate. It's easy to get along with people from the same culture. In the garrison there were Russian, Armenian, Georgian, and Azerbaijani soldiers, but we all understood one another well. I had already lived in Germany a few years, but I didn't have any German friends.

Chapter 14.

"Posledny god uchyoby" or "My Last Year of College"

The following year we were already getting ready for our thesis defenses. It was spring, the most beautiful time of the year, and everything was in bloom. The first cucumbers and tomatoes were appearing, and the cherries and strawberries would be ripe any day. It was sunny and warm. And it was Navruz!

Navruz

Navruz is an ancient pagan celebration of New Year's which is set on the vernal equinox (March 20-21). With Zoroastrian roots, it spread through Central Asia, the Middle East, Russia, India, and even China. Today it is an official holiday in over a dozen countries, including Uzbekistan, where it survived in spite of centuries of Islamic belief and Soviet rule.

On the eve of Navruz, families in Uzbekistan prepare ritual foods such as "sumalyak" (sprouted grain prepared with spices on a wood flame). Making this delicious and nutritious dish is very labor-intensive and time-consuming, so everyone joins in to help, while listening to music and songs, and even dancing! In other words, making the food is an important part of the celebration. Mainly women make the *sumalyak*, but men also help.

So we, too, decided to make *sumalyak*. We needed the whole family to be there to do it, because you have to boil it for a long time and constantly stir it. Thus, a bunch of family members gathered around the *kazan* (a large pot), and it was fun: we talked and laughed. It seemed like the pleasure came not from the *sumalyak* itself, but from the process of making it.

261

Right before Navruz, community clean-ups are organized in Central Asia. The streets and squares are cleaned up, flower gardens are spruced up, trees are whitewashed, and the soil in vegetable gardens is turned. During the celebration of Navruz, there are street festivals, which usually include concerts, souvenir booths, and theater performances. Our entire extended family would go to town to have fun, and we would always run into people we knew. It was a completely different life than the one we had in Germany. This life, unlike the one in Germany, was my life.

I was also in a good mood because I was pregnant with my second child. Everyone already knew that I was married to a German – it was pointless to hide it. But my relatives and neighbors pretended that they didn't know. No one spoke of it openly, but I knew my family's reputation had suffered. My sisters were already of marriageable age. The potential suitors from our community, whose parents had formerly wanted to join their families with ours, suddenly disappeared. My parents were naturally worried about my sisters' futures.

One of my sisters had been dating a guy for several years and they loved one another, but his parents categorically refused to allow their son to marry her. In the first place, it was unclear who her older sister was married to; in the second, although we were descendants of an ancient family, we weren't small tradespeople, like his parents. They were interested in money, and the people who had money were those engaged in trade. Plus, my sister didn't really fight for her happiness. We girls had been brought up with the idea that in our culture you had to give in on everything, including your parents' decision about your choice of a partner. Apparently, it was easier to go along with it and not fight or stand out from the crowd. Plus, it's just easier when everything is decided for you. That's how all the other girls in my age group behaved. I could never understand how feudal ways and socialist ideology could coexist. The Soviet school I was forced to go to propagandized freedom for women, a higher education, a career, and independence. We lived in a dual world, a world which I didn't accept and which I wanted to run away from.

After successfully defending my thesis at the end of June, I returned to Germany with a heavy heart. Nonetheless, I still hoped that we would soon return to the Soviet Union. When my son was born in October, Juergen was told that he would be reassigned to Russia in the near future. It actually took two more years before we were able to go back.

Carl Zeiss

After getting my degree, I was offered a job at one of the major companies in East Germany, "Karl Zeiss Jena". I was welcomed by the workers there in a reserved, but friendly way because I was from a country that was considered their big brother, and officially they had to be friendly to us. All graduates from Soviet institutes were generally given good jobs. After all, in socialist countries you basically didn't have to look for work; instead, the government would assign you to a company where you were supposed to work for 2-3 years. In other words, your education was free, but you had to work off the money the government had invested in you.

I had a youngish, good-looking boss. After a while he disappeared, and no one would openly explain what had happened. There were rumors going around, and finally one of my colleagues said that he had been significantly demoted because he had applied to leave for West Germany. She advised me not to ask any more questions about him and told me to not even say "hi" to him if I were to run into him in the hall.

Well, I guess they didn't know me very well. I did exactly the opposite and purposefully sought him out. I found him in the company cafeteria, where he was sitting alone and eating. I noticed how the people around him were talking and pointing at him. I decided to sit with him. My colleague advised me not to, but I sat down with him anyway. He was pleasantly surprised. I asked him where he was working now, and he said he was a freight loader in the warehouse. When I started to get upset, he said, "Dildora, don't you know what kind of country you live in?" I said that I knew quite well, and therefore I planned on having lunch with him every day. I could tell he liked having a friend in such hard times.

So we started having lunch together, and later he told me that after he had applied to leave for West Germany, for all intents and purposes, all his friends, family, and even parents had stopped talking to him. Everyone turned away from him in an instant. His father was an important person at the same firm and tried over and over to get him to withdraw his application. He told me that even if he were to do so, his life and career were over. I asked if he actually thought there was any chance that they would let him leave the country. He had no idea – they might let him go or they might put him in jail. He pointed out two people sitting alone off to the side. One had applied to leave three years ago, and the other had been refused a visa. It was terrible: that meant that he had no future whatsoever in East Germany.

Of course, the Party leadership called me in and asked me not to have anything to do with my former boss. They just asked; they couldn't forbid me to interact with him. After all, I was from the Soviet Union. But no, out of basic human decency, I had to keep hanging out with him. I couldn't stand seeing how everyone pointed their fingers at him, how they avoided him, and how no one would talk to him. It wasn't that I felt bad for him; rather, I think we were very much alike, and we understood one another. Later I found out that he had to spend three years in complete isolation before leaving for the West. And there were hundreds of people like him in the GDR, who had applied to leave and didn't know what the future held for them.

It is a well-known fact that East Berlin was separated from West Berlin by a huge concrete wall, which became known as the "Berlin Wall". Its construction was approved in 1961 by Khrushchev and built by East German troops. The Soviets did not participate.

Before 1961, people could move freely from one side of Berlin to the other; then, one day, the city was suddenly split in two. The East Germans built an elaborate series of walls and fences, which were guarded by armed soldiers and dogs. The Berlin Wall, which was ten feet tall, three feet wide, and 100 miles long, took two weeks to construct. Only three checkpoints existed, where people could go back and forth between East and West Berlin: Alpha, Bravo, and Charlie. Many people tried to escape from East Berlin, but doing so was very dangerous, and nearly 200 in the attempt. Only 5,000 successfully made it to West Berlin.

Although in the GDR you weren't allowed to talk about people who wanted to leave the country, everyone knew about them. After all, you could easily watch Western TV in East Germany. Even though we were forbidden to watch it in Juergen's parents' house, we always watched it in our own apartment. This led to yet another conflict between me and Juergen's parents. We were having a political argument, and I bolstered my points with facts I had learned from watching western TV. They saw us almost as traitors because we watched western TV and listened to western radio. They didn't understand an important fact: almost everyone in the GDR was watching western TV – after all, the forbidden fruit is sweet. Even our local TV had a political show that attempted to repudiate the information presented on western TV. And they did so with good reason: the government knew that people were watching western TV and listening to western radio. In the Soviet Union it was easy to jam western media, but here in East Germany everything was being broadcast right on the other side of the wall, and, furthermore, in German. Many of the people I knew in the GDR watched western TV.

Chapter 15.

Dubna

In February 1985, we went to Dubna, Russia as expats. Before 1985 I had never heard of it, because it was a "closed" city.

Founded in 1956, Dubna was a beautiful city located approximately 80 miles north of Moscow, between the Volga, the Dubna, and the Sestra Rivers. Built around a proton accelerator for nuclear research, it became home to the Joint Institute for Nuclear Research, an international nuclear physics research center and one of the largest scientific foundations in the country. Some of the best scientists from Warsaw Pact member countries came here to work alongside their Soviet counterparts. This was sort of the Soviet response to CERN – the European Organization for Nuclear Research, which had just opened in Geneva. Among other claims to fame, Dubna's world-famous scientific center added five new elements to the Mendeleev Periodic Table.

Since the city housed sensitive military and defense institutions and factories, it was classified as a "closed" city. Access was strictly controlled by the government, and the city was guarded by the KGB. Nonetheless, and rather ironically, the scholars and engineers working in Dubna had freedoms and privileges that the majority of Soviet citizens could only dream of.

Dubna welcomed us with yellow two-story buildings, Stalin-era apartment buildings, little Finnish houses in an urban forest, cottages for scientists of the institute, and modern high-rises. We arrived at the very peak of winter, and winters here were harsh and cold. The temperature sometimes dipped to as low as -40°.

We were housed in a typical three-room apartment, furnished in Soviet style: a big wall unit in the living room and hard soft furniture, a couch with armchairs… typical, varnished furniture. It was very warm in the apartment, and I felt like I did in childhood in the apartments of my Russian girlfriends in Tashkent. In Tashkent, Uzbeks usually lived in houses, whereas Russian-speakers lived in apartments. For some reason, when I was a child, I always wanted to live in such an apartment, and finally my childhood dream came true!

The furnishings in Soviet apartments were all the same. People stood in line for imported furniture from friendly socialist countries like Romania, East Germany, and Czechoslovakia. Furniture from East Germany was considered to be the most prestigious – probably because of its quality.

When you go into a Soviet apartment, you pretty much know where each piece of furniture will be. The setup was standard. In the living room there was always a wall unit. You would see the pride of the house displayed on the shelf of honor: a collection of books (or Madonna dishware). Books were in short supply in the Soviet period, and it took a lot of work to get good books – even collecting recycling. In other words, you would walk around and collect paper – either old newspapers and magazines or tattered books. Then you would take them to the recycling center, and they would give you a coupon you could use to buy books. Don't forget that the Soviet Union was a nation of readers.

In Jena right after we got married, I found a huge Russian section at the downtown bookstore. I bought books there every time I went; books in Russian which it was impossible to buy in the Soviet Union, except on the black market.

As I already said, it was impossible to live without becoming involved in the black market. You had to have *blat* (connections) everywhere; you even needed *blat* to get a good book. Books were cheap in the Soviet Union if you could find them in the bookstore, but on the black market they cost up to 10 times the normal price. Western books translated into Russian usually cost no more than 4-5 rubles in the bookstore, but you would pay 25-30 rubles for the same book if you were to buy it on the black market. You can imagine how expensive it was to buy a book, if a pound of meat cost just one ruble.

In the GDR, Russian books were imported goods. Only Russian speakers were interested in them, so I was happily able to buy the best books (high quality ones with attractive covers) published in the Soviet Union. Soon there was a huge quantity of books in our little apartment in Jena. I was spending all my money on books. After all, you could simply walk in and buy any book you wanted. I couldn't even imagine having such books in the Soviet Union. How many pounds of recycling would I have had to collect to get them there?

Besides a wall unit, there was always a rug (usually made of wool) hanging on the wall. Such rugs were always in short supply, and if you managed to buy an expensive, large rug, you would most certainly display it on the wall so all your guests could see it. Sometimes you could judge how well-off a person was by the quantity of rugs in the apartment. In the middle of the room there would be a lacquer table with chairs and a couch with an armchair. Usually apartments came furnished – maybe because the apartments were small, or because there was a lot of furniture. So, we moved into a typical three-room Soviet apartment. Foreign specialists were given apartments in good neighborhoods.

As I said, in the apartment it was not just warm, but hot. Apartments had central heating, and you couldn't regulate the temperature in your own apartment. Heat wasn't very expensive, so it was cranked up all the way. It was so hot, that many people kept their windows open all winter long. After Germany, where even on the coldest days, they would only heat one room in a house in the villages, and you would sleep in cold bedrooms, all this seemed like a pointless waste of resources. It was typical poor Soviet management.

The next day we met the neighbors. In our section of the building there were families from a variety of Eastern European countries: Hungary, the GDR, Bulgaria, and Poland. My daughter because friends with a girl from Germany who babbled in perfect Russian and went to a Russian kindergarten.

The institute was international. Every country had its own administration, and the head of each delegation was usually the secretary of the communist party. We were supposed to check in with this organization immediately upon our arrival. They had regular communist gatherings, and everyone was supposed to participate. They controlled the workers more than in the GDR itself. We later found out that there were many Stasi agents (like KGB agents) in the delegation.

There was a German school in our little East German community, which our daughter started attending in April. Children of foreign workers would attend Russian schools in the morning and Germany schools in the afternoon. I also started working; I was offered jobs in the German group and in the international group, which was headed by a local scientist. Naturally, I chose the international group, and immediately made friends with workers from Hungary, Georgia, and Czechoslovakia. One of the Russian workers, Olya, became a close friend.

It was a big deal to have a good, genuine girlfriend in the Soviet Union. A girlfriend was everything: an advisor, a psychologist, and the person you told all your secrets to. In fact, you would tell more secrets to your girlfriend than to your own husband. That's why we didn't need psychologists: whenever you had a problem, you would talk to your best friend. And even if you got pregnant by accident, you wouldn't run to the doctor, but to your friend. An accidental pregnancy was a typical thing in our country, where even condoms were in short supply. Going to get an abortion was as normal as going to the dentist.

Abortion

In the Soviet Union, contraception was a problem. Soviet condoms were of very bad quality and had holes in them even before you used them. There were no birth control pills, and if somebody managed to bring them from an East European country, people thought that they would harm your health. IUDs were commonly used, but you could only get them if you were married and had kids. They, too, were of bad quality – sometimes they would fall out, and some women got infections from them. Therefore, abortion became the main method of birth control. It was typical for Soviet women to have several abortions in their lifetime, and it was the same in East

Germany and other East European countries. Even when they had contraceptive pills, it was very common for women to have abortions.

I remember how when I was young, my female relatives would often come home all pale after their most recent abortion and would lay down to rest until evening. In the evening, they would get up as if nothing happened and start to make dinner or do other domestic chores. When someone asked one of my friends why she didn't rest after her abortion, her family members said she had abortions frequently (like, incidentally, all Uzbek women), and that she was used to it. How could you get used to that kind of surgery, which was done without anesthesia? Without anesthesia!!! Of course, if you had *blat* (as with everything else), you could at least get a local anesthetic, but that was considered a luxury and wasn't available to everyone. I remember how our young, healthy neighbor quickly died from loss of blood after an abortion, and the ambulance took too long to get there. This healthy young mother left behind three orphans. And there were thousands of such incidents.

On top of that, the poor women didn't have any sort of sex education. No one told them how to properly protect themselves. Gossip and conversations with girlfriends were our main source of information about sex. And Uzbek women, thanks to their so-called Muslim culture, had no idea whatsoever before marriage as to where children came from.

Soviet women

Soviet women were treated terribly. We didn't know what tampons were, let alone have the opportunity to buy to any sort of feminine hygiene products in stores. Women used cotton wool, and if there was a shortage of that, they had to use old rags. And this in a country where women were highly educated. And Socialism had been achieved. What a system…

You couldn't buy attractive clothes; that's why seamstresses were so popular. There was a small dressmaking shop on every corner that would produce special order dresses, blouses and skirts. Usually, the customer would provide the material. Even in these dressmaking shops you had to have connections; otherwise the item might not be made well. And because of the terrible service culture at that time, the dressmaking shop owner was always right. Relationships between dressmakers and women were crucial. To have a good relationship with dressmakers, we had to bring them small gifts of perfume and flowers on International Women's Day and on their birthdays.

So here you can see some of the worst consequences of the Soviet system's attitude towards women.

My friend Olya

A day didn't go by that Olya and I didn't talk; plus, we worked together. I had also become her close friend. She was going through a hard time in her life. She had married a specialist from Czechoslovakia who had come to Dubna as an expat. They had an affair and then got married. When his contract ended, he left, promising to send Olya all the necessary documents to follow him, but then disappeared. There were a lot of cases like this. Naïve Russian girls so easily trusted men, that it wasn't unusual for foreigners to promise them the world, then just leave. Olya was so upset – after all, the Czech had taken advantage of her kindness and innocence. He used her, then just up and dumped her and left. When she started looking for him, she found out that he was married – to someone well off, and after his contract ended, he had returned home to his wife. The paradox was that Olya couldn't divorce him. She needed his formal consent, which she had no way of getting. I started to help her and witnessed many similar cases. After all, it is well-known that Russian girls are very beautiful, charming, and trusting. Many men took advantage of their trust in the most despicable way.

There were many specialists from Georgia and the Caucasian republics whose wives had stayed back home, and they had unofficial Russian wives here. It was typical macho behavior. Men from the Caucasus, just like those from Central Asia, were considered macho. And Russian men weren't any different – it was normal for them to have lovers. My other friend, Alina, was miserable after she found out about her husband's affair, but was afraid to get a divorce, because she didn't want to spend the rest of her life as a single mother. Russians looked down on single mothers.

272

There were tons of young, beautiful, and educated women who couldn't find husbands. Alina was sure that no one would look at her if she were a divorced single mother, and with a child, she would have no chance of getting married again.

And yet there were lots of single mothers. Many women who couldn't find husbands had children with married men. Therefore, Alina decided not to leave her husband and just tolerate it.

Alina was beautiful and always elegantly dressed. She was a fashion-designer and had graduated from a prestigious school of fashion in Moscow. Her husband, on the other hand, was a short, unkempt man. This was so typical for Russia, where women were generally very attractive, feminine, and tastefully dressed, but sometimes you didn't even want to look at some of the men. Paradoxically, women would actually choose to marry them. Alina would always justify herself to me, saying, "Well, look at how many men cheat. It's no big deal!"

Poor Russian women... they had to endure not only alcoholic husbands, but their lovers as well. The statistics put them in this bad position: there were more women than men in Russia. In the Soviet Union girls would get married early, and by 25 they would begin to panic, worrying that they had missed their chance to get married. So, then they would do whatever they could to have a child by 30 – even by getting pregnant by married men. I was surrounded by tons of such friends – people who could carry on interesting conversations about anything. They knew a lot - about fashion, literature, and film, and we often got together and cooked.

In short, life in Dubna was never boring. I liked it in Dubna. I started to dress very feminine again, as was customary in the Soviet Union. After all, the way you looked was very important to Soviet women. You would always be judged by your clothes. Even if a Russian woman was just running to a neighboring store to get bread and milk, she always had makeup on and at the very least was wearing heels.

So, after dressing in rather masculine fashion for seven years in the GDR, I again began to wear makeup and dress nicely. It was easy for me to do, as I had a much better chance to buy stylish clothes in Germany, clothes which were unavailable to the women in Dubna.

I again started wearing high heels and wasn't afraid of snow drifts or icy roads. Like everyone else, I wore boots with high heels. Maybe according to German logic that is not practical or comfortable, but it is attractive! I constantly got compliments, which is something I had not had for a long time in Germany.

Russian – or, more precisely, Soviet - men had a talent for giving compliments to women. And really, isn't it nice to hear men say, "You look great!"?

People in Dubna had trouble figuring out where I was from – no one ever thought I was Uzbek. Typical Uzbeks are of Turkic origin. Their copper-colored skin, almond-shaped eyes, and dark black hair make them look as though they are from Iran, Afghanistan or Northwest China. I didn't look like an Uzbek woman. When I said where I was from, people were always pleasantly surprised. For the first time in my life I didn't experience discrimination because of my looks. And at long last, I was seen not as a foreigner, as Germans in the GDR had often called me to my face. Nor was I a "Saryk" ("non-Uzbek") or a "Russian woman", as I often heard myself called in Uzbekistan. Now I was a beautiful young woman.

One day my sister had an interesting experience in Dubna. She came to visit me in a panic because she was already 22 years, wasn't married, and was almost an old maid. A lot of young specialists from Uzbekistan worked in the Nuclear Physics Institute, and when I saw a few nice-looking young Uzbeks in the store, I suggested that my sister talk to them. Who knows – one of them might be interested in her. She didn't want to – once again that Uzbek modesty, so I said "hi" to them in Uzbek as I walked by. They were in shock, especially as I continued talking to them in fluent Uzbek. You should have seen the expression on their faces! It turned out that they couldn't have imagined that I was Uzbek. One of them said that he had seen me more than once in the laboratory, but with a blond male. It never occurred to them that an Uzbek woman could be married to a man who wasn't Uzbek, not to mention a foreigner from Germany. That's how our progressive young Uzbek nuclear physicists thought. But I think that they lost interest in me and my sister, as a family

274

with a renegade like me wouldn't be of interest to them. My sister was a beautiful and intelligent girl, but she also didn't look very much like an Uzbek, so her chances of getting married to an Uzbek were nil.

In the Gorbachev era, the image of the Soviet woman began to change radically. We began to see Gorbachev's wife Raisa on TV a lot, which was very unusual. Before Gorbachev, you would never see the wives of general secretaries, and we didn't even know anything about them.

In comparison to the wives of other Politburo men, Raisa Gorbacheva was an intellectual in her own right, a university graduate who even had a PhD, and she always appeared in stylish dresses! It seemed that Raisa had a mind of her own, and she always smiled naturally. Perhaps this is why Raisa aroused so much personal curiosity among the Soviets.

I remember my mom talking with her friends about how Raisa dressed. I think my mom's generation wasn't ready for it. I think they were jealous that Raisa was dressed so stylishly, and that she acted like an independent woman. I guess they wanted to be in Raisa Gorbacheva's shoes. Everyone everywhere criticized her manners, and at first, she wasn't accepted by Soviet society, because she was different from previous Kremlin wives. She was very instrumental in changing the image of the Soviet woman. Eventually many women began to imitate her and copy her fashion style. The expression "Gorbacheva's style" even appeared. I remember well how my mom and her friends discussed every detail of her clothes and desperately wanted to look like her.

In Dubna, we were surrounded by indescribable natural beauty. Perhaps it was because of urgent deadlines or it was a conspiracy, but in those years, builders didn't put a lot of effort into dealing with nature when it was in the way, and would leave entire wooded areas between city buildings. Pines and birch trees grew in our yards, between university buildings, and even on sidewalks. In the Spring, streets and squares would drown in a white-lilac haze, in which the smells of blossoming apple trees, jasmine, and lilacs intermingled. This special city atmosphere – quiet, peaceful, and refined – is more typical of European cities than of provincial Russian ones.

The Cultural Center, city administrative buildings, and the JINR ("The Joint Institute for Nuclear Research") were designed in the classical style. The city was very small and cozy; people tended to know one another. All the children and I had to do to get to a small wooded area was walk out our door. Since then I have never lived in a place where civilization was so closely intertwined with nature.

Gradually musicians and artists appeared among my friends. In the city there were a lot of cultural figures, and the city was called the "city of physicists and lyricists". Our friends invited us to their concerts and exhibits. The cultural life of the city was bubbling over. Since Moscow was close, famous theater companies were brought in to perform. There were also gatherings with prominent cultural and artistic figures.

In the center of the city there was a huge Cultural Center with an enormous amount of dance, musical, choir, and theatrical activities for children and adults. There was also a good ballet school, which I immediately registered my daughter at, as I wanted to realize my own unfulfilled dream of being a ballerina. In fact, however, she didn't manage to hold out in that school for long. Ballet is hard. The instructors are strict, and the initial selection of students was harsh. It was not easy to get into that school. Those few lucky ones who managed to get in had to work hard physically, and that was no fun, as they say in western countries. Not all children could endure the physical demands and the strictness of the instructors. After a year of ballet, my daughter refused to continue. At the same time, I started sending my children to a musical school. They had to practice every day and weren't very happy about that.

The system of instruction was authoritarian. There were a lot of lessons, plus you had to practice every day for an hour. But all the children around were as busy as mine; some went to choir lessons, some did sports, and others went to art school.

Even I started to attend the re-opened School of Fashion, where my friend Alina, the artist-fashion designer who I wrote about above, taught the Basics of Fashion Designs. She also discussed the history of fashion, different styles, as well as famous world-class

276

designers. We made clothes based on our sketches and even modeled them at our fashion show.

We were all busy with our favorite thing: talking, visiting, and going to concerts. In the summer I went on picnics and sang songs in the evening by the campfire with friends from around the world.

In Dubna we would drop in on one another without a phone call or warning. Our life was full, and I didn't even want to think about my boring, monotonous life in the GDR, where for 7 years I had no friends save the Russians at the military garrison.

It seemed that the international specialists from Eastern Europe also really liked this way of life, and they happily interacted with everyone. Everyone tried to extend their contracts and stay longer in Dubna. After all, it was interesting to discover one another's cultures through intensive interaction. For example, I had never known any Hungarians before. Hungarians had more freedom than we did, and they knew this, so they were rather haughty about it. They were allowed to visit Western countries, and in the summer, they would go on vacation to Istanbul in Turkey and to Italy. We couldn't wait for them to return and hear their stories about places we would never be allowed to go.

Hungarians had a relatively high standard of living, a more liberalized economy, a less censored press, and less restricted travel rights than other countries in the Eastern Bloc. Hungary was generally considered one of the better communist countries. For East Germans to go on vacation to Hungary was a luxury, because visiting Hungary was almost like visiting a Western country.

Uzbek Food

It's true that at the very beginning we had a mishap. Most of Juergen's coworkers were Soviets, and I decided to invite them over so I could meet his colleagues. No one said they weren't coming, but only one actually showed up. He tried to delicately explain that his Soviet colleagues were forbidden from fraternizing with foreign specialists, even if they were from socialist countries. When I understood what had happened, I realized that in the future I should hang out with the artsy types – they were freer and untethered by official bans. As a result, we developed a circle of friends that included artists, singers, pianists, and liberal, free-thinking scientists who were more or less independent. People were always over at our house. We made music, discussed things openly, and weren't afraid to talk about politics or dissidents. Everyone liked the food I prepared, and I was happy to cook for everyone.

I really loved to cook and had done so since I was 10 – as is typical in an Uzbek family. At home we had cookbooks published in the 1930s and 40s with pictures of interesting-looking dishes with unfamiliar names. I wanted to make the recipes in those books, but it was simply impossible to get most of the ingredients. There were even shortages of basic things like eggs, and they were very expensive. To get an egg for breakfast was a luxury in our house, as in everyone else's. And when I wanted to bake something and the recipe required several eggs, my mother would have a conniption. There was no way my mom could let me have several eggs for a dish; it was even considered a luxury to add butter to dough, and so we had to improvise and replace these hard-to-get ingredients with available products. Since we made traditional Uzbek dishes at home, I was interested in making Russian, Georgian, and Armenian dishes. Instead of praising my cooking, my mom would constantly yell at me for always using up expensive products. But that in no way tempered my desire to cook and, especially, to bake. You have to understand that there was a major shortage of the most basic food products. People would stand in line for hours for them.

Sometimes I would justify my love of cooking to my mom by saying that it would be a plus if I were a good cook, and it would give me better chances of finding a good husband. My mom would be happy when my future mother-in-law would say to her, "You did a good job raising your daughter, and she cooks so well!" One of my aunts was great at making Uzbek flour-based foods, and I wanted to learn how to roll dough as thin as parchment, just like her. Or learn how to make flatbreads in a tandoor oven as only she could. We always invited her over when we had guests. And when we were expecting guests, for several days in advance an amazing, pre-holiday atmosphere would fill the house. We would have guests over for a few days in a row; first my mom's colleagues would come. They were highly educated scientists and scholars, for whom we had to roll out the red carpet. The next day our relatives would come

278

over. And we had to make so much food – on average over 20 different dishes. We would ask my aunt to make "naryn".

In Uzbek cuisine, *naryn* is a fresh homemade noodle dish, which is served as a cold noodle dish or as a hot noodle soup. Homemade noodle dough is rolled very thin and cut into long strips, then boiled and served with horsemeat. The dish is served as a part of any extended meal after *samosas* and before *plov*. Cutting the noodles into strips is tedious work, and it was always fun to sit together in a big group and chat while doing so. We always had fun when preparing this dish.

One day my aunt was supposed to come over and make *naryn,* which was my favorite dish. I decided to pretend I was sick so I could stay at home. When one of us was sick, one of our relatives, who was a pediatrician and lived nearby, would come over. She was an intelligent and well-educated woman. She immediately understood what was going on and decided to punish me appropriately. Since she understood that I was faking to stay home, she put me on a diet: for a few days I couldn't have any sweets, couldn't eat anything, had to drink disgusting castor oil every day, and was confined to bed. It was the most awful punishment I could have had at that time. Imagine staying in bed when there are guests, lots of noise, lots of things going on, and tons of great food. The whole house was full of aromas. From the kitchen wafted the smell of parsley, cilantro, dill, celery, and basil.

Another one of my favorite dishes is "manty", or filled dumplings. *Manty* are made with a water-based dough which is rolled out and cut into squares. The squares are filled with minced meat, vegetables, and/or herbs, then pinched together at the top. The dumplings are slowly cooked in steamers and served with sour cream.

Food

Contemporary Uzbek cuisine is the culmination of centuries of interaction with neighboring nations, as well as those located further away, whose influence came via the Silk Road, which passed through modern-day Uzbekistan.

The meats consumed in Uzbekistan are lamb (the most popular), as well as beef, horsemeat, chicken, and fish. Pork is not consumed much due to the Muslim history of the region.

Vegetables and fruits are plentiful in Uzbekistan and are central to Central Asian cuisine. Pears, apples, grapes, lemons, pomegranates are just some of the many varieties of fruit you will find in the region, and tomatoes, eggplants, and peppers are just some of the many vegetables which grow there. Sesame seeds, pepper, cumin, and coriander are just some of the spices frequently used in Uzbek cuisine.

Popular Uzbek dishes include "plov", which is a rice dish with meats and vegetables cooked slowly on an open fire. No occasion is complete without it! Other famous Uzbek dishes include flatbreads filled or topped with sesame or black cumin seeds, "shashlik" (shish kabobs) and "samsa" (baked pastries with meat and vegetable fillings), and soups like "mastava" and "shurpa" made of meat and vegetables.

As with most Muslim peoples, meals are great social occasions, whether consumed at home or in the local chaykhana. In rural and more traditional settings, Uzbeks eat sitting on the floor, and the food is served either on a cloth spread out on the floor or on a low table. Eating with ones' hands (instead of utensils) used to be typical, although this practice is not so common today. As a result of how different segments of Uzbek society have responded to Russian culture, there is now a broad spectrum of practices, from those who maintain the traditional ways to those, especially in an urban context, who have totally discarded them, and eat at the table like Russians.

Most meals are accompanied by "chai", or tea. The tea ceremony, which includes special rituals related to the preparation, serving, and drinking of tea, is one of Uzbekistan's most beautiful traditions. Green tea is predominant in most parts of Uzbekistan, but black tea is the favorite in Tashkent.

The tea-room ("chaykhana" in Uzbek) is another important element of traditional Uzbek culture. A place for friendship and socializing, it is always located in a shady place, preferably near a cold creek. At the *chaykhana*, Uzbek men enjoy *plov, shashlik,* and endless bowls of tea, while gathered around low tables placed on "tapchans" (wide low beds which create a seating area).

When traditional Islamic restrictions on drinking were removed during the Soviet era, the consumption of alcohol became very normal, even among women.

Kids and Different Cultures

In Dubna, our children were friends with children from other countries – and simply by attending German and Russian school, they started to absorb different cultures – not to mention learn several languages well. Moreover, every summer I took them to Uzbekistan so they would get to know my culture better. When we lived in the GDR, our daughter, who spent all day in a German kindergarten, didn't want to switch to Russian when she came home. Unlike all the other Russian-speaking moms who, like me, had German husbands, I had no intention of speaking with our children in poor German and, moreover, with a strong Russian accent! It never entered my mind that my children wouldn't speak Russian. Knowing any language is a treasure, and knowing Russian, specifically, would give my children the ability to speak with my family in Uzbekistan. The only way they could truly understand my culture was though the language. It wasn't easy – children always want to do what is easiest and never voluntarily do things they don't like to do. Every time my daughter started speaking with me in German, I pretended that I didn't understand her, and she had to force herself to speak Russian. Moreover, from early childhood I not only taught her words in Russian, but the alphabet, and we started reading together, syllable by syllable. I realized that if you introduce young children to their letters and numbers in a fun way, they learn them instantly. My daughter could say words in three languages without getting confused. She learned to read in Russian very early on. When she and I arrived in Tashkent when she was 5, she could read books on her own in both Russian and German, and all the neighbors came to look at this miracle child. It was no problem for my daughter to speak and read in different languages. By 5 she knew her numbers well, so we started working on her counting and adding very young. We also made her physically strong – she always took cold baths, and we let her climb on high ladders.

A sports complex was built in our apartment building. The children were able to climb on the ladders and ropes and wear themselves out completely! In our gym you had to be more careful: the children could jump from the ropes hanging from the ceiling, and you could swing on the rings from wall to wall and jump on the trampoline as much as you wanted. There were two monkey bars, a half-moon rung climber, kettlebells, hoops, a whole corner with wooden bricks, and a few shelves with dolls, toy animals, building sets, and games.

I remember how, when it was nearly -20°F degrees out in the winter in Dubna, people on the bus would stare at my daughter Indira, who was in a thin coat and light hat, and accuse me of being a careless young mother. Everyone said that my daughter would get sick and I needed to take care of my children better. But I knew she wasn't cold. How could they know that running in the snow barefoot and in her underwear was her favorite thing. We would let her go out on the balcony, and she would stand there in her underwear for 10 minutes at a time. She would squeal and squirm when we tried to bring her back into the house. She was never sick and when she started school, we were supposed to bring her medical records from the clinic, but she had never been to the clinic, so there were no records. Everyone was surprised that a school-aged child had never been sick; all her childhood illnesses had been mild and had passed without her having had a temperature, and we had never had to go to the doctor.

It was clearly advantageous that we were young parents and weren't surrounded by grandparents, who wouldn't have let us temper our children in such a way or give them complete physical freedom to move around freely. We gave our children more and more freedom of movement and the ability to decide when they wanted to eat and sleep, and how long they wanted to spend on walks – in a word, we trusted nature a lot. Luckily, as I already wrote, Juergen and I were raising the kids independently. In Soviet families the grandma played a huge role in raising the children, and that meant that she stuck her nose into everything. And not listening to the grandparents was even worse – there would be fight after fight, and in that culture, people don't contradict their parents and elders. We had been brought up to respect our elders. In Uzbek culture, often the grandma decided how to raise the grandchild, and even the parents didn't dare object. Even the name of the child had to be approved by the grandparents. The elderly in our culture always had the last word. I can imagine how hard it would be to live with a mother-in-law and be completely in her power.

I was once again grateful to fate for being able to live as I wanted and, most importantly, to raise my own children as I thought best. It was already overwhelming when I came to Tashkent, and my family would spoil my children. The kids loved the attention and being spoiled, and they would change right before my eyes. If I was strict with them, they would immediately go crying to grandma, and of course grandma would immediately hug them, pity them, and kiss them. Try to raise your kids properly in these conditions! I couldn't even dress them as I thought necessary: my mother would suddenly start wrapping them up warm – for some reason she thought that my children, who were used to running around in their underwear, would freeze. She would touch their little hands and feet and exclaim how cold they were and that I needed to put clothes on them right away. In Russia children were wrapped up so tightly that sometimes they couldn't move. In the winter, children were dressed in several layers of thick clothing, hats, and scarves. Apparently, this is why those children were always sick, whereas mine weren't.

Other parents would be horrified that I let my children walk through puddles and get wet. How could I deny my children the pleasure of discovering water and puddles? I knew that even if I forbade them to do it, they would anyway. Can you really keep children from discovering the world? And whereas my mom had warmed up ice cream for us even in the summer, I bought my children ice cream in the coldest weather, and we would eat it outside when it was below freezing. I remember how foreign tourists couldn't understand how people in Russia could eat ice cream outside when it was freezing cold. And I have never eaten such delicious ice cream as "Plombir" (sweet cream ice cream), "Leningrads" (chocolate-covered ice cream bars), and "Eskimos" (chocolate-covered ice cream sticks) anywhere else in the world. I have tried ice cream in many different places, but I have never found ice cream as good as what they had in the Soviet Union. You can enjoy eating that kind of ice cream even on the coldest days!

Even in -10 to -20°F weather, the children played outside, and everyone cross-country skied. In Dubna our children learned to stand on skates without falling and to ski. Even when it was terribly cold, it was impossible to drag them back inside the house. Not far from our house there was a large skating rink, and on the weekends, they played music and hundreds of people would skate there. Usually entire families would go skating together. They would bring a thermos of hot tea and savory pastries, so they could have a snack together.

Almost all of our friends spent the weekends either skiing or skating. Our favorite thing to do in the winter was to ski. People who lived in big cities would leave town on the weekends and go to the forest to ski. Almost all Russians are taught to ski and skate when they are young.

I finally decided to learn to skate, too. I managed to stand up on my skates and even start skating the first time I tried. It felt good to skate with my friends. Usually when my family went skating, I would stay at home, so I decided not to miss this opportunity to be with friends and family. On the first day, when I had just learned to skate and didn't fall once, I slipped on the ice in front of our entryway. In the Soviet Union, no one cared about the condition of the streets and roads. An icicle could simply fall on your head from a building. And no one was responsible for the damage caused to the nation's citizens, although government services were responsible for cleaning the roads and sidewalks. And why should they try to do a good job? They knew full well that no one would hold them responsible for any problems.

When I fell, I broke my arm. It was particularly upsetting that this happened not on the rink, but in front of my house.

When friends fall sick, Russians go to enormous trouble to help them, however inconvenient that may be. My friends and neighbors immediately showered me with attention. My neighbors made aspic especially for me, as it was believed to help heal fractures. Another no less popular healing method was drinking "Mummy", a medicinal compound made of hard-to-get herbs that grow so high in the mountains of Central Asia, that climbers had difficulty getting

284

to them. It was also very expensive; nevertheless, my parents sent me a couple small packages of it.

In general, Soviet people preferred medicinal herbs and grasses and "gorchichniki" (or "mustard plasters") over modern medications. Every day, friends would come to visit me. I was spoiled by this attention, which I missed when I was living in Germany.

I had friends from around the world in Dubna. Our neighbors from Hungary became our good friends. Through this friendship, I learned a lot about the Hungarian culture and mentality. People from East European countries stick together. Most of my neighbor Juja's friends in Dubna were Hungarians. We liked to go together to the Russian *banya,* which is a Russian sauna, but also a sort of health club. My friends and I would spend hours together chatting, gossiping, eating, and drinking beer. Despite the differences in our cultures and languages, we always had a lot of things in common to talk about – especially things of interest to women. It was fun for me to spend time in the *banya* with Hungarian women.

Russians like to meet at the *banya*. Russian men would often make business deals there. But it was not just a place for getting together; it was a health spa. As the Russian saying goes, "The *banya* cures most diseases". People spend hours at the *banya* and observe some special rituals there. First you soap up, then steam yourself, the rinse off and repeat the process several times in a row. You can rent "veniks" - bundles of leafy birch twigs - to beat one another with and help the steam cleanse your body. The steam in the Russian *banya* is so hot that the air burns your nostrils when you breathe. The idea is to make you sweat a lot and thereby flush the dirt out of your system through your pores. When you leave the steam room, you feel wonderful! Then we would get together with our friends in the lounge area, where we would enjoy beer with "vobla." *Vobla* is dried, boney, salted fish that you chew and suck on. It's sort of like salted pretzels, potato chips, or salted nuts. I liked the Russian *banya* because it was segregated and women never mixed with men, unlike in Germany, where men and women were naked together in same small steam room. I hated that. It violated my culture, and I could never ever accept it!

285

Soviet people weren't spoiled by electronic entertainment as in western countries. You could always see people playing outside in the yard. Men, old and young, would be playing chess, checkers or dominos. Russian also like to play cards.

Russians also have a passion for their countryside. City people usually take the "elektrichka" (or commuter rail) to the countryside on Fridays. On weekends, trains are crowded with people carrying backpacks, headed for the countryside to hike and sleep in the open air. We would also go with our kids and our Russian friends to spend the night in the forest. We would sleep in tents. But most of all we loved cooking on a campfire, playing music by the fire, and singing. The next day we would go off to find mushrooms. This is another favorite Russian outdoor activity. In the morning, everybody sets out with pails, satchels, or makeshift containers and starts scanning the ground for hidden mushrooms. I would always pick the wrong ones, because I grew up in Central Asia, where people didn't have any clue about mushrooms. My friends tried to teach me the difference between poisonous and edible ones, but unfortunately, I always picked the wrong ones. When my friends' pails were full, we would sit in a circle and clean the mushrooms while chatting. Meanwhile, we would have a picnic. In the evening we would make mushroom soup on the campfire with fish caught in a local creek. How much pleasure we got from hunting for mushrooms, talking, and enjoying the beautiful countryside around us, while surrounded by the intoxicating smell of pines. I was always amazed by the endless forests edged with beautiful birch trees. It was like one of Russian artist Aleksey Savrasov's landscapes.

Gorbachev

In Dubna, you could feel the liberal atmosphere. I think that it was fostered by Gorbachev's policies. Gorbachev's *perestroika* was in the air.

When Leonid Brezhnev died on November 10, 1982, he was one of the oldest government leaders in the world. The target of countless jokes, he had become the laughingstock of the nation. Then Yuri Andropov, who had been the head of the KGB for 15 years, became the new general secretary. He began his tenure in office with a campaign against corruption and absenteeism in the workplace, but he wasn't in office long enough to make any major long-term changes. I remember one of his first acts as general secretary was to have the authorities check people in movie theaters and supermarkets, as well as on the streets, to make sure they weren't skipping out on work. He was only in office 15 months. Everybody knew that he was sick. After his death on February 9, 1984, another elderly man, Konstantin Chernenko, was elected as general secretary. The Soviet people didn't take this news seriously; they were already asking who would be next. Chernenko passed away in 1985, and the Central Committee elected Mikhail Gorbachev as the new General Secretary. At this time nobody knew who Gorbachev was. They knew absolutely nothing about him.

The 27th Party Congress in 1986 had a "revolutionary character". Gorbachev's first speech was different than anything we heard since the October Revolution in 1917. We couldn't believe that he actually talked openly about economic problems, low labor productivity, and shortages of consumer goods and food. He also said the country needed radical changes, including political changes, and he proclaimed that there would be a choice of candidates in future elections. Russians were not accustomed to democracy in action. Gorbachev kept repeated the words "perestroika" (restructuring), "glasnost" (openness), "socialist pluralism", and "democratization," but nobody knew what these words meant in practice. Still, the slogans sounded very familiar: *perestroika* guaranteed the extension of democracy to the working masses, socialist self-government, the strengthening of discipline and order, an increase in transparency, as well as a critical assessment of all facets of society. We had all heard speeches before, speeches full of promises, but this time it was different. For the first time we believed that Gorbachev would change our lives.

Gorbachev had excellent ideas, such as private enterprise and freedom of the press.

Under the leadership of journalists like Vitaly Korotich and Yegor Yakovlev, magazines such as *Novy mir* and "*Ogonyok* and newspapers such as *Argumenty i fakty* and *Moskovskie novosti* started publishing previously suppressed works. For example, the atmosphere of the Stalinist years was recreated in Anatoly

Rybakov's novel *Children of the Arbat*. In 1989, the magazine *Novy Mir* began publishing *Gulag Archipelago,* Solzhenitsyn's book from the early 1970s about the Gulag, for which he was deported from Soviet Union in 1974. In this book, he described his own experience in the camps as well as that of hundreds of others, based on their oral stories and letters. These subjects had been completely taboo until that time. The average citizen didn't have a clue about what had happened under Stalin; we didn't even know what was actually happening in the country during our own lives. Everybody was shocked when they read *Gulag Archipelago*. The magazines and newspapers were taking a pro-Gorbachev stand by printing anti-Stalinist materials. People lined up at the newspaper kiosks to buy the latest editions, and they sold out instantly. They knew that they would find interesting material in the publications which had so suddenly become liberal and begun publishing previously unavailable literature. They even published Bulgakov's works and Pasternak's *Dr. Zhivago*, which had been banned for decades. I remember that some friends said to me, "These days reading is more interesting than living!" Suddenly we were able to get our hands on any kind of literature, including works by famous Russian writers that we were unfamiliar with. We found out about writers, musicians, and dancers who had emigrated to the West, like Nabokov, Berdyaev, and even Stravinsky and Balanchine. Now, at last, they were fully recognized. We also started hearing about Russian stars living abroad, such as Baryshnikov, Rostropovich, Nureyev, and Brodsky. We were blown away by all this information. As Gorbachev said, *glasnost* and *perestroika* had taken off!

We regularly met with our friends to talk about all this. Everyone was disappointed about our nation's past and the system in which we lived. We had gone through decades of strict censorship and strict government control of information, but now we could talk openly (even at work!) with our colleagues and friends. We weren't afraid, as we had been in the past, that someone would report on us. In my group, there were scientists from North Korea. When the Gorbachev era began, they began to feel very uncomfortable. When my colleagues and I began to emotionally discuss what was going on, they would quietly disappear from the room. They were even afraid of one another. If I stayed in the office to talk to one of them, they would always first open the door to make sure there was no one in the hallway, and then start speaking to me in a whisper. They always followed one another and reported on each other. Sometimes my friends and I would mess with them by criticizing the leadership. Oh god, how their faces would change. They would immediately grow pale and run out of the room. Like us, the North Koreans are the product of a collective society and would always do things in groups, even going to the store. They were all dressed in the same gray-black clothes and had pins with the portrait of the leader of North Korea, Kim Jong-Il on their chests.

I knew that the Soviet Union was multicultural, but my knowledge about my own country was largely from books. As a child I didn't have a chance to travel; now I wanted to use this opportunity to see as much of the country as possible. I hadn't been to many of the 15 Soviet Republics, so Olya and I decided to go to the Baltics. Our first stop was Riga, the capital of Latvia. I had heard a lot of positive and negative things about the Baltic republics during my childhood. When my friends traveled to the Baltic states, they would say they were "going west". Because the Baltics had a higher standard of living, people liked shopping there. Everything was up to European standards. But after coming back, people complained about how unfriendly the Baltic people were to Russians. When my dad spent some time in the Baltics on a business trip and brought back beautiful, high-quality children's things, it was as if he had gone abroad. He was thrilled with his experience there, but he couldn't understand how the Baltic republics managed to retain so much freedom. He felt as if he had been abroad, not just in the Baltic republics of the Soviet Union.

When a tall, pale woman, as he told it, met him in the Tallinn Airport, he was surprised at how cold she was. On TV he was greeted in a manner best described as distantly polite. At first, he thought it was because of disdain for Central Asians, but later he realized it was just Baltic aloofness.

The main director of Tallinn TV spoke Russian with a strong accent; my dad had trouble understanding him. My dad was also surprised when his colleague offered him cognac in the middle of the workday. My dad of course refused to drink during work, but his colleague continued to drink the cognac gulp by gulp. My dad, who, like the Russians, was used to drinking a glass of cognac down all at once, believed his colleague must be drinking like a European. After that, people treated my father with respect.

Judging by the questions his TV staff asked him in Tallinn and Riga, he could tell that they knew very little about Central Asia, and they basically had nothing but scorn for the Soviet Union. Dad liked the fact that everything there was nothing like things in Uzbekistan: the architecture and the clean streets were just like in a foreign country.

In Tallinn they said that they were going to do an interview with him and told him in advance what kind of things they were going to discuss. He was concerned about the frank questions they were going to ask, which would have been impermissible in the Soviet Union, and had to get permission from his boss in Uzbekistan to answer them. The most astonishing thing was when, on his first day there, they showed him Finnish television, which the local population was able to understand because their languages were so similar. When my dad returned, he told us that he had at last made it to the European border.

Olya and I didn't have any friends in the Baltics we could stay with, and hotels were a luxury for Soviet citizens, so we decided to take a night train and arrive in Riga in the morning. We would then spend the entire day walking around town. There were two rather pleasant-looking young men from Riga with us in our train compartment, but they turned out to be very cold, and were more European in this respect than Russian. It turned out that one of them was Russian, and the other a Latvian, who spoke Russian with a strong Baltic accent. We talked to them for a long time. You could tell they loved their republic and told us the sights we could see in one day. When we talked about politics, they kept quoting Finnish television. Their opinions about the Soviet Union were much different than the ones Russians held. They spoke more openly and had no reservations about criticizing the Russian occupation of the Baltics. I was surprised that even the young Russian was a Latvian patriot who disliked Moscow. In the morning we said goodbye to them and went to walk around the city. I immediately felt like I was in Europe or, more precisely, in Germany. The cobblestone streets of Riga, which exuded a European spirit, reminded me of German cities.

The Balts were uncomfortable with Russian immigration to their small countries. This is why they were not really happy when Russians visited. Olya and I personally experienced this. When we went to a café to drink coffee, no one would serve us; we went to another café and the same thing happened. At last we realized what was going on. They didn't like Russians - although I was not Russian at all and Olya and I had no relationship whatsoever to the Russian occupation. Then Olya suggested that we speak to them in German; otherwise we would never get any coffee. A miracle happened: when I addressed the waiter in German, I got service. Even though no one in that establishment spoke German, the main thing for them was that they didn't want to hear any Russian.

After eating in silence, since Olya and I couldn't speak Russian there, we left the restaurant feeling rather down. Olya couldn't understand how Russians could live there. Apparently, you could only live here if you had power; after all, the Russians held all the leading positions and were in a privileged position. After such treatment I was not in a great mood and no longer wanted to continue our trip through the Baltic republics – after all, they all had the same attitudes toward Russians. And it might be worse in the other republics – after all, there were a lot of Russians in Latvia. I really didn't want people to treat me poorly based on my ethnicity; I had had enough of that my whole life! Olya completely agreed with me and that very day we returned to Dubna.

We had colleagues from Georgia. Georgians are a very friendly people, and they would always lovingly and passionately tell us about their homeland. They ultimately convinced me and Olya to go to Georgia. They organized the whole trip and enlisted their relatives and friends to put us up and show us Tbilisi. In the Soviet Union, Georgians were famous for their delicious food and wonderful wine. They were the only nation in the former Soviet Union with a wine culture. During meals, Georgians would make an endless series of colorful toasts to their guests. Even if you were just an acquaintance, they would make such toasts in your honor, that you would start feeling like the closest family friend.

Like Italians, the handsome Georgian men were talented at being gallant with women (but not with their wives). They would give beautiful compliments to women, have romantic dinners, and always be well dressed. Knowing all this, Olya and I wanted to see the Caucasus. But suddenly the political situation radically changed and on April 9, 1989, when Olya and I were supposed to go to Tbilisi, Soviet troops broke up a peaceful demonstration at the government building there. Twenty Georgians were killed, and hundreds were wounded and poisoned. Everybody was shocked, and of course, we didn't go.

In the Brezhnev period, rock and roll was forbidden. Suddenly with *perestroika,* hundreds of amateur groups that imitated Western groups appeared in the cities. There were also professional and original Russian language rock bands like "Mashina Vremeni", "Akvarium", "DDT", "Nautilus Pompilius", and "Auktsion". In Dubna, we had several rock festivals where big Russian stars like Viktor Tsoy performed. These groups sang songs that expressed a cry for help, exhaustion from living in such a system, and a desire for freedom. It only became permissible to sing about such things during *perestroika.*

We were all overwhelmed by the sudden freedom of the press and our new ability to freely express our thoughts. Everyone was criticizing the system, and we finally began to hear the truth about the last 70 years. The revelations about the Stalinist system and 70 years of political oppression were very scary. Many people couldn't believe that the horrors of the GULAG actually occurred in our country. It is not surprising that no one had spoken about any of it. Fear was in our genes; we had been conditioned to fear the regime. For the 70 years of communism we were not allowed to speak the truth. I remember how, when I was little, my uncles would come over. They would go into a room and close the door, then quietly, always in a whisper, discuss something, and I remember them saying Stalin's name.

Now, with *perestroika*, a lot of information came crashing down on us. It was definitely an interesting time to live through, but we also felt so disappointed about everything. It was particularly difficult for the older generation to realize that their lives had been a lie. They asked themselves, "Is everything I believed in a lie?" After all, when they were younger, they had even believed General Secretary of the Communist Party Khrushchev's prediction in the 1960s that by 1980 we would have achieved communism. We were supposed to overtake the US in terms of *per capita* output, and by 1980 we were supposed to be producing enough of everything to make communism possible.

The Soviet people believed all this, because they had no concept of what the situation was abroad. They were happy because the Soviet government guaranteed employment, health care, housing, clothing, and pensions. The citizens were brought up to respect the general interests of society and to avoid selfish individualism. But there were people who knew what was really going on in the country. Many were silent. They had already been scared into silence by a system in which the least bit of criticism or independent thought could land you in prison, a labor camp, or to a psychiatric ward for the crime of anti-Soviet propaganda.

It takes enormous courage to fight your own people for their own good, and to accept being pilloried by the very people, whose freedom and rights you are defending. Three individuals stood out among the dissidents in Russia: Andrey Sakharov, Alexander Solzhenitsyn, and Roy Medvedev. They were unique and outstanding individuals who were not broken by the enormous material and psychological pressures brought to bear up them. And in spite of state resistance to them, their main ideas seeped into the minds of thousands of Soviet citizens.

I am pretty sure there were more people who were unhappy with system, but they were taught that if they were to speak out openly, they would put their families and loved ones at risk. The Soviet system had managed to root out everyone who dared to openly express their opinion. 70 years of stupid silence, and then suddenly - *perestroika* and *glasnost!* Now even leading liberal dissidents like Sakharov were allowed to leave their places of exile, return to Moscow, and even lead political movements.

293

When Gorbachev start talking about "democratization", only a few people knew what it meant.

New laws made it possible to open private businesses, and suddenly in Dubna there were new "co-ops" – small, privately-owned businesses and shops. The problem was that most of the new businesspeople were interested in trade rather than in production, and many of them were also involved in crime.

Anyway, it was an interesting time, a lot was going on, and, as I said before, we were constantly getting together with friends and having emotional discussions about what was happening. We all believed things would get better and there would be a bright future for us.

But not everyone believed in Gorbachev's promises. For example, there was my boss, Valentin Pavlovich, who was the head of the laboratory and a brilliant physicist. In spite of his brilliance, he was not allowed to go abroad to international conferences and was not promoted because he openly expressed his political views, which were very different from those of the heads of the institute and the government. The only people who were allowed to go abroad were members of the leadership of the institute, and they had to be members of the communist party. Like all geniuses, Pavlovich had never had to depend on anyone and apparently wasn't afraid of the Soviet regime. He had also never joined the communist party. After one of his many conflicts with the leadership, he apparently committed suicide by jumping to his death out the window of his ninth-floor apartment. My colleagues and I were in shock. He was a rather young man and a very kind person, who always had a smile on his face. So because he had independent ideas and was unable to agree with official government policies, this brilliant physicist perished. And there were many such people! Of course, the official cause of death was not published anywhere, just short condolences to his family, which lived in Moscow. The families of many of the scientists working in Dubna lived in Moscow or in other cities; apparently there were not enough apartments in Dubna. As I already said, the Soviet Union didn't have a free market, where people could buy their housing; apartments were given out by the government. Therefore, scientists in Dubna lived in dorms in spite of their great service to their country, and they lived in conditions more appropriate for university students.

The multi-storied dorm for scholars across from our house is the one Valentin Pavlovich jumped from. Specialists lived in small rooms there. Once I went into one of those rooms to see a colleague and was shocked. A man who had a PhD and who had published a large number of scientific articles was still living like a student! This once again demonstrated how the Soviet government treated its citizens. Again, the newest communist motto, "Everything for the good of the Soviet citizen!" was contradicted by the reality of Soviet life. Although the institute in Dubna was considered to be a privileged place to work, people lived in absolutely deplorable communist conditions.

At that time there were shortages of everything, even basic foodstuffs. But in Dubna there were special stores for expats, where you could buy not just basic foodstuffs, but even luxury items on major holidays. You could buy as much as you wanted of some items, and I tried to help my local friends by buying food for them in this store. At that time, when the supermarkets were empty, you easily could buy several different kinds of sausage and meat, and even Czech beer in the special orders department. I knew that the local people didn't like this system – even though Soviet citizens were used to certain people, like members of the government, having privileges, such as access to special stores and cafeterias. Everyone who managed to get into these places was surprised that you could get anything you wanted, even black caviar. And what surprised them most was not the quantity of items, but the insanely low prices. This once again demonstrated what a hypocritical country we lived in!

I was not very comfortable being seen going to the special orders department for the privileged, so I ordered items for myself and my colleagues by phone and had them delivered to my house. They usually brought the food in open baskets, and when they entered the building, I saw some of the other residents, who were sitting by the entrance, looking at the contents of the basket with envy. Expats also had the ability to buy a car (a Soviet one, of course) without waiting for years, as Soviets did. One of the privileges of being an expat was that you could get a Soviet Lada in just a year. In the GDR, people would wait 20 years to buy a car. We had no chance of buying one there. People even joked that as soon as a baby is born, you should get him on the waiting list for a car.

In East Germany, Soviet cars were considered a luxury. Germans could generally only get locally produced Trabants, which were practically made of plastic and slightly bigger than a Wartburg. In East Germany, you had to be part of the elite to have a car, so we took advantage of this opportunity in Russia and bought a Lada, which had just been released and was modeled after the Italian Fiat. Even in Russia few people had one of these cars, and there were a limited number in Dubna. Since the garage was on the other end of town, we would park the car in front of the house (just like everyone else). Imagine our surprise, when one day we woke up to find our car was gone. We couldn't believe our eyes. We were in shock, because how could you steal a car with expat plates from such a quiet neighborhood? All sorts of scenarios went through our minds. Some of our Russian colleagues were jealous and irritated that it was so easy for foreigners to buy Soviet cars, when Soviet citizens themselves had to wait for years. I thought that maybe one of these jealous people had decided to take revenge by stealing the car and doing something to it. In short, over the course of the year that it took them to find the car, we were very anxious, and began to suspect the people around us. It turned out that the car had been stolen by a man from a typical nearby provincial town. Since he couldn't drive it openly for fear of getting caught, he took it apart and sold it for parts. When he was caught for stealing another car, parts of our car were found in his garage. If he hadn't been caught for stealing the other car, we would never have found ours. After all, we all knew that the Soviet militia always took bribes and never tried to solve a case unless you paid them off or had connections.

Escaping to the West

Once we understood what kind of system we were living in, we decided to radically change our lives. We also were concerned about our children's future and didn't want them to have to live in a hypocritical system. We really became aware of this when, in the summer of 1988, we went to the GDR for summer vacation. They had "Red Fascism" there – even the Russian press was forbidden, because of fears that Gorbachev's reforms would influence the GDR. We realized that we couldn't return home to Germany, and began looking for any and all ways to escape to the West.

After giving it lots of thought, Juergen and I decided to appeal to the West German embassy in Moscow. It was a risky thing to do. It's scary to think what would have happened if anyone from the East German community had found out about it. An embassy official let us into the German consulate without any problems, and we warned him that if any Russian officials in the consulate were to find out about our visit, there would be trouble. He understood and took us along empty corridors to his office. There, we explained our situation: that we couldn't return to the GDR, and that thanks to *perestroika* we knew the whole truth about the system in which we lived. He knew very well what had happened in the GDR. It was a terrible letdown when he told us that he couldn't help us concretely in any way, because even with GDR passports and a western visa, we wouldn't be permitted to leave Moscow. He told us to try to leave through Hungary, saying that there are places along the Austrian-Hungarian border where it is easy to cross from one country to the next. This was our only chance to escape to the West. In parting, he said, "Don't be afraid. Throw your heart over the barrier, then jump over it yourselves! But don't be under the illusion that everything is perfect in the West."

Our Hungarian friends happened to be returning to Budapest at that time. We got in touch with them, and they said that they would help Juergen. So in June, Juergen decided to cross the border in Hungary. If he succeeded, then he could invite us, as family members, to join him, and the kids and I would leave. We never considered having the whole family flee together and subjecting the children to danger. Juergen arrived in Budapest and went to the West German embassy, where they tried to convince him not to try it: "You can get shot trying to cross the border. Even if you try to cross through the marshes, you could be accidentally shot." And so he returned to Dubna without achieving anything.

297

In the summer of 1989, our contract had ended, and we were supposed to return to the GDR.

When Juergen and the rest of us arrived in Dubna in 1985, we were sure that we would stay there permanently, but Gorbachev had changed our feelings about the Soviet Union.

For the first time, I consciously lived in Russia among Russians. I was shocked by the poverty around me, and you only had to leave Dubna and go to the neighboring cities to see surprising squalor. For example, as soon as you entered the neighboring city of Kimry, you felt as if you had taken a time machine back to the 19C. There were old, collapsing wooden houses and drunken men lying under fences. There was cussing everywhere and constant articles in the newspapers about drunk young men getting into fights.

People were dissatisfied with things, but they couldn't express this openly; nor did they do much to make them better. It was no doubt impossible to try to change the way the government operated, and thus not surprising that most people didn't attempt to. However, it's much harder to understand why people didn't lift a finger to improve everyday things around them. For example, to get to his apartment, the average person had to pass through dark, graffiti-covered wooden entryways, which were creaky and painted some horrifically ugly color. I could never understand why the smells and dirt in those entryways in the buildings didn't seem bother the people living there. Was it really so impossible to take turns taking out the trash or repaint them a nice color? After all, people were capable of it! This was apparent when you walked from the entryway into someone's apartment: you would find yourself in a completely different world. You would be met with great warmth and smiles. You wouldn't notice the disarray in the apartment, which was typical in Russia. You would usually be invited immediately to the kitchen table, which occupies a central place in the Russian home. Usually it's a small table covered with way too many dishes of different sizes and from different sets. The table is laden with very simple food: different types of pickled vegetables, sauerkraut, black bread, meat patties, boiled potatoes, and buckwheat porridge. And there would always be salted fish - like salted herring, and sometimes lunch meats and cheese. People would spend hours sitting together at the kitchen table. Usually they would drink lots of strong, sweet, hot, black tea. The kitchen table was the gathering place in the house. It was a center of social life, and a place for community. Family and friends would sit at the table sharing their laughter, sorrows, and secrets, with an intimacy that was very open and not at all self-centered. To ease the pain of life, Russians have to have someone to whom they can pour out their hearts or talk to about their family problems or lovers. Russians expect total commitment from their friends, something people in the West don't understand. If a Russian's friend falls ill, they will go all out to help. Normally in official life, Russians hide their emotions; they only take them out to share with family and friends.

Chapter 16.

Escaping to the West

Return to the GDR

In August of 1989, when we returned to the German Democratic Republic, the country was getting ready for its 40th anniversary. There were slogans displayed everywhere praising the country, the achievements of socialism, etc. You could feel what I always called "Red Fascism". And you can imagine how we reacted to this "Red Fascism" after experiencing *perestroika* in the Soviet Union. *Glasnost* opened our eyes to the horrors of the communist system we lived in. And now we were shocked that it was impossible to buy Russian newspapers in the kiosks. General Secretary Honecker was doing everything he could to isolate his citizens from the changes going on in the Soviet Union. In the past you could buy Russian newspapers in any East German kiosk, but now you couldn't find them anywhere. The leadership of the GDR was critical of the changes going on in the Soviet Union. The chief ideologist in the GDR made a comment to the tune that just because Russia had changed its wallpaper, that didn't mean the GDR had to do so.

The German press even began publishing anti-Gorbachev articles, highlighting how much the changes taking place in the Soviet Union irritated the GDR government.

In September, our son Alishér was supposed to start first grade. I decided to stay at home and pick him up after school so I could do his lessons with him. When I spoke with the principal, she was very upset about this and categorically forbade me from doing so, saying, "Like all other children, he should be in after-school care and do his homework in the community of his peers."

No one was allowed to be different in this country. Everyone was supposed to be exactly like everyone else in every way. The collective was an important element of society, including collective education in kindergarten and school. There was after-school care in every school, where the kids did their homework collectively and played together.

Ideological education began early - in kindergarten. Once our son came home after school and said that a police officer had come to their class and told them that there was a good Germany, East Germany, and a bad Germany, which was called West Germany. Juergen and I were horrified; we couldn't believe they started brainwashing children at such a young age.

In a socialist society everyone has to work; there was even a "parasite" law that said that if you didn't work, you could be put in prison. And I had decided not to go to work, pick up my son right after school, and help him with his homework. But it was not to be. I was summoned by the government, and they demanded an explanation as to why I didn't want to work. I said that I wanted to stay at home and do my son's lessons with him. They responded, "You are behaving like a petty bourgeois woman. You are highly educated and should use your knowledge for the good of society!"

There was nothing I could say in response. I knew that in this system, society was more important than the family. When they threatened me, saying I would have problems if I didn't go to work, my husband and I decided once and for all that we would escape to the West.

Escape to the West[3]

Our friends from Hungary (our former neighbors in Dubna) helped us make the decision to flee. We called them, and they said that the border between Austria and Hungary had opened in September. A new law had been enacted in Hungary allowing Hungarians to travel to Austria, and on June 27, 1989, the electronic fence on the border with Austria was turned off.

Hungary was a popular vacation spot for East Germans. All summer long, people would pile into their two-cylinder plastic Trabants and set out for Hungary. We had our Russian visa and decided to escape to Hungary. It would be no problem to go Hungary and when we arrived at the border, show our passports and tell the East German police that we were heading to Russia.

We had to do this, because it was impossible to live in a country where "Red Fascism" was blossoming, and the government was pompously preparing for the 40th anniversary of socialism. We warned our Hungarian friends that we were leaving, and for their part, they promised to find out who we should talk to in Budapest. The first East Germans had already begun fleeing to the West via Hungary. Hungary had opened its border with Austria not only for its own citizens, but for the citizens of the GDR.

After gathering all the belongings and documents we needed, we set out at night in the direction of Czechoslovakia. We told the children that we were going back to Dubna, and they were very happy, because they missed their friends in Dubna a lot. We left at night and were very nervous when we got to the border. The German

---

[3] Map source: Wikipedia

and Czech police were beating and arresting people if they had the slightest suspicion that they were trying to escape. Beatings and arrests were a constant issue at the Czech border.

When we left the country on September 29th, we decided to leave behind all our belongings, except for our documents. We realized that if the border guards saw all our things, they would immediately guess that we were planning to flee. We warned the children that if asked, they were to tell the police that we had been on summer vacation in Germany and were now returning to Dubna. At the first checkpoint between the GDR and Czechoslovakia, they questioned us ad nauseum about where we were going and why. Here the Russian visa in our passports helped. Next we had to cross the Czechoslovak-Hungarian border. We went way out of our way to get to a border crossing with less traffic. When Juergen was showing his passport at the border, I thought I would die from fear. It was scary, because they could arrest us and send us back, and if they sent us back, they would definitely put at least one of us in jail. Everyone who was picked up at the border was put in jail. While they were interrogating Juergen, scenes from WWII films, where people were fleeing from Nazi Germany, flashed before my eyes. I was shaking in terror. Thankfully, the children were sleeping, and they didn't have to deal with our anxiety. And luckily, without asking us to open the trunk of the car where all our documents were, the border guard let us into Hungary.

So we were in Hungary before midnight and set off for the German Embassy. We called, and they said to come in the morning. We stayed with our Hungarian friends, who received us warmly and said that 1000 refugees from the GDR were being held in a special camp in Budapest. In the morning, the embassy sent us to the camp. They said that in principle, Juergen could go further and that he would automatically get a West German passport at the Austrian border. Since I didn't have an East German passport, they said I would get a special visa to West Germany.

The camp was on the hilly side of Budapest on the site of a pioneer camp [like a boy scout camp]. The conditions there were good. Every family got a room with amenities. They fed us three times a day for free, provided us with clothes, and even gave us

Hungarian money so we could go into town. All of this humanitarian aid was organized by Malteser International, the worldwide relief agency of the Sovereign Military Order of Malta for Humanitarian Aid.

By that time, there were already hundreds of people in the camp, and many had children. Tragically, members of some families had been arrested by the Czech border patrol and sent back to the GDR, where they were immediately put in jail. There were many people in the camp with broken arms and legs in casts. People were being beaten at the border, and family members were being purposefully separated from one another. There was one Russian woman with a daughter whose husband had been taken off the train by officials three weeks before, and she had no idea what had happened to him. Many women had similar stories: they had lost their husbands along the way and didn't know what to do. It was a dramatic situation.

In our case, no one could tell us how to get a visa so that Juergen and I could cross the border. No one in the German Embassy or the aid organization that was helping in the camp could give us any real guidance. Then our Hungarian friends advised Juergen to go by himself to Germany and apply for a visa for me there. They promised to support me and the children in Budapest while he was gone. We decided to do it that way, with him going and me staying in the camp with the children – after all, the conditions there were good. Juergen left, and the children and I stayed behind waiting to hear something.

There were a lot of people like us. Many had lost their partners along the way and were trying to somehow get at least a little information about their loved ones. Some people couldn't take it and returned to the GDR. People in the camp were fleeing either for political reasons, in search of freedom, or for economic reasons. It was hardest of all for people like us, families whose members fell into different legal categories. If you didn't have a German passport, you had to wait in the camp for god knows how long for a visa.

It was beautiful fall weather. The city of Budapest was gorgeous, and we fell in love with it immediately. Every day the children did their lessons with me so they wouldn't fall behind in school, and then, after classes, we would go to town. We would walk along the streets of the city and stop in museums. The children loved the zoo. Our friends frequently invited us over. They took us to their country house, where we made the famous Hungarian goulash together.

One day when my son was running around in the park, he was bitten by a dog. The people from Malteser immediately took us to the hospital so he could get a shot. Later they took us to McDonalds to cheer him up. This was a real treat for us. McDonalds was a window into the world of capitalism. Alishér long remembered his milkshake and hamburger. The kids were particularly excited about the little toys in the bright McDonalds wrappers.

Only a couple of the refugees knew anyone in West Germany. Many had no one there, and were fleeing, just like us, into the unknown. Many were optimistic about the future, but many were terrified by the uncertainty. We were also scared – after all, we had small children and no idea how we would be able to start a new life. We had left everything in East Germany: our apartment, our furniture, our loved ones, and our most treasured belongings. What would become of us?

In West Germany, Juergen was told that since I was a refugee, I didn't need a separate visa and could enter the country with him, so he came to get us. By that time, we had made friends with several people who unfortunately still didn't know the whereabouts of their family members who had been arrested on the train. Most families in the camp had members with different political statuses, just like us: a husband or wife was German, but their partners were from different countries. Everyone was waiting for an exit visa. There were a few women from Ukraine and Russia. One woman, named Tatyana, was always upset and nervous. When they were travelling on the train, Czech border guards came on board and, without even questioning anyone, asked some people, including her husband, to leave with them. And that was it. Since then she hadn't heard anything about him. No one could help her. She cried every day. Malteser couldn't help – they didn't have any Czech contacts, not to mention any GDR police contacts. She was worried about his health – he had diabetes and all his medicine was with her. Another woman from Ukraine had had her 18-year-old son arrested and for two weeks hadn't had any news about him.

When anyone new arrived at the camp, everyone would surround them and ask them if they hadn't happened to have seen any of their loved ones.

Some people had trouble sitting around and waiting. There were family conflicts, where a husband or a wife would get tired of waiting, gather their belongings, and go back to the GDR. They would honestly admit that they had reached their limit and that it would be better for them to return home to their lives. One day my friend Tatyana also decided to go back home and wait for her husband there. She told me that they had a house, they had work, and that she didn't have the strength to run off to an unknown situation. So there were people who, after losing their partners and their children and spending 2-3 weeks waiting for an exit visa in the camp ended up going home. Incidentally, it was also risky to go back home. You would have to go through the same border checkpoint from Czechoslovakia to the GDR. We heard rumors that they were arresting people who went back for attempting to flee. Every day someone would return with arms or legs in casts and would tell us terrible stories about how they were treated by the East German and Czech border guards – how they were beaten, and how a few were even thrown from moving trains. Sometimes lost family members would turn up, and those were very happy moments. Sitting with these people, we would hear heartbreaking stories which the newly arrived person had witnessed. It was unbelievable that during peacetime, people could be treated so terribly. This was all reminiscent of the Nazi period.

As I said above, in September 1989, Hungary opened its borders with Austria, allowing East Germans to leave via Hungary. East Germans then began taking refuge in West German embassies in Poland, Czechoslovakia, and Hungary. At the same time, the Hungarian government stopped enforcing East German visa restrictions. In the first three days after these changes were made, thousands of East German refugees passed through Hungary to West Germany, where they were given asylum.

In October 1989, pro-democracy demonstrations began in Dresden and Leipzig. The communist leader Erich Honecker was forced to resign, and there were anti-communist protests in East

Berlin, drawing more than a million people demanding democracy. Consequently, the East German government resigned.

On November 9, people were permitted to cross from East Germany into West Germany, and mass celebrations ensued.

When Juergen and I went to Berlin, the sight of the Berlin Wall made us sad. We knew full well that the free world was just beyond that barrier, but you couldn't go there, even if you wanted to. At that spot, you really felt like a hostage of the system. I always thought about how hard it was for families who had members on the other side. You would sometimes hear about parents living on one side and children, who for some reason happened to be on the other side of Berlin the night that they built the wall, on the other. There were a lot of these family tragedies. Finally, on October 9, 1990, the two parts of Germany were formally reunited. How many families were reunited after the Berlin Wall came down?

Freedom

After saying goodbye and good luck to those who were staying in the camp, we anxiously crossed the Austro-Hungarian border. The border guards turned out to be friendly and gave me a visa; Juergen already had a West German passport from the first time he had crossed the border. Besides giving people leaving East Germany visas, they also gave them money for travelling expenses and assigned them to different sections of Germany. We really wanted to stay in Bavaria, so they put us in a refugee camp in Ulm. At the same time, the GDR was celebrating the 40th anniversary of the creation of the socialist republic.

Mikhail Gorbachev arrived in East Berlin on an official state visit in connection with the GDR's 40th anniversary celebration. On October 7, the GDR held its customary torchlight parade on Karl Marx Alley. The several thousand counterdemonstrators who were chanting "Gorby" were beaten. Demonstrations broke out in all the major cities, including Dresden, Karl-Marx City, and Leipzig. Ultimately, the East German government had no choice but to open the border. Within a week after that, 2 to 3 million people had crossed into West Berlin.

Within two weeks Juergen got a job at the Siemens company, but it was in the small city of Amberg. We moved there, and our kids were happy. Everything was new for them, and their favorite thing was to eat at McDonalds. I remember going to the McDonalds in Ulm for the first time and paying 20 German marks for dinner for 4. It was the most expensive dinner in our life! We didn't have enough money to do that at the time, but we wanted to celebrate our arrival to West Germany.

The kids easily adjusted to school and, as refugees, we were surrounded by nice people from churches and other organizations. We were also invited to various people's houses for dinner. Sometimes I had feeling that East Germans were something exotic for West Germans.

You could easily see the differences between East and West Germans. The West Germans were more friendly and actively interested in our story. They offered help to everyone. At that time, East Germans were comparatively less open. The West Germans saw the East Germans as different – and that was natural. They had been separated from one another for 40 years. The East Germans were living in a communist country with no contact with the outside world and had a completely different mentality. At some point I realized that the East Germans had an inferiority complex vis-à-vis the West Germans.

Within a short time, we managed to make new friends who were interested in Uzbekistan. They were in awe of our escape and wanted to know all the details. At the same time as we were getting to know the local people, we were going through the process of getting our papers in order. We had to file a bunch of documents and go to a variety of different government offices. In the window of one of the government offices, on the list of wanted terrorists, I saw the face of a woman I knew. I pointed it out to Juergen. He confirmed that that woman had lived in Dubna as an expat with her husband. We were in major shock, especially when we found out that she was involved in the murder of her uncle, a banker.

Suzanne Albrecht was a member of the Red Army Faction (RAF) terrorist group who was trained in guerilla warfare in Yemen. She and other terrorists murdered the chairman of the Dresdner

Bank and attempted to assassinate the NATO commander-in-chief. After that, Albrecht fled to the GDR, where the Stasi gave her a new identity.

She came to Dubna as the wife of a German scholar and kept to herself. We were always surprised by how unkempt she was: her long hair was always greasy, and she dressed slovenly, whereas her husband was attractive and genteel. They had two children. Later we found out that the GDR was hiding terrorists. They would give them new faces and passports with new names. She was sent with her family to Dubna because people around the world were looking for her. Even her husband didn't know that she was a former terrorist. After the reunification of Germany, she was arrested and put in jail. So we lived in a hypocritical country. We had heard rumors that the GDR was training Palestinian terrorists, but we didn't want to believe it.

This incident proved to us yet again what kind of country we had lived in.

Chapter 17.

Radio Liberty

Because of Juergen's job, we moved to Amberg, which was not far from Munich. I had always dreamt of working for Radio Liberty, which was headquartered in Munich at that time.

Radio Free Europe and Radio Liberty were US government-funded radio stations established in 1950 in response to censorship in the Soviet Union and Eastern Europe. Their mission was to broadcast news that was otherwise unavailable from their headquarters in Munich into the countries of Eastern Europe and the Soviet Union. They provided citizens of these countries local news in their native languages. The Soviet government responded by attempting to jam the broadcasts, but they were only partially successful.

After his release from prison camp in 1953, Solzhenitsyn used his first paycheck to buy a radio receiver, and then listened continually to all the Western broadcasts available in Russian. He learned to piece together information from partially jammed broadcasts.

Dissidents inside the country were the first Soviet citizens to break the wall of silence and mutual distrust with the West. They were followed by a significant number of cultural figures who left the country, giving a new impulse to Western broadcasting into Russia.

Victor Nekrasov, Vladimir Voinovich and other popular writers and artists appeared regularly on Voice of America, RL, the BBC, and Deutsche Welle. They spoke to a huge audience of fans and initiated a dialogue that helped overcome cultural obstacles. This genre of frank and intimate conversation was new to Soviet listeners.

The broadcasts created new stars like writer Sergey Dovlatov, who emigrated to New York from Leningrad in 1979. In the Soviet Union almost none of his prose made it into print, while in the US his works were published one after another - first in Russian and then in English - in the most prestigious publishing houses.

Since Radio Liberty was jammed in the Soviet Union, many people were unable to listen to it. I remember how my dad would try to catch different voices on his small transistor radio at night. The first time I heard Radio Liberty in Russian was when we were trying to find out what had actually happened in Chernobyl. I tried to catch the bits of information that made it through government jamming. We had first heard about what happened in Chernobyl from our Hungarian neighbors, who themselves had found out from Western radio. I managed to catch some details from Radio Liberty on our transistor radio in Russian. After that I started regularly listening to it. I even tried to catch the Uzbek programming, but when I heard programming that was purportedly in Uzbek, I was confused. The language sounded sort of like Uzbek, but sort of not. It was then that I started dreaming of working for this radio station. Most likely it was thanks to my background and growing up in a multicultural society that I was interested in international politics, and the life, culture, and languages of different countries.

When we finally made it to the West, the first thing I did was write a long letter to Radio Liberty expressing my desire to work for them. The next day I received a telegram from them inviting me to visit for a week-long interview. I jumped from joy! I had been invited for a whole week to the famous Radio Liberty. And there I was in Munich. I had always dreamt of going there, after all, for me Munich meant Radio Liberty. The radio station was in the center of Munich near the English Garden. It was surrounded by a fence, and you couldn't just walk in. This was for their security. There had been attempts to blow it up and some of their workers had even been killed by secret service agents from Eastern Europe.

At first, I had trouble understanding what language their Uzbek employees were speaking in. It was clearly not the Uzbek language I knew, and I thought that maybe it was some sort of archaic Uzbek spoken by their ancestors who had fled to Afghanistan during the

312

October Revolution. None of the Uzbek employees had been born in Uzbekistan. Half of them were ethnic Uzbeks from Afghanistan, and the other half from Turkey. None of them spoke the Uzbek language I knew.

The employees of the Uzbek Language Service met me rather coolly. Later one of their colleagues admitted that they thought that everyone who came from Uzbekistan was working for the KGB, and apparently they took me for a KGB agent too. They were very reserved and cautious with me. For them I was apparently some sort of sensation because I was an Uzbek woman with a higher education who spoke several languages, including real contemporary Uzbek that was actually spoken at that time in Uzbekistan. I don't think that it was common in Afghanistan to meet women who had graduated from college, learned several languages, and violated Islamic traditions by marrying an infidel.

Almost all the employees were descendants of the Basmachi who fled Russia after the October Revolution. The term "Basmachi" comes from an Uzbek word meaning "one who attacks." The Basmachi movement (an early precursor to the mujahedin) was organized in early 1918 in Central Asia to oppose the Soviet Red Army. In the 1920s, the Basmachi movement led a large-scale uprising against the Soviets that was eventually suppressed by the Red Army. The Fergana Valley was one of the main areas of support for this movement, which had largely died out by 1931.

There are probably over 36 million Uzbeks in the world. The majority of these live on the territory of the former Soviet Union, but many live elsewhere. During and after the Bolshevik Revolution, more than half a million Uzbeks fled south to join relatives in Northern Afghanistan. Their descendants form the bulk of the Uzbek population in Afghanistan, which numbers over a million. During WWII, many Soviet Uzbeks, along with other Central Asians, deserted the Red Army and joined the German army. Some of them escaped to the West after the war, later to be joined by Afghan Uzbek refugees after the Soviet invasion of their country in 1979. Still others fled from Afghanistan to Pakistan.

Another significant group of Uzbeks (numbering in the thousands) lives in the Xinjiang province of the People's Republic of China, which is adjacent to Soviet Central Asia. A couple thousand Uzbeks live in Turkey, and there are Uzbeks communities in various Western countries, including Germany, Britain, Canada, and the U.S.

It was very interesting for me to meet these people. Previously, I had had no idea that such groups of ethnic Uzbeks were living outside of Uzbekistan; in fact, I was certain that all Uzbeks lived in Uzbekistan. After all, we lived in a closed society where you couldn't get that kind of information.

They suggested I spend a whole week at the radio station and gave me various tasks, such as translating from Russian and German, reading texts into the microphone, and writing short essays. I found all this very interesting. Over the course of the week, I met my future colleagues. They were from a totally different world. Their mentality and culture were very different from the ones typical of Uzbeks where I grew up. Over the course of that week, so much interesting information was poured into me. I think that I was a major discovery for my colleagues, too. They were surprised at how much I knew, that I spoke a number of languages, and that I acted like a European. In their culture, women would get married, have children, and stay home with them. Most of the employees had just a high school education, no more.

After spending a week at the radio station, I knew that I wanted to work there. To be with Uzbeks, to be swimming in a huge amount of information, and to be up on political events. I always dreamt of having a job like this. I received a job offer a few months later and became the editor and moderator of the Uzbek Language Service for Radio Liberty.

Because I was the only native speaker, I was appointed moderator and program director. In other words, when my colleagues read their material into the mike, it was my job to correct their mistakes in the Uzbek language and pronunciation. It was hard – at first I didn't even completely understand them when they spoke, and it was awkward to have to correct them all the time. They were all older than me, and you are supposed to respect your elders in Uzbek culture. But I had to do it - it was my professional duty. I tried to explain to them as diplomatically as possible that in modern

314

Uzbek it was better to say it this way, etc. Of course, none of them liked this – after all, they had worked there for decades and no one had corrected them before. And then this young and inexperienced girl who, moreover, had grown up in a communist country, was trying to teach them. Gradually storm clouds began to gather over me.

On top of that, they didn't like the fact that I was always talking to our Russian-speaking colleagues – even though they were also dissidents who had been exiled from the Soviet Union and stripped of Soviet citizenship for political reasons. In spite of all this, in the eyes of my colleagues from the Uzbek Language Service, they were the occupiers of their country. They didn't want to understand that their Russian-speaking colleagues were just as much victims of the communist regime as they were. Just like other national editorial boards, the Russian editorial board was staffed by people who had been forced to leave their country.

In the last ten years of the Brezhnev regime, emigration to the West was permitted. In this new third wave of emigration, there were a lot of talented people, like Viktor Nekrasov, Vasily Aksyonov, Vladimir Voinovich and other popular writers and artists, who regularly appeared on Radio Liberty. They now had an opportunity to get published in the Soviet Union. They could speak to their Soviet audience via Radio Liberty. This is was new for Russian listeners. The famous dissident writer Sergey Dovlatov was tall, good looking, and charming. He was also a wonderful storyteller. It was an honor to have a cup of tea with these Russian cultural intellectuals.

My colleagues accused me of not being a serious person, because I was happy sitting and drinking coffee with the Russian speakers and, moreover, speaking the language of the enemy (Russian). People started making caustic comments to me. I tried to explain to my colleagues that our Russian-speaking colleagues had also suffered and had also had to leave their homeland. They were victims of communism just like us. They would reply that a real Uzbek woman didn't have the right to sit alone with men and drink coffee. O Lord, I felt like I had landed in the Middle Ages. These people had clearly gotten stuck in the past. I started to realize that if the Bolsheviks hadn't taken over Uzbekistan in 1917, all Uzbeks would be on the level of my colleagues – or even worse, and I would be walking around in a burka. For the first time in my life, I thanked the Russians for bringing progress to my country along with their Revolution.

It was paradoxical to me that while I was working for an American radio station in the center of Europe, I was surrounded by people with very backwards views. I had to appeal to the American managers for advice. I needed their support. They shrugged their shoulders and advised me to put up with it – or at least behave diplomatically. And I tried to.

The director of the editorial board also took a dislike to me from the very beginning. He saw me as a threat and, moreover, they hadn't hired his brother-in-law because of me. And thus I fell into the world of eastern intrigues.

In Russian there is the word "dedovshchina", which means hazing in the military. That's what I was going through. With 12 uneducated men from Afghanistan and Turkey against me, a woman, you can only imagine what I endured. They were irritated by my independence, my education, and my self-confidence.

I continued to enjoy talking to my colleagues from the Russian service. After all, they had an entire group of extremely fascinating people from all over the Soviet Union: former dissidents and intellectuals who had been stripped of their Soviet citizenship and exiled. I was grateful for every minute I had with such people. When I was with them, I felt at home. When I went back to the Uzbek Language Service, I would find myself in the world of macho, khans, and ignorance. My mentality was extremely different than that of my colleagues, even though we more or less spoke the same language.

Never having spent a day in Uzbekistan, they had no idea what high-level women there were there. They had no idea that women were educated, had equal rights with men, and had important jobs.

My coworkers would tell me negative things about the Russians – that they were our enemies and that they were infidels. And that by talking to them I was damaging my honor as an Uzbek woman.

Their idea of an Uzbek woman was someone who could do nothing more than produce children. They had had no contact with Uzbekistan for the past 70 years. They only knew stories about it from their fathers and grandfathers, who had fled the country in the 1930s. Moreover, they were uneducated. Before working at the radio, they were driving cabs and trading at the market in Istanbul. In the 1950s, when Radio Liberty created the editorial boards for Uzbekistan and other nations, they couldn't find any native Uzbeks, Tatars, or Kazakhs, so they took people from Afghanistan and Turkey who claimed to be native speakers. Their level of education wasn't important, as they didn't have to do anything except read a text into a microphone. Furthermore, none of them could read the Cyrillic alphabet, which was the alphabet currently used for the Uzbek language. They created an incomprehensible Uzbek-Latin alphabet for themselves, because, of course, they used the Latin alphabet in Turkey, and that's what they knew. In all those years they hadn't managed to learn the current Uzbek alphabet, the Cyrillic one.

For many centuries Uzbek was written in the Arabic alphabet. Then, under Stalin, the Uzbek language was Russified and literally transcribed into the Russian Cyrillic alphabet.

Without knowing the Cyrillic alphabet, it was impossible to follow events in Uzbekistan, or read the press or literature. For the past 50 years all Uzbek literature, daily newspapers, and journals were written in the Cyrillic alphabet.

It seemed to me that these people paid lip service to being patriots of their former homeland, but had no interest in what was actually going on there now.

The goal of the radio station was to transmit objective information to Uzbekistan. The information came from the Western press, which my coworkers at the editorial board were supposed to translate and read into the microphone. Since almost no one in the Uzbek section spoke Russian, English, or German, everything was first translated into Turkish, then they translated it from Turkish into incomprehensible Uzbek. The spoke the Uzbek language of their grandfathers, but (of course) with Turkish and Afghan words mixed in. That is why, when I had tried to catch Radio Liberty on my

317

transistor in Uzbek, I had trouble finding it, because the language the Uzbek program was broadcast in was incomprehensible. Each program was broadcast multiple times at different times. First, they aired the news, then they talked about different topics. When I looked at what they were broadcasting, I realized that 80% of it was of no interest to the modern Uzbek listener. The topics were basically about Turkey and Afghanistan.

I had a lot of ideas, but my boss, Mr. Turan, turned them all down. He thought there should be more topics related to religion. Who cared about religion in atheist Uzbekistan? The people there didn't have any concept of Islam, and you couldn't even buy the Quran! I suggested having programs where social and economic issues were discussed, as well as questions relating to women, the family, and the foundations of democracy – after all, the Soviet people had no idea what democracy was.

In 1990, when I started to work at Radio Liberty, the Soviet Union was beginning to fall apart, and in 1991, the 15 Soviet republics suddenly and unexpectedly became independent countries. This was a very challenging and stressful time for these newly born nations.

There were a lot of topics to cover in our program. I created a network of independent journalists in different parts of former Soviet Union. Under Gorbachev, some Uzbeks became more outspoken, and it wasn't hard to find independent journalists in Uzbekistan to cover all the different regions of the republic.

But I still had problems with my colleges. They were jealous of me and complained to the American management that I didn't even speak proper Uzbek and that I was strongly influenced by Russian culture. Sometimes they hid the tapes of the programs or arrived late to the studio when I was the producer. They came up with different intrigues, and sometimes even refused to talk to me. They also spread gossip about me, because I was still having coffee with my infidel colleagues. I tried to be polite and respect the elderly, as was customary in my culture, but I couldn't believe all this was happening in Munich, in the center of Europe, in the 20C.

After my boss had repeatedly forbidden me from creating programming that would be relevant to people in Uzbekistan, I was forced to turn to the American management. But they always gave me the same answer: "Hang in there. Don't pay any attention to them." But how could I "hang in there" when my heart bled for my homeland, Uzbekistan. Although my colleagues called themselves Uzbeks, they had none of the feelings I did for my homeland.

Beginning in 1990, the major Muslim republics in the Soviet Union became politically independent, but in many other respects their dependence on Moscow continued or became even stronger. The new, post-Soviet leadership was poor, and the ideology that had faded was partially replaced by Islam and Islamism.

The collapse of the Soviet Union aggravated the situation, particularly when it became clear that the oft-invoked "friendship of the peoples" was not, to put it mildly, deeply rooted. Millions and millions of ethnic Russians left the Central Asian republics, where they were made to feel unsafe and unwanted.

Suddenly ethnic conflicts flared up in various parts of the Soviet Union. In 1989, more than one hundred people were killed - and another thousand wounded - in the ethnic bloodbath in the Fergana Valley. Uzbeks attacked the Meskhetians, a Turkic people from Soviet Georgia that Stalin had exiled decades ago to Central Asia. The situation was out of control for a few days. People were in shock, and the government was powerless to help. Radio Liberty correspondents had trouble getting accurate information.

Since the local Soviet news didn't cover the tragedy in Fergana Valley at all, broadcasts from the West were particularly important. Foreign broadcasts were the only way people could get information about what was happening in their own countries.

In an attempt to get information about what was really going on in Fergana, I contacted Sanobar Shermatova, an Uzbek journalist in Moscow. Sanobar was working for a leading Russian newspaper and was a highly qualified specialist in the Central Asian countries. Her interviews and articles contained thoughtful analysis and played a significant role in the development of democracy in Central Asia. She was a strong, courageous person, a person with principles, which she never abandoned. Although she still had family in Uzbekistan, she bravely criticized the government. At that time, it was dangerous to speak and write openly about what was really going on in Uzbekistan. Although it was the era of *perestroika*, people were still very scared; they were also afraid of putting their relatives in danger. Sanobar and I worked well together. She was our correspondent in Moscow. Even now I remember her unique throaty voice and ringing laughter. I am saying all this in the past tense because she died suddenly in the spring of 2011.

My work on the radio resulted in problems for my parents. My father was called into the KGB, where they asked him unpleasant questions and threatened him. My sister, who worked for the government, was suddenly fired for no reason. My parents didn't tell me about this. They knew I liked my job and that I was genuinely concerned about my country.

Of course, my boss didn't like the material Sanobar and I were writing. I had the feeling that Mr. Turan was afraid to openly criticize the authorities in Uzbekistan, because in these broadcasts we openly discussed the problems in Uzbekistan.

My boss started to raise his voice at me for no reason. Sometimes he would even scream, behave in a macho manner, and treat me the way he would treat women in Afghanistan. I couldn't allow myself to be demeaned while working for an American radio station, when I had been demeaned enough in my own country.

When I was on sick leave, Mr. Turan fired me for some unknown reason. I was in shock. He fired me according to the American "Hire and Fire" principle. But he forgot that he was in Germany, where there were socialist laws which usually upheld the rights of the workers. I ended up having to sue the radio station, and nine months later I was reinstated. When I returned, they had a new director, Kevin Klose. He had worked for a long time as a correspondent for an American newspaper in Moscow. I decided to talk to him and explain the entire conflict I had been having with my boss. I also asked him to let me run my own programs. When I told Mr. Klose about who I was working with and under what conditions, his hair stood on end. He immediately ordered Mr. Turan to leave me in peace and said that in the future I would be in charge of my own programming. Hurrah! It was another victory over backwardness and the macho culture.

After that, everyone in the editorial office immediately started respecting me and treating me radically different. After all, people in this world love the strong!

Independence of Uzbekistan

On June 20, 1990, Uzbekistan became the eighth Soviet republic - and the first in Central Asia - to declare its independence.

The first thing the new Uzbek government did was to immediately start restoring prerevolutionary names that had been changed by the Soviet regime, and naming streets in honor of Central Asian folk heroes, like Tamerlane. For example, all the statues of Lenin and Karl Marx were replaced by statues of Tamerlane.

In those days, there were already two major political parties in Uzbekistan: "Birlik" (which means "unity") and "Erk" ("liberty").

While the Baltic nationalist movements were winning elections, defying Moscow, and proclaiming independence, the Uzbeks were merely pushing for the reinstatement of the Uzbek language. Other republics were ahead of Uzbekistan in demanding economic sovereignty; in 1988-1989, the main Uzbek economic demands were a reduction in quotas and the opportunity to diversify agriculture.

The leader of Birlik was a young scientist named Abdyrahim Polatov. Birlik's first priority was not only to address the most pressing issues in Uzbekistan, but to rouse Uzbeks from their political passivity and create a new, self-consciousness nationalism. "The main goal of our movement is to educate people, to raise their social consciousness and their political activism," Polatov explained. "Only the people themselves can stand up for their own rights. Our movement will be virtually powerless if the people keep on hibernating politically. So our main goal is to awaken the people and create a politically active society." Their national movement was fairly modest in size and in ambition.

The Erk party leader, Mohammad Solikh, was a poet and a writer. He advocated conservative pro-Islamic nationalism, which played on traditional themes, and was less secular and modern than Birlik.

I met both of these men when I went to visit my family in Tashkent in early 1990. The excitement over *glasnost* and democracy could be felt everywhere. People had started openly speaking and criticizing the government. Everyone was talking about Uzbek independence, but no one had any concrete idea as to what freedom and independence were. My Afghan colleagues on Radio Liberty had more of a sense of freedom than the Uzbeks. They couldn't understand that you can't develop a sense of freedom or democracy; you have to grow up with it. It's no accident that Moses led his people around the desert for 40 years, so that a new generation, which had never known slavery, could be born. Freedom, as Spinoza defined it, is not an external condition, it is a state of mind. Freedom is not outside of us; it's inside of us, if it exists at all. And if a person is free, no external forces can change or transform his thoughts and actions.

But Uzbeks have a particular national trait: they are yes-men. This is a very Eastern trait. People pay attention to what their higher-ups want and never say "no" to them. "So long as the Communist party is in power here, there will only be small changes in Uzbekistan." Unfortunately, Uzbekistan still has a communist government.

Never in my conversations with Uzbek activists did I hear any talk of secession from the Soviet Union. Uzbeks still felt dependent upon the Russians. Unlike their peers in Georgia, Moldavia, or the Baltic Republics, Uzbeks had not really broken out of their colonial mentality. Central Asian republics were far more conservative politically than the other republics. When independence was new, people were ecstatic about all the new things they could say and do and see. But today people are noticing that in fact, nothing in their lives actually changed. Ultimately, people become disenchanted.

At the same time, Uzbekistan was moving toward a market economy. You had to spent hours and hours to find things that were necessary for daily life, like food, soap, sugar, and even salt. There were no supermarkets or department stores as there are in Western countries. You couldn't do all your shopping under one roof. Instead, you had to go to numerous small kiosks all over the city to find even the basics. People would stand in line for hours to buy something at the store. There were shortages of staples such as sugar, flour, and eggs, which would disappear from the shelves for several weeks at a time.

Despite the privatization of many state-owned enterprises - from major industries to small stores - land couldn't be privately owned and the agricultural sector was still controlled by the government. People were also suffering from hyperinflation, which wiped out the savings of many people who had spent decades putting aside their hard-earned rubles.

Moreover, like many other Uzbeks, those of my family members who worked in both the public and private sectors were not paid for months at a time. Sometimes they would receive their salaries "in kind" – i.e., they would be paid in goods which ranged from soap to underwear, which they, in turn, sold at the market.

Fortunately, most Uzbeks had gardens where they grew their own food, and since they had big families, they could support one other. Nonetheless, most people would still go to work in the hope that they would get their salaries on time.

When I came back, I decided to organize a series of round tables, to which I would invite western specialists, politicians, and the Uzbek opposition leaders to discuss ecological problems, women's issues, and a number of other topics relevant to Uzbekistan during that time.

I had a very good relationship with both opposition leaders, and they were happy to participate in the round table discussions. Because Polatov and Solikh were competing all the time, I gave both of them equal opportunities to express their opinions on the air.

The Aral Sea

I prepared a series of programs on the topic of the catastrophe of the Aral Sea. The Aral Sea is the greatest tragedy of the Uzbek people. Once a great inland salt-water sea, the Aral Sea is dying for lack of water. At one point it was 26,000 square miles in size - more than the combined sizes of the states of Massachusetts, Connecticut, Rhode Island, and New Hampshire. Since then, it has decreased in size by 70%. The pervasive cotton monoculture destroyed Uzbekistan's water cycle – and the human cycle of life as well.

Uzbek Women

On top of ecological problems, I was convinced that the problems of women and mothers should be addressed.

For many years, you see, women were told how wonderful life was in Soviet Uzbekistan, how happy our women were at work, how many doctors and engineers there were among them, and how joyfully they picked that magnificent snow-white cotton.

In other words, seventy years of Soviet rule had not ended exploitation.

Uzbek women, not Uzbek men, slaved away in the blazing sun for 10 or 12 hours at a time. They performed backbreaking labor, weeding the parched, dusty earth with small hand-scythes, or hunched over, dragging long harvest bags between their legs, and plucking cotton, boll by boll.

The suicide rate among women began to rise in 1990. Hundreds of young Uzbek women committed suicide by setting themselves on fire out of despair over their lives. They were protesting the exploitation and misery foisted on the poorest, most vulnerable segments of Uzbek society by cotton colonialism, as well as the conservative, macho ways of Uzbek and Islamic culture.

Understanding Islam

Suddenly Uzbeks returned to the mosque.

Organized by emissaries from Saudi Arabia and other Arab and Muslim countries, Uzbeks built hundreds of new mosques, launched various religious nationalist organizations, and reintroduced the hadj, the pilgrimage to Mecca. Even the newly elected president and former communist, Islam Karimov, visited Mecca.

Other important revivals were taking place among Muslims. In Samarkand, a mosque which was attended by 200-300 people back in the seventies was packed with 1500 worshippers on Fridays at noon in 1989. The number of students in the Islamic seminary in Bukhara tripled. In 1989 alone, 80 mosques were reopened in Uzbekistan. (Stalin had closed 26,000 mosques after the October Revolution.)

These days, religion is everywhere in Uzbekistan: in politics, in the stores, on the plane, in taxis, and now even in restaurants – everywhere, except where it should be, in people's hearts, telling people how to behave in those places.

I started a new series with a religious scholar on "Basic Islam", because, as I said, people at that time had no idea about religion. People start to go to the mosque because it was fashionable. There was also the danger of being brainwashed by orthodox religions, especially Wahhabism, which came to Uzbekistan from Saudi Arabia and Pakistan. In the early 90s, they attracted a lot of young people (mainly unemployed young men from the countryside) to radical Islam by paying them large sums of money.

I invited different religious scholars from different countries to a roundtable, where they discussed the Qur'an and the role of women in Islam.

Beside the series on religion, I prepared a cycle of programming related to democracy and the market economy. I invited specialists from western countries to explain the concepts of democracy and the market economy to listeners in Uzbekistan.

During my work at Radio Liberty, I had the opportunity to meet some very interesting people. In Germany, there were a lot of Uzbeks who had fought in the Soviet Army and ended up as POWs in German concentration camps. The Nazis created special groups for former Soviet soldiers. All the soldiers from the Muslim regions of the Soviet Union were brought together in the Turkestan division to fight against the Russians and liberate Kazakhstan, Turkmenistan, Uzbekistan, Kyrgyzstan, and Tajikistan. Vali Kayum Khan and Baymirza Hayit were appointed the leaders of the Turkestan division. Both of these men enjoyed respect among Uzbeks abroad.

When I met them, these interesting men were old and very private. They seldom gave interviews to people they didn't know.

325

They had to be careful, because they were sure that KGB agents were after them. I was lucky to meet them, especially Vali Kayum Khan, who was a well-educated person. Born in Tashkent to a rich family before the October Revolution, he was sent by his parents to study in Paris and Germany. During WWII he was captured by the Nazis and became the president of Turkestan in exile. He hated the communists because they nationalized all his family's belongings, and a number of his family members disappeared during the Stalinist era. He told me a lot of things about his life and what he had gone through. I was fortunate to be able to record a conversation with him.

Even today it's impossible to say Vali Kayum Khan's name openly, but it's unclear why. He seemingly fought for the liberation of Uzbekistan, although it is true that he did so on the side of the fascists, and Uzbekistan was already free. When my dad came to Germany, we visited Vali Kayum Khan. He tried to write an article about him during Gorbachev's *glasnost* period, when the press was relatively free, but the authorities wouldn't let him.

The same thing happened with Baymirza Hayit. He became the only Turkistan scholar in Germany and published a number of books about the history of Central Asia, but was not even allowed to enter his own country in the early 1990s. I was happy that I was able to meet such interesting people. Unfortunately, they died before they were able to fulfill their last wish - to visit their homeland, where their families, which they hadn't seen for over 50 years, were still living.

I was successful at this job and enjoyed organizing all these programs and meeting these interesting people. I was independent and my colleagues started respecting me. They would even ask me for advice.

In 1990, Radio Liberty was able to hire journalists from the newly independent countries. The Kyrgyz and Tatar services hired young women. I was excited, thinking I would have colleagues who shared my outlook on things. But I soon realized something was wrong. When I greeted them in the hallway, they were very unfriendly. They refused to speak Russian with me, and I finally understood why: they were victims of the same "dedovshchina" (military hazing) as I had been in the beginning.

One day I invited the three of them for a cup of coffee and told them my story. They admitted that they were having the same difficulties I had had at the beginning: problems with their Turkish and Afghan colleagues due to language and mentality. Their colleagues warned them not to interact with me, because I had a bad reputation and was very independent. I laughed and offered to be their friend, because we were from the same background, and I told them that they didn't need to be afraid of these people. It was hard for them, because this was a job that all young people in their countries were dreaming of. They had been chosen from among hundreds of candidates, so they were afraid of having a bad relationship with their bosses and being sent back. I understood them well and told them to let me know if they needed any help. After a while, we are all became good friends.

The early 1990s were a very challenging time for everyone in the former Soviet Union. For Soviet citizens born and bred in an economy with "full employment" and where social services were guaranteed by the government, unemployment became a terrifying part of the reality of the new market economy. More and more factories and plants went out of business, and all of the state-owned businesses closed their doors. Organized crime, money laundering, pyramid schemes, racketeering, corruption, inflation, a lack of clear commercial laws, and the collapse of many of the new banks took a toll on the former Soviet economy.

During my work at Radio Liberty, I no longer suffered from the nostalgia that had plagued me ever since I moved abroad. I always missed my big family. I missed spending time sitting with my friends in the kitchen over multi-course meals, and spending hours drinking amber-colored strong black tea by candlelight in Dubna. But at Radio Liberty, I was surrounded by interesting people from all over the former Soviet Union. Numerous actors, musicians, and writers came to Radio Liberty. It was no longer dangerous for Soviet citizens to visit the enemy's radio station, as it had been before.

In 1995, the US Congress decided to move Radio Liberty to Prague in the Czech Republic. I couldn't follow them to Prague because of my family, and I was very sad to lose this job. At the same time, the BBC was opening a Central Asian Service

Department in London. I applied for the job, and one day I got a call. Two people from the BBC came to Munich to meet with me. During our conversation, they want to know my ideas for a new radio station in London. I shared my experience and ideas with them, because I was pretty sure that I would work with them in the future.

I didn't hear from them for a month - no thank you letter or anything. Then, one of my friends who had interviewed for this position in Tashkent told me about a woman named Dilorom who had started working for the BBC. She went to Tashkent to hire people for this service, and mainly chose her friends and acquaintances. I was disappointed by the unprofessional behavior of those in charge of hiring for the BBC.

Beginning in 1990, it was easy to hire journalists in Uzbekistan to work for former "enemy" stations, like Radio Liberty, Voice of America, and the BBC. In Prague, Radio Liberty had all new people in the Uzbek department. In Tashkent, Radio Liberty hired young professional journalists. In March 1995, I was in Tashkent where I met and interviewed some of these journalists, and when I came back, I recommended them to the Radio Liberty management.

In June, the radio station moved to Prague, and a very painful period began for me. I would spend the whole day at home and was very lonely. I looked for a new job, but it was impossible to find anything with my background. Even though my knowledge of German was satisfactory, I was not German. I continued on as a lecturer in International Studies in the Turkish Department at Munich University, where I had started teaching when I was still working at Radio Liberty. I lectured on the culture, economics, literature, languages, and politics of Central Asia (especially Uzbekistan) once a week. But this was not enough, and sometimes I didn't know how to keep myself busy. During the day, the kids were at school. At the employment agency, they suggested that I continue my postgraduate education. I started taking classes during the day at the International Business Academy. That kept me busy, but I missed my job, and I started to get nostalgic for both my job and my family in Uzbekistan. In the morning I would wake up with pain in my heart, but I couldn't do anything - my family was here. My kids were busy teenagers, and my husband worked during the day. I attended the business school 8 hours a day. Almost all my friends had moved with the radio station to Prague; we visited them there several times. Prague is a beautiful city, and Radio Liberty had a facility right downtown.

In November 1996, my husband was offered a position in the US. I was very excited about this.

I was looking forward to moving to the New World. In 1994, I had gone to New York to visit my friends and fell in love with this city. I liked everything about it. There were so many opportunities there!

During the 10 days I was there, I saw a Broadway show, visited museums, and met with some friends. When I came back, I told my husband that I would like to live in America. I wanted to escape my boring life in rural Eching, where I didn't know any of my neighbors. Like all Germans, the people in Eching were very reserved and not very friendly. When we bought our house in early 1990, I didn't expect that my next neighbors wouldn't even greet me. To see my friends, I had to drive over 10 miles to downtown Munich. Since Radio Liberty had moved to Prague, I missed all my friends and was miserable in boring Germany. Moreover, my kids were constantly having problems with the authoritarian style of the school system. If you were lucky and the gymnasium accepted you, you had to excel in all subjects. That, of course, is impossible; I have never met a person who was talented in both science and languages. If you weren't good at all those subjects, you might have to repeat the year. My daughter was talented in languages, literature, and the humanities, but was not good in science. She got top grades in the humanities, but bad grades in science. Problems with the school constantly soured our family life. I remember a conversation with my son's English teacher, who told me: "I promise you, your son will never ever learn English!"

I never ever heard a good word from my kid's teachers about them, but I always heard complaints: they were unable to learn this or that. Both my kids hated their school and their teachers.

This one was one of main reasons I wanted to go to America. I didn't want the German school system to spoil my kids' childhoods.

Meanwhile, I finished my postgraduate program at the Bavarian Academy of Economics. In July 1997, we sold our house and were ready to move to Michigan.

Chapter 18.

America

When we arrived the Detroit airport, it was very hot and sunny. The first thing that impressed me was the ethnic diversity. It was unusual for us to see Asians, Africans, Hispanics, and ethnic blends, since we had come from an ethnically homogeneous place. People were very friendly; everybody around was smiling. We rented a car and set off for our apartment.

The streets were very wide, just like in the Soviet Union. There were no cities at all, just countryside. I was looking for a city, as I was pretty sure that our apartment was located in a city. After driving for almost 40 minutes, we ended up at an apartment in a subdivision in Lake Orion. We easily found the townhouse which Jurgen's company had rented for us. Here this type of residence is called an apartment, but by German standards, it could easily be considered a house. It was furnished, with 3 bathrooms, and every bedroom had a bath. What a luxury! We were surprised to find a welcome cake on the doorstep. It was very nice.

The apartment was furnished in a style that was old-fashioned by European standards. Everything looked antique: the sideboard, the covers on the sofas and chairs, and the fake flowers, which were considered to be in bad taste in Europe. We didn't feel very comfortable with this furniture. It was a pain to have to jump into the tall American bed every night. The thin sheet covered by the bedspread was constantly slipping off of us. I couldn't even imagine how we would sleep in the cold of winter under such a thin blanket. But we really liked the fact that each of us had his or her own toilet as well as a bathtub or a shower, where you could stand under a strong stream of water as long as you wanted without worrying about how much it cost. It wasn't surprising that Americans took baths every day.

331

In the morning it was finally time for us to discover America! We decided to go out for breakfast. We didn't know where to go, so we stopped into the first supermarket we saw, Farmer Jacks. When we asked where the nearest restaurant was, two employees suddenly looked at one another, then, raising their brows in surprise, asked, "You all need to go?"

We later found out what had surprised them: instead of saying "restaurant," we had said "restroom". This was just the beginning of our adventures in English.

Along with amazement came disappointment. Our first breakfast was terrible. The coffee was made out of god knows what – it was some brown-colored liquid. The more we went to restaurants in the US, the more we were disappointed in American food.

After I arrived in the US, I was upset because of several cultural differences. The more I compared the new world to the old, the more I wanted to go back to Europe. It was awful to have to get used to streets without pedestrians, there was no public transportation, and the food was bad. One day we went to Detroit, and instead of seeing a city like Chicago or New York, we saw empty streets and ruins. At first, we thought that we just hadn't found the downtown, but imagine my disappointment when I realized that this really was Detroit. I cried for two days as I couldn't imagine having to live in the countryside. At that point, I could never have imagined that exactly 20 years later I would open what would become a successful Detroit tourist company, would passionately show visitors the city as it was coming back to life, and would be madly in love with Detroit.

Nothing was as I had imagined it would be; moreover, we found out that I wouldn't be able to get a job in the near future, because getting a work visa would take a lot of time. I was ready to go back!!

But then Alishér started school and for the first time ever, he liked it! He was attending the International Academy, which had an International Baccalaureate program.

A few days after we moved in, I went to sign Alishér up for this school. The principal was a man named Bert Okma. Later, when I became the coordinator of the International Center of this school, Bert and I would become good friends. But when we first met, I was under the impression of all the Hollywood movies I had watched, and I bombarded him with questions, which he would later recall with laughter: Did they have police in the school? Are there shootings? How many kids were doing drugs? Etc.

Alishér now had an unusual reason to go to school, then come home and work until late on his homework: he suddenly had a lot of friends of different ethnicities. There were a lot of Germans students whose parents had come here like us to work. The majority of them were supportive of him and eventually became close friends.

I later realized another reason why, in spite of his weak English, he was suddenly interested in school: the teachers constantly praised him. When children are told that they can do something and that they are trying, they start believing it. Here, unlike in my country or in Germany, teachers weren't allowed to yell and swear at the children. Only praise was allowed, and this is not only pleasant, but, in my opinion, motivational.

I knew the Soviet and European educational systems well, but after a while, I concluded that the American educational system is one of the best. The system was created to work with children whatever their level of ability. I really liked the fact that they would draw up individualized programs for children based on their competencies. And children could move to different levels of difficulty in any given subject, if they so wished.

If, for example, a child knows computer science well, then he doesn't need to sit bored in the same class with his fellow 9th grade students – he can go study with the 11th graders. This is possible because you have your own class schedule in US high schools, just as you would in a university. I liked the fact that this educational system was extremely flexible, that the schools offered a wide variety of classes, and that the students got to choose the ones they needed. The flexibility of this educational system allows students to specialize in certain disciplines. Seeing how much Alishér liked the school, I knew I had no choice but to reconcile myself to the situation and get used to this new life. What else could I do?

I decided to change my attitude and to look at everything as an adventure. In other words, I would act as if I was lucky to have come to this country and remember that I had to discover America for myself, which I had already begun to do. I immediately felt better! And I started liking a lot of things! For example, Americans are very friendly people. They introduce themselves and others right away and ask questions out of curiosity. They always say, "Nice to meet you" when parting. They start conversations with small talk and compliments. During conversations with Americans, you will hear them say things like, "Not bad," "Ok," "Great," "Awesome," "Amazing," and "I love it" a lot. You hear such things from the cashier at the supermarket, from the realtor, and from others. I like that Americans are confident, self-assured, and empowered.

Americans are very free, but in a communist society, behaving as if you are free is always viewed with suspicion. We couldn't allow ourselves the luxury of being free. We couldn't think freely, behave freely, express our reactions freely, or do or say what we wanted. We couldn't allow ourselves the luxury of being ourselves. Psychologically, we were slaves.

I started liking Americans and their optimism more and more. I liked that the core unit of American society is indeed the family. Americans are constantly asking about one another's families, and this reminds me of Uzbek culture. According to Americans, "We are a family that welcomes everyone who shares our family values." For me, that's what America is: a large family which anyone can belong to, as long as you accept those values. This was very different from Germany, where no one invited you to be part of their country, and that is why I never felt at home there. When anyone moves to the US, the local people say, "Welcome to our country! When are you going to apply to citizenship?" If you move to Europe, they usually ask, "Where you from and when you are going back home?"

It took me two years to understand Americans. In spite of the differences in mentality and culture, I eventually became comfortable living in this country, and I realized that it suited me better than Europe. People here are just as open, welcoming, and social as in my native land, plus it is very easy to make friends. Moreover, a large number of Russian speakers lived nearby, and with time we became friends with a lot of them. Unlike the Russian-speaking immigrants in Germany, the immigrants in the US had jobs in their professions: some were doctors, others were engineers, and others were business owners. Millions of immigrants in Germany are highly qualified professionals (for example, doctors, engineers, and highly qualified workers), but their degrees and certificates aren't recognized. Most migrants to Germany are forced to take jobs that don't correspond to their professional qualifications. So, for example, every other taxi-driver in Germany is probably better educated than his passengers.

Migrants to Germany have fewer opportunities in the educational system and on the labor market. Migrants are nearly twice as likely as Germans to be unemployed. Teenagers from migrant families are much more likely to end up in "Hauptschule" (a second-tier educational track for weaker students) than children from German families, and are nearly twice as likely to drop out of school. Thus, many are deprived of the opportunity of getting a higher education. And as education is often not valued very much in immigrant families, the cycle continues, and many second-generation migrants live on government assistance, despite isolated instances of success.

A significant percentage of migrants, especially Turks, live in what is practically a "parallel universe". Not only do migrants have a lower educational level and higher rates of unemployment, they also participate less in public life than the German population. Insofar as many of those from Turkey tend to live "among their own" - and there are established Turkish neighborhoods in many German towns – they have less contact with other ethnic groups. That makes learning German, and, ultimately, integration, more difficult for both children and adults.

Nonetheless, there is a widely held belief that migrants are taking jobs from Germans. Right-wing extremist groups use this misconception in their campaigns against foreigners. The flip side of the coin is this: a country that doesn't take advantage of the knowledge and professional skills of its migrants is passing up opportunities for development.

I remember the release of the book *Germany Abolishes Itself,* written by the well-known German politician Thilo Sarrazin. The main idea of the book is that the country is getting progressively stupider because the only people having children are Muslim immigrants and the unemployed. He also wrote that "all Jews share a certain gene," as do members of the French and Spanish Basque communities. Judging by the extensive excerpts from this book in the press, the author is basically saying nothing new. He is, as he was in the past, fixated on the "excess number" of foreigners in Germany who, in his opinion, bring nothing but harm to the country. He was especially hard on Turks and Moroccans - and basically any and all Muslims - who he sees as complete welfare bums and who, instead of working, do nothing but bring "girls in headscarves" into the world. Buying and selling vegetables doesn't count. And the German taxpayer is paying through the nose for this lopsided "demographic". Moreover, in the opinion of the author, the country is getting increasingly stupid thanks to the overwhelming number of Muslims.

In Germany, there was always an atmosphere of "ingrained racism," and the government doesn't work hard enough to eradicate this problem. I don't even think the creation of a multicultural society in Europe is possible! Even the German Chancellor, Angela Merkel, admitted at one point, "Of course the tendency had been to say, 'Let's adopt the multicultural concept and live happily side by side, and be happy to be living with each other.' But this concept has failed, and failed utterly."

Let's ask ourselves the question – what exactly "failed" in Germany? Multiculturalism? Democracy? Or something different, something that purported to be these ever so important things? Let me remind you that multiculturalism presupposes peaceful coexistence and cooperation in a single society with different cultural communities. In "classical" multiculturalism, the minority has the ability to express its ethnic characteristics not only at home, but on the street and in social life, create relevant social organizations, not hide its religious beliefs, etc.

Multicultural societies have in fact existed for the entirety of human history. Ancient Rome and Muslim/Orthodox-Christian

Constantinople, the Golden Horde (until its official adoption of Islam under Khan Uzbek), and the Russian Empire, which is simultaneously the heir of Constantinople and the Golden Horde, were multicultural. Even my homeland Uzbekistan was multicultural. Over a hundred ethnic groups, including Greeks, Ukrainians, and Uyghurs, lived next to one another. I see America as a multicultural country, because many different ethnic groups peacefully coexist. There are lots of other examples.

In big German cities like Berlin, Koln, Rostock, and Hamburg, there is intense "ghettoization" of immigrants. Immigrants have trouble renting apartments, and thus are often forced to live in specific neighborhoods, and this interferes with their successful integration into German society.

This even happened to me. When I needed to rent an apartment in Munich, I had to call the owners of the apartment time and again for weeks, because as soon as they heard my accent, they would hang up. I will never forget how my daughter, who speaks perfect German, managed to get someone to show us an apartment, but when we got close to the house, she asked me not to speak so they wouldn't know I was a foreigner. At that moment my anger pierced my heart like a dagger. It was then that I decided to move to America and never return, because I wanted to live in a country where I was respected as a person irrespective of my ethnic background!

In America, immigrants and their children drive the country. Unlike monocultural Europe, which doesn't allow immigrants to assimilate, multicultural America gives them the opportunity to blossom.

The situation with the immigrants themselves is also different in the US, too. Second-generation immigrants want most of all to become Americans and to be accepted as Americans. Many of them purposefully try to get rid of the vestiges of their ethnic heritage, which is why the children of first-generation immigrants usually don't speak their parents' native language. In other words, immigrants in the US assimilate far better than their immigrant counterparts in Europe.

Immigrants in the US would also say that they are very happy here and that don't want to go back home, because America offers their children opportunities that were unthinkable where they came from. This is different from the way immigrants in Germany behaved; there they were constantly complaining. Immigrants would come to Europe to work and send their money home, thus remaining cultural and emotional foreigners for generations.

Germany is one of the few countries in the world that still largely bases its citizenship on "blood". For example, immigrants from Russia, Romania, and Poland who have never been to Germany, who can't speak a word of German, and who are totally unfamiliar with the German way of life can come here and automatically lay claim to German citizenship because their forebearers emigrated from some German territory centuries ago. On the other hand, a Turk, Italian, Croat, Spaniard or Yugoslavian who was born and bred in Germany, who has never seen his or her parents' homeland, who speaks fluent German, and who would be like a fish out of water living in any other country, doesn't qualify as full-fledged German citizen. It's the opposite in the US: irrespective of ethnic background, anyone can become a citizen.

In the US, my friends' children, who are part of the second generation of immigrants, became doctors and lawyers, and full-fledged members of society. They would proudly call themselves "Americans" and consider themselves to be real patriots of this country. I never met a Turk in Germany, even a third- or fourth-generation immigrant, who legitimately considers himself a German.

American Patriotism

Everyone probably knows that Americans are patriotic. I was first annoyed by the flags on every house and in every lawn, because it was unusual to see German flags flying on flagpoles and hotel roofs. You don't see the German flag often, and in fact, since 1945, Germans have rarely allowed themselves to fly their flag.

It took me a long time to understand the importance of Independence Day, and why it is such a major holiday, as well as why, beginning in kindergarten, everyone in the country sings the national anthem, sincerely, and with their hands on their hearts.

Yes, that's how it is. And it seems to be very simple and straightforward. It seems like you hang the flag on your door, learn the words to the anthem, and that's it – you are also a patriotic American. Americans really and truly love their country, their homeland. Yes – country and homeland!

But they don't love the government, the president, or Congress. Unfortunately, for many of those who lived in the countries of the former Soviet Union, the words "country" and "government" mean the same thing. And that's not surprising, because for years we were taught to love the government under the guise of our country. Consequently, for millions of people these two words came to mean the same thing.

And that is the difference. And it is precisely for this reason that Americans are truly patriotic, whereas we aren't. Americans wave their flags because they love the city where they were born and the school they attended. We had "Red Patriotism", because, I repeat, we were taught to love the government and the leadership under the guise of country and homeland. That's why we – and the Europeans – don't understand the concept of American patriotism, and it often annoys us, because it is genuine.

Why I Decided To Live In America

The Things Which I Couldn't Accept In Germany, Even After Living There For Many Years

Friendship

For Germans, the word "friend" is a special status conferred only on special, very close relationships. Germans would consider what Americans call "friends" as merely "gute bekannter" ("good acquaintances"). I am very social and a people person and like to make friends easily.

It is known that the Germans are complicated people. To be friends with someone in Germany is to have achieved a very special status that took a lot of time and emotional investment. When I moved back to Germany in 2009 for 2 years, I was unable to make any friends. The only people I made friends with were Americans living in Germany.

339

Smiling

The German attitude toward strangers is one of coldness and suspicion. If you stroll along most German streets, it is easy to get the impression that smiles are a rationed commodity around here. I remember when I moved back to Munich from the US, my neighbor, who lived next to me, tried to avoid me when we ran into each other, because I would smile when I greeted her. Apparently, it would have been a lot of work for her to do the same in return.

If you are looking for a place where the vast majority of people are friendly, helpful and warm, as well as open and considerate, you've probably chosen the wrong country.

Pessimism

A deep capacity for gloom is one of the qualities a dark history has bequeathed to this people. They know all too well that things can go terribly wrong.

Germans also worry a lot. And if they are not busy worrying about some problem, they are probably worrying about why they are not worrying. This is typical of Russians and Uzbeks too.

Time

Germans plan everything; they even have to make plans if they just want to spend an evening at home. One thing to always remember is the German obsession with time, and the fact that there is a proper time for everything. You can never be late; even if you are invited for afternoon coffee or dinner, you are supposed to be on time. Being late by even one minute is considered rude. This habit became so deeply engrained in me, that my American friends would sometimes laugh at me and say that they could set their watches by me. It took me a while to adjust to this; because in Uzbek culture it's just the opposite: being on time especially if you are the guest, is considered to be rude.

FKK

FKK means "Freikorpekultur", or "Free body culture". The idea of "Korperkultur" or "body culture" was developed at the end of 19th Century to encourage comfortable, urban middle-class

Germans to get out more and loosen their collars. At the dawn of the 20th Century, Germans developed a national urge to get naked.

In the former East Germany, where there was once no freedom of movement or speech, being naked was one of the few possible expressions of freedom. With my background, I couldn't accept this part of German culture. I couldn't be with my in-laws on the same beach naked. I couldn't enjoy being naked with my friends or coworkers in the sauna. No, no, and no!!!!

What I Miss About Germany

Bread, Cake, and German Hospitality

But there some nice things I miss from Germany! Like Coffee shops with Kaffee und Kuchen. In Germany, when you want to get to know someone better, the next step isn't getting together at home for cocktails, as in France, or for dinner, as in the United States, but for cake and coffee on a weekend afternoon. Like coffee, kuchen probably came to Germany from Austria.

When I lived in Germany, there was nothing more enjoyable than coming home to visit my husband's parents and grandparents and getting together over a cup of coffee and some delicious cake made by my in-laws. I also liked to meet up with friends in coffee shops, which ranged from elegant to cozy, to catch up. You would often see elderly, nicely dressed ladies sitting in the café and chatting, as well as young people, who like their afternoon cake.

When I went to visit German family members and friends at home, I knew there would be a nice spread of pastries, cream cakes, fruit flans, and biscuits. Whether it was a Sunday, a holiday, a birthday, or just a regular weekday, there was always time for a tasty afternoon break!

You can find so many different varieties of cakes in Germany. In the summer, most *kuchens* are made with the fruit that's in season - particularly strawberries or rhubarb. In the winter, cakes are made with dried fruits, along with such standbys as chocolate, custard, and poppy seeds. Unlike in the US, with its easy-bake brownies and muffins, German cake recipes aren't always quick and easy. They are often complicated affairs, with multiple layers of cake and cookie bases, cream and fruit or jam fillings, plus a special topping.

I always liked watching Juergen's mother and grandmothers make these dishes. I am glad that I was able to hold onto all my old German cake recipes, and from time to time I spoil my friends by making them.

One of the other things I miss most is good hearty German bread. The Germans take bread making to a whole new culinary level, and for many Germans, bread is their favorite dish in the world. My mouth waters at the memory of delicious *Walnussbrot, Kuminbrot,* and other baked German delicacies.

Bread in Germany is more than just a part of the daily meal; it's part of the culture. Germany is thought to be the country with the widest variety of breads, and each region has its own variations. Some bread is made of wheat and rye flour and, quite frequently, whole meal, as well as whole seeds such as linseeds, sunflower seeds, or pumpkin seeds (*Vollkornbrot*).

The first thing I usually do when I go back to Germany is get my morning rolls, known in Germany as *Brötchen*, which is a diminutive of *Brot* ("bread"). I enjoy them cut in half and spread with *Butterkäse* (butter cheese), honey, jam, cold cuts such as lunch meat, or fish. At lunchtime I get *Laugenbrezel*, pretzels with Bratwurst, *Fleischkäse* or a pair of *Weißwurst*, Bavarian white sausage.

Nonetheless, for me the plusses in Germany were outweighed by the minuses. And most important of all is the fact that in the US, I felt at home for the first time in my life. I wasn't always being insulted, as I was in Uzbekistan, because I had fair skin. Or as I was in Russia and Ukraine, just because I was Uzbek. In the US, I finally stopped feeling like a stranger.

Chapter 19.

"Ташкент или ностальгия по городу которого нет"
or
"Tashkent, Or Nostalgia For A City That Doesn't Exist"

Many years after I left Uzbekistan, I found myself back in Tashkent. As I expected, from the moment I arrived in the airport, Tashkent smelled not of fried onions and pastries, as in the past, but like some other foreign city. And of the huge community that had once lived in this city, in my city, a city that had been home to tons of my relatives, friends, acquaintances, and neighbors, only those family members who had gotten stuck here for one reason or another still remained. Over the years of my absence, the people of Tashkent had been scattered around the world. The majority of them had gone to Moscow, Jerusalem, St. Petersburg, New York, or Germany.

I instantly realized that the Tashkent I remembered was gone, and in its place, there was another, unfamiliar city. My favorite places in Tashkent had disappeared, the names of streets and squares had changed, and suddenly there were different faces. Even use of languages had changed. People no longer spoke Russian much in Tashkent, it was used less, and the generation of my nephews doesn't know it at all. The Russian spoken in Tashkent used to be purer than the Russian spoken in Moscow; it was literary Russian. It was unclear if this language had managed to survive anywhere.

Everyone in Tashkent used to speak proper Russian, because year in and year out there were more and more Russian White Army officers, and many members of the Russian elite had graduated from

343

Oxford and Cambridge. In a word – they were all part of the Russian elite. In the 1920s, they all poured into the young republic of Turkestan and founded entire dynasties of doctors and scholars here. And how many evacuated writers, cinematographers, actors, and scholars lived here during the war? The level of the intelligentsia per capita in Tashkent was much higher than average in the country.

And in spite of all this, the native language of the majority of people was still Uzbek. But Uzbeks easily went from one language to the other, playing with words.

Even today my sisters and I speak a mix of Uzbek and Russian; it's a deeply ingrained habit.

This was an unfamiliar city with renamed streets and full of crowds of uniform faces. I vaguely recognized some intersections and clearly remembered the events of my life that had taken place there, the people who had lived there, and why I felt such a pleasant sensation at the sight of the gigantic sycamore near the gates. Near some vacant lots in downtown Tashkent, I was inundated by the smells of Tashkent courtyards, the smell of fried onions and meat, sour milk, freshly baked bread in a tandoor oven, and blossoming trees. I instantly recognized neither the streets nor the places near and dear to my hart, but moments, episodes from my life that had taken place on these streets. Episodes of all kinds: happy, sad, and melancholy.

As I was approaching an old neighborhood in the city – a "mahalla", I saw an almost completely rebuilt Muslim complex with mosques and madrasas. Even today you could see the narrow alleyways with adobe houses and dikes, which could be found on almost every street. I remember how, in childhood, cool air came off the dikes on hot days and you could hear the sound of running water, which was very calming.

Suddenly I remembered the days during my childhood when it snowed, and we would run and slide down the hill here for hours, until we could feel clay, instead of melting snow, under our butts.

Or how I would wake up at 5 am from the deafening sound of *karnays* and *surnays* (traditional Uzbek instruments) signaling reveille at Uzbek weddings and inviting people to morning *plov* in a neighboring house. It was here that real Uzbeks, the native inhabitants of Tashkent, had always lived. I saw men in Uzbek robes and embroidered skullcaps. They were sitting on ledges, smoking, and gather in the evening at the teahouse. It seemed that time here had stopped a few centuries ago. I was filled with longing for a Tashkent that was now gone...for my Tashkent.

The people of today's Tashkent don't even know that this city was like Babylon. A city where everyone was friendly with one another, and where people would fall in love and get married. Will the Tashkent Babylon ever exist again? Today the city is very uniform and lacking diversity. The departure of different ethnic groups has been a great loss for Tashkent. Aren't young people around the world trying to be multicultural? And in my Tashkent, we were multicultural. From childhood on we grew up surrounded by many different cultures and languages. Our culture was formed by the intermingling of these different languages, ethnic groups, rituals, and mentalities. Such lovely, utopian form of coexistence really existed at a certain point in history, but it is gone now.

The Tashkent that was built after the major earthquake in 1966 will always live in my memory. Much of the city was reconstructed then thanks to the efforts of ethnic groups from the various Soviet republics. In my Tashkent, there was a lot of greenery, parks, and squares.

It was so painful to realize that none of that exists any longer. I wanted to cry for my lost city.

The next day I decided to go look for the remnants of the city of my childhood with my sister. We naturally decided to start with the markets.

Alay Market

We went to the Alay Market, which is the oldest and most famous market in Tashkent. The history of the Alay Market goes back to ancient times, when Central Asia was part of the Great Silk Road. The name of the market ("Alay") comes from the "Oloy" Mountain. The local inhabitants (Kazakhs, Tajiks, Uzbeks, and Kyrgyz) who had settled around it traded here.

I so wanted to try flatbread freshly baked in a tandoor. It's not accidental that Tashkent is called the "City of Bread." This is true both literally and figuratively: the tastiest flatbreads made out of wheat flour are baked here. People buy them right on the street; each resident has his or her own favorite bakery street vendor. Whenever I would come home to visit, my mom would run over to the neighborhood baker to bring me freshly baked flatbread every morning. I am certain that I will never forget the smell of that flatbread. I have tried freshly baked bread in many countries around the world – from Bavarian pretzels, to French baguettes and croissants, but I have never tasted anything better than hot fragrant flatbread with sesame seeds exuding its amazing smell. I will probably miss the hot aroma of Uzbek flatbread till the end of my life. And probably only people from Tashkent can understand this!

But this place no longer bore any resemblance to my Alay Market at all! It had been completely rebuilt out of concrete and was colossal, with tons of jewelry and hard currency stores. I felt like I had been misled and brought to the wrong place. It would have been better if I hadn't come here at all, and instead, had preserved in my memory the market I used to pass through every day after school, deeply inhaling the aromas of fruits and shashlik (shish-kabobs), and hearing the endless calls of the local vendors inviting people to try all the eastern foods being sold.

Shakhantaur

We continued along our path to another part of the city, Shakhantaur. The Tashkent TV station where my father had worked was located there. I knew every corner of this neighborhood. There used to be a huge grocery store there, where you could buy anything you needed, and for 10 kopecks you could drink a glass of grape or tomato juice. There was no trace of it anymore. They had rebuilt everything, and on the spot where there used to be beautiful little Tashkent houses, there were now huge structures built in some incomprehensible style, along with cupolas, arches, and giant marble squares. What happened to the District Officers' Building and the Young People's Theater (TUZ), where I went many times to see children's shows? It used to be located on the square where the monument to the great Uzbek poet Alishér Navoi stood. The

346

only thing left in Shakhantaur was the old mosque. Now it stands like a gate to nowhere – to the city that disappeared when I left.

Beshagach

For me, Beshagach has always been associated with the Beshagach Market, the Lenin Komsomol Park, and Komsomol Lake, which was in the park. Together they created a certain unique atmosphere. And now I find out that that park is no longer there. Beshagach was the only place in the city that "Ear-Throat-Nose" pastries were sold for 4 kopecks at a certain time. You would have to arrive early because there would be a line. I will never forget the time when you could buy five whole pastries for 20 kopecks and treat your brothers and sisters. I was so proud of this.

And they were now doing something ostentatious and commercial with the lake. Well, what of it? Someone else's life will begin at this lake. The time of old Tashkent and the old park with its Komsomol Lake had passed. That generation was gone – some had left, and some had died. This is why many things die a natural death. But why so mercilessly destroy everything?

The Square

I realized all at once that the heart of Russian Tashkent, my beloved Revolution Square, was gone. In the mid-1990s, all the monuments in Tashkent to Russian writers (with the sole exception of Pushkin) were removed.

The authorities, under the cover of police cordons, had chopped down the trees on Revolution Square.

The central square of the former capital of Turkestan (first named Konstantinovsky Square, then Revolution Square, and now Amir Temur Square) was filled with beauty and powerful energy thanks to an alley lined with century-old sycamore trees and hundreds of historical oaks, chestnut trees, ash trees, and Ailanthus trees ("Trees of Heaven"), which were planted in the 1880s on the initiative of the second Governor-General of Turkestan, Michael Grigorievich Chernyaev. And then it turned out that all this had disappeared in an instant. The square, which had provided reliable shade in the hot months and fed the largest megapolis in Central

Asia with oxygen, had now been "cleansed" by the authorities of the heritage of the Russian period of history. Instead, in its place they erected an enormous equestrian colossus of Tamerlane ("Timur the Lame" or "Amir Temur"), the cruel and despotic conqueror of Asia, who had fought Khan Tokhtamysh of the Golden Horde and threatened Moscow.

Amir Temur (who is called Tamerlane in Europe) was victorious in the battle for power in Central Asia, and for nearly 40 years successfully ruled a vast state, whose borders he extended to the Mediterranean Sea, India, Chinese Turkestan, and Russia. Amir Temur transformed his capital Samarkand into a genuine "Rome of the East", adorning it, as well as other major cities in his empire (including Tashkent) with prominent buildings and other structures. At that time, a romantic atmosphere reigned under the crown of trees which attracted the broadest range of people, from amorous couples to prostitutes. But the main attraction on the square was neither the people, nor the café with fountains, nor the seed vendors, and not even the monument to Marx. It was the century-old sycamores. The trees were impressive. They were several yards around and old enough to remember the first governors of Turkestan, the 1917 Revolution, the 1966 earthquake, and the amorous pair Rodion Nakhapetov and Anastasia Vertinskaya from the famous movie *The Lovebirds*.

For me, the most important parts of the square were the Pinocchio Café and the Tashkent chimes, where people would meet for dates, business, and just get-togethers. Back then life was more carefree. Today everyone is busy, but back then we would just go hang out, and the starting place for us was often the chimes. The famous Tashkent chimes were on a tower that was 100 feet tall. They were a monument to the victory over the Nazis, and there is a legend that they came to Tashkent from the city hall building in East Prussia. How many meetings and dates took place under these chimes!

At one time the Snowball Café was located on the square. We could only buy 1/3 cup of the crème ice cream, which was served in shiny little metal vases, at a time. Shaped like balls, the ice cream melted quickly in the merciless sweltering summer heat in Tashkent. Two minutes after the ice cream was served, you had to drink it out of the little vase!! They also served milk shakes for 10 kopecks. I have looked all over the world for a similar milk shake, but never found one.

I so miss the scent of the real Tashkent, which left with its people.

The "30 Years Of The Komsomol" Movie Theater, Or "The Thirty"

We often skipped our classes and went to our favorite place: the squat old building of the "30 Years of the Komsomol" Movie Theater.

Every generation watched its movies here. During the showings, young people would kiss and press against one another in the back row. It was often a place for dates. The theater was the only place where you could be alone with a young man and not be noticed by your neighbors or relatives. When Juergen came to Tashkent, we went to this movie theater more than once. It was safe for an Uzbek girl to be in this neighborhood with a German.

I was told that they couldn't find sponsors for the restoration of the ruins of the famous "The Thirty" building, the phenomenal example of Art Nouveau architecture in Tashkent. When I saw an empty lot where the theater had once been, I realized that my city had simply disappeared off the face of the earth.

Karl Marx Street

You can now find vendors with long, unpronounceable new names selling their new handicrafts to tourists along the former Karl Marx Street. Now, this street is known to almost all residents of the city under its unofficial name, "Broadway," because it was made into a pedestrian mall in the late 1980s. Tashkent artists exhibited their works here, and there were numerous types of cafés and other similar establishments along it.

In Soviet times, Karl Marx Street was one of the streets most loved by Tashkent residents.

From November 1941 to March 1944, when she was evacuated to Tashkent during the war, the poet Anna Akhmatova lived in house No. 7.

The merchant Zakho built a grocery store at the corner of Karl Marx Street and Irdzharskaya Street (formerly Kirov Street), which was the central grocery store until 1966; now the Zarafshan restaurant is located at this site. After my music lessons, I loved to peek into this deli with my mother, which had such a huge selection of sausages. My favorite pastime was to wander aimlessly around Children's World [a children's store], which was located nearby; my grandmother, after much persuasion, bought me my very first German doll there for 5 rubles.

Suddenly I realized that the streets and squares, parks and squares of that "Babylonian" City of Tashkent had passed into oblivion. The city had entered a new chapter in its history.

I think people are characterized by their attachments to the places of their childhood and youth. Maybe because the image of you during the years when you were happy is captured in these places, like in a mirror or on the surface of a lake. But if the mirror is no longer there? And if those streets and buildings, trees and people who would remember you have disappeared from the face of the earth? Things should change gradually and majestically, they should be built thoroughly and not hastily, streets and squares should be named once and for all; their names shouldn't be changed to please a new ruler. It is bad when the memory of a person survives longer than the memory of a city, especially when that city was as charming and gracious as Tashkent was. The city protected and took care of all of us, but we did not save it! It was the end of a very strange civilization, which existed in a certain place in Central Asia for a short time due to a series of coincidences. And then it disappeared! It existed and then stopped existing... May that old, delicious, bright, peaceful Tashkent live on at the very least in memory.

Although the city does in fact live on - and it is probably flourishing - but now with different streets and squares, and with different monuments and idols. Perhaps a different text will be written in the new City, but this time it will be one that is outside of Russian literature, culture, and language ...

Chapter 20.

A Letter to My Grandchildren

A Letter From Sunshine Girl To Her Beloved Grandchildren

My Dear Grandchildren, Anni, Maxmilian, Milena and Rosalie, if you only knew how I love you!

My dear grandchildren, I don't know what things will be like by the time you read this, and I am not sure I have anything of value to help you navigate the world you will be living in, a world that I imagine will be both fantastic and frightening.

I was once a little girl, and, just like you, I was full of dreams and wanted to conquer the world. It wasn't easy, but I conquered it! In spite of all sorts of difficulties, nothing could stop me. You should always believe in yourselves and never give in.

Live life on your own terms. Do what you enjoy, and enjoy what you do. If you do, trust me: great things will follow.

Don't allow your head to always rule over your heart. Life is more fun when you say "yes" – so dream big and say "yes" to your heart's desires. The ability to dream is one of our greatest gifts. So look at the world with wide-eyed enthusiasm, and believe you are more powerful than the problems that confront you.

I always dreamed of traveling around the world. I remember sleeping outside in the summer when I was a little girl. I would look at the starry sky and make a wish to go far, far away and see different countries. I made that dream a reality. I have been to many countries around the world. I've lived in Europe, and now I live in the US. It wasn't easy. First, I went away to school in Odessa, then I followed my beloved to Germany. And I never gave in. Despite all the difficulties, I simply could not betray my dreams.

351

Never betray your dreams for the sake of fitting in. Instead, be passionate about them. Passion will help you stay the course and inspire others to believe in you and in your dreams. The world's greatest innovations have been driven by passionate people – those not willing to give up on their dreams. Passionate people spur the change that moves the world forward!

Each of us has special gifts and talents, so embrace everything that is unique about you. As you grow up, you will come to recognize these talents, and you will develop passions, and those passions will give your life goals and purpose.

If you want to be a singer, then sing. If you want to be a teacher, then teach. If you want to be an entrepreneur, then do that. Decide what is important to you and do it.

Whatever you do – throw your heart into it and listen to your heart's song.

I always wanted to be a ballerina or journalist, and life gave me the chance to realize one of those dreams, when I worked at Radio Liberty. I enjoyed every single day I worked there.

Never betray your dreams for the sake of fitting in. Every time I would watch a ballet or meet ballet dancers, I would admire their beautiful posture. I deeply regretted the fact that I hadn't fulfilled my wish to become a ballet dancer, and I still regret it today.

Don't hold back on dreams, love, or relationships.

Whatever you decide to do, it is important that you put your whole self into it. Give it your all. Take the brakes off and embrace your life and all that you do. You will find that it makes life much more fun, and you will get so much more out of it. Pursue your hopes and your dreams no matter how difficult or "different" they may seem to others.

There are beautiful people everywhere! Remember to treat people as you would like to be treated.

I have moved many times and to different places in my life. I always felt a certain sense of sadness when I left the familiar and replaced it with the unfamiliar. It was hard saying goodbye to friends, acquaintances, and support systems. It was challenging to start afresh and to meet new people. But I have learned that there are amazing people everywhere you go. People who will inspire you and who will become close friends. You will find people who you will love and who will love you. There are wonderful people no matter where you go. There are people in the world who you will simply adore. Just like that. For no reason whatsoever. You will be happy simply because they exist. They can be very far away, in different cities or even in different countries, but you know that they love you too. There will be people who take some time to get to know, and others that you will be good friends with right from the start – and these friendships will last for many years.

And when you have made friends with people, it will feel like you have always known them.

I remember how, right after I lost your grandfather, I was driving and crying bitterly for the umpteenth time, when I heard an interview on the radio with the Dalai Lama. The journalist asked him, "What has helped you continue living after all the difficulties you encountered in your life?" To which he replied, "I try to find something positive in everything." I thought, what positive thing can there be in my tragedy? And I was suddenly struck by the thought that it was my friends who were with me day and night during the hardest times in my life. There were a lot of them, real friends who had proved true in times of trouble. It's not for nothing that we say, "A friend in need is a friend indeed."

I was pleased to realize that my value is my friends. Thank you to Riva, Nellie, Zhenya, Nina, Lina, Sasha, Lyusya, Ann, Diane, Azar, Farah, Shameem, Gabriela, and Barb for being with me, supporting me, and helping me at my worst time of my life. The thing that brought me the greatest comfort was when my friends came by to talk and spend time with me. Even though they didn't necessarily know exactly what I was going through, they offered their time and attention when I needed it most.

Life has a way of bringing all of us a great deal of happiness, but it also has a way of hurting us. I was badly hurt when I lost your grandfather. It was as if my life had come to a standstill. I lost everything in an instant. I lost a beloved person, my economic well-being, and my house. I found myself in a completely hopeless situation. I didn't see any sort of future for myself. I felt pain and loneliness all the time. I was in hell!

I tried to process everything, but my emotions kept creeping up on me. I don't know about other types of grief very well, but dealing with suicide feels like being in a hole. You want someone to come and help you out of the hole. Then you learn that even if someone throws you a rope, you still have to climb out of that hole yourself. You still have to find a way to climb up the rope. The healing process isn't quick. It takes a long time. There are moments when light shines through briefly, but then things get cloudy again. I was surrounded by bad weather, and there was wind, darkness, and rain everywhere I looked. It takes a while to figure out how to get out of that hole, so you end up spending some time in there. Years pass and you never forget what happened, but you eventually begin to smile again. The pain doesn't disappear, but it recedes into the past.

When I met Master Lee from Buddha Temple, she talked to me about being positive and trying to find hope. It took a while for me to find hope, but I knew that the bright and sunny parts of me could still surface, even in the darkness of that hole. I didn't forget that I am Sunshine Girl!

I always prayed that if tragedy were to hit, that it not hit in Germany. Because I knew that in Germany I would be alone. And that's what happened. None of my so-called friends in Germany, not even the Russian-speaking ones, were there for me. The people who came to support me were Riva from Vienna, and Ann and Martin from France.

Then I had to make a difficult decision: where to live. Should I stay in Germany with my children or leave to be with my warm circle of friends in America??? Steeling myself, I made the difficult decision to leave for America.

It's not for nothing that they say, "Life is 10% of what happens and 90% how you handle it." When I arrived in the US, I was immediately surrounded by close friends, and I understood that I had made the best decision in my life. In the US I didn't even anywhere to live, but Barb and Roger generously offered to let me live in their house until I got my own place. I will be grateful to them until the end of my life. I had to start from scratch: I cleaned houses, babysat, packed boxes in the basement, and cooked, and was happy that I was able to make money one way or another. My friends were proud of me. It seems to me that this could only happen in the US, where any kind of work is respected.

When I bought a condo and went to the furniture store to buy furniture, I was devastated that the person I treasured, and with whom I had always done everything, was not beside me. I was crying my heart out, but then, all of the sudden, I realized that I could pick the furniture out myself, and that I could make all the decisions about my life on my own from now on.

When I was searching for religion in the hopes that it would help me deal with the pain of losing your grandfather, I met with Master Lee at Buddha Temple. She told me that looking at the bigger picture of my life, I had actually been given three lives. The first was before I met Juergen, the second was my happy life with him, and now I should live for myself and accomplish the things I had always dreamt of.

I realized that I could now take responsibility for my life and start figuring out how to achieve the things I had always wanted. I had to extricate myself from the past and move on to a better place. And I did.

My dear grandchildren, if you take responsibility for your lives and take control of them, you will see new possibilities and be able to figure out what you want for yourself. This will make a profound difference in your lives.

Always expect the best!

Say "yes" to life and be open to new experiences. You may not always get what you want, but you will generally get what you expect, as I did.

It seems that life was now giving me a chance to realize myself and move closer to achieving my dream of opening my own business.

My first success was when, while teaching my International cooking class, I was featured on Fox News and MSNBC News.

Imagine being on TV with my own cooking segment. I was so proud of myself!

Then I started a home care business for seniors from different countries. I started teaching them English and American cultural values. They had moved to the US in old age and barely knew the country they were now living in, so I decided to show them Detroit.

The more I was in Detroit, the more I was attracted by this city.

I came to love Detroit as a parent comes to love an adopted child.

A city cannot speak, so you must get to know it slowly and methodically, which I began to do. There was something about Detroit that didn't belong to me, and I couldn't quite figure out what it was, but it was definitely attractive to me. Maybe thanks to the unique positive energy in this city. Slowly I started to appreciate and love this new home even more. More and more I liked the fact that Detroiters are optimistic and self-confident, but not arrogant. I began to appreciate how much history there is in this city, and that even if you have lived your whole life here, you still have more to learn and appreciate. Detroit bewildered and captivated me... I don't even want to try to convince people to like it, especially those who have never been here. This city isn't for everyone. But it's possible that this city, with its creative spirit and Motown soul, is just right for me.

The positive energy that exists between everyone in this city is magical, addictive, and contagious. There are so many different cultures, races, and personalities here, all of which have a great passion for their city. You can't help but feel a sense of pride when you know that you live in and/or work in one of the greatest cities in the USA.

Suddenly, Detroit became a home for me, even though it's thousands of miles away from my roots.

The regular excursions for the elderly that I led around Detroit resulted in my creating yet another business. Detroit had offered me a wonderful opportunity! I started a new business offering tours around the city. Soon my company became one of the most successful in Detroit.

On a beautiful day when I was showing around a group of government advisors from DC, one member of the group made an interesting comment: "How interesting that a woman from Uzbekistan is leading tours around Detroit." To which I replied that I was madly in love with this city, and each time I go into a beautiful building in the classical art deco style – like the Fisher and Guardian buildings – I'm surrounded by so much positive energy that I am certain that I lived in Detroit in a previous life. How else can I explain why I am so in love with this city? And why is it that I feel myself at home specifically in Detroit, and not in Odessa, Jena, Munich, or any of the other places where I have lived? Home is where you are welcome and feel warm and comfortable, just like in your mother's womb. Every time I stroll along the streets of Detroit, I am infected with such a powerful wave of positive energy, that I am simply overwhelmed. It's not for nothing that they say that the most wonderful city is the one where you are happy, and your hometown is not the one where you began your life, but the one where you hope to end it.

Grandchildren, you can build your future from anything you like. From some crumb or from a spark. Out of the desire to move forward, slowly, step by step.

I will miss seeing you all grow up, but I feel very, very lucky to have met you, and lucky to have had the chance to spend time with you.

Life is really beautiful! Live it!

Made in the USA
Columbia, SC
14 July 2021